Paul's **SAT**® Math 800

Paul Kim

For the Redesigned SAT

Paul Academy
INTERNATIONAL

Contributors

Written and edited by the talented test prep professionals at
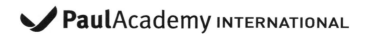

PaulAcademy is a publishing arm of one of the industry-leading test prep organizations in Asia. PaulAcademy is a dedicated test prep organization that has helped thousands of students to realize their potentials and achieve their dreams. As a leader in test prep & strategy development specializing in SAT, ACT and AP preparation, PaulAcademy teaches pragmatic problem-solving skills that will ultimately help students obtain successful academic results. PaulAcademy aims to spread its expert knowledge to students worldwide.

Editor-in-Chief
Paul Kim

Head of Publishing
Saeyeun Kim, Sieun Lee

Material Development & Editing
Jaewoo Lee

Marketing
Byeong Kook Kim, Paul Jae Woo Jung

PaulAcademy INTERNATIONAL

Email: books@paulacademy.net   Website: http://www.paulacademy.net

ISBN : 978-15-307005-8-5

Paul's **SAT**® Math 800

Paul Academy International

The Tiger Mom's Secret Weapon

How Asian Students really achieve SAT success

While teaching the SAT, I hungered to find the same quality of SAT test questions as the real College Board test, because the practice questions of leading test prep companies were slightly different from the real thing. They didn't match the real content or they were just too easy. The difference was so big that I had a hard time accurately predicting my students' scores. I decided to make new SAT books with new principles for success.

1. Fully Comprehensive

I have created comprehensive vocabulary lists based on how frequently each word has appeared in previous tests. I didn't want students to be forced to purchase three or four vocabulary books in order to get all the information they needed, and I didn't want them to have to study words they would never need. My grammar book provides concise, efficient coverage of every grammar rule that has been tested, and contains 16 top-quality practice tests. My essay book has a full list of released questions and a strategy that quickly allows any student to reach their highest possible score. My math book focuses more on the advanced tactics for students wanting to perfect their scores to 800.

2. Question Difficulty Level: CollegeBoard

Previously, there were only a few prep books on the market aimed at Advanced Learners (scoring over 700 in each section), but even though the questions in the book were difficult, the skills they taught were irrelevant to success in the SAT. My book strictly adheres to the topics, skills, and reasoning that CollegeBoard actually tests.

3. Linking Concepts to Real CollegeBoard examples

When I explain a concept in my books, I find example questions in both the Official SAT guide and my own practice tests to drive the concept home. Students always know exactly what to expect and how to use what they are learning.

Using these three principles, my students' scores skyrocketed. I received many requests to make my strategies public, and so here now they are finally being printed. It has become the number one choice for reliable, comprehensive SAT success in the Asian market, and it will no doubt work for you, too.

Paul Kim

CONTENTS

This is the Redesigned SAT

Introduction to the 2016 Redesigned SAT

Implemented since March 2016

1. Major changes in the Redesigned SAT

A. Score
- Full score 2400 → Full score 1600 (Reading + Writing & Language 800, Math 800)
- Essay is now optional and graded separately. It is scored from 2 to 8 for each of the three criteria - reading, analysis, and writing - with the full score being 24.
- Even though the essay is optional, it is virtually essential for students aiming for the top universities.

B. Section
In the previous SAT, the sections were divided into Essay, Critical Reading, Writing, and Math. Now, they are divided into Evidence-based Reading & Writing (Reading + Writing & Language), Math, Essay (optional).

C. Exam length
The total length has been reduced from 3 hours 45 minutes to 3 hours. (3 hours 50 minutes with essay)
1. Evidence-based Reading & Writing: 65 minutes for reading, 35 minutes for writing
2. Math: 55 minutes with calculator, 25 minutes without calculator

D. Number of questions
- Critical Reading: 67 questions → 52 questions
- Writing: 49 questions → 44 questions
- Essay: 1 question (no change)
- Math: 54 questions → 58 questions

E. Exam method
– There are now 4 answer choices instead of 5.
– Paper and pen (no change)

F. Scoring system & criteria
– Essay: focuses more on the student's analysis and reasoning than the essay's overall consistency
– No points are deducted for wrong answers: wrong answers and unsolved questions do not affect the score

G. Original SAT and New SAT

Original SAT			Redesigned SAT			
Section	Exam length	Number of questions	Section	Exam length	Number of questions	Exam method
Critical Reading	70min	67	Reading	65min	52	4 LP 1 DP
Writing	60min	49	Writing & Language	35min	44	4 Passages
Essay	25min	1	Essay	50min	1	1 EP 1 RP
Math	70min	54	Math	80min	58	Calculator / 38 questions NO Calculator / 20 questions
Total	225min	171	Total	180min (230 min with essay)	154 (155 with essay)	

※LP: Long Passages, DP: Double Passages, EP: Essay Prompt, RP: Reading Passage

2. Specific changes in each section

A. Reading Test
1. Focuses more on context rather than the difficulty of the vocabulary
– No more questions that cannot be solved without knowing the original word's meaning
– Finding the word's tone from extended context is more important
  ex) how word choice shapes tone/impact
– No more sentence completion
– Fewer questions that directly ask for a word's meaning or a fragmentary detail

2. Analysis & evidence use
– In addition to finding the answer, you also have to find which part of the text supports that answer.
  ex) Which portion of the passage best supports the answer to the question?
  CB: "There will be at least one question asking them to select a quote from the text that best supports the answer they have chosen in response to the preceding question."

3. Passages about real-world topics
- No more fiction and essays about random topics
- Passages including charts, graphs, and figures (equally applied for reading, writing, and math)
- 1 history/social science passage and 1 science passage

4. New passages
- American/World literature passages kept; history/social science/science passage added
- Founding documents, global conversation passage included

Study Strategy

The Redesigned SAT places an emphasis on Evidence-based reading, so you have to carefully check the passage summary, main idea, and tone while comprehending the passage. Instead of relying on your gut to solve reading questions, always check which line you used to find the answer when studying for the reading section.

B. Writing and Language Test

1. Passages about real-world topics
- Passages about history/social science, science, humanities, career
- More than one graph or chart question: questions asking you to smoothly integrate given information into the logical flow of the passage

2. No major changes to grammatical error questions
- Development of ideas
  ex) adding relevant supporting details, improving focus and cohesion
- Careful & purposeful use of words
  ex) improving precision or concision
- Rhetoric and conventional usage
  ex) fragments & run-ons, parallel structure, modifier, tense, pronoun & number, verb agreement, logical comparison, idioms, punctuation
- Diction

3. Linking the given text to a chart or a graph
  ex) fixing an incorrect interpretation of the chart

4. Increased passage length
– No more one sentence grammar questions
– Passages providing extended context

> **Study Strategy**
>
> Think of the new writing section as the Improving Paragraph questions from the original SAT Grammar section, except with more focus on the grammatical aspects.

C. Essay
1. Changed from essential to optional

2. No more short prompts asking for your opinion
– The original prompt relied on background knowledge and experience; whether you used real facts or fiction didn't matter as long as the logical structure was correct. In the New SAT essay, you have to read a passage that is 600~700 words long, and analyze and explain its argument. You cannot use your own examples or state your own opinion.
  ex) instead of stating your own opinion, state specific evidence from the text to explain how the author leads his argument
– The key is to analyze the writer's rhetorical strategy, logic, and argument, and then put it into your own words.
3. Scoring system & criteria
– Instead of a scale ranging from 0 to 12, the essay is now scored from 0 to 24 based on the scoring criteria.
– Reading: understanding the source text and main idea is critical; how accurate the details are, and how well you use the evidence from the text are key
– Analysis: how well you understood the given task, how effective the various elements the author used in his/her argument are, and how effective the evidence the author used to present his/her argument is
– Writing: is there a central claim, are the organization and progression effective, is the sentence structure varied, are words being used accurately, are the style and tone consistent, are there any grammatical errors, etc.

4. You have now 50 minutes instead of 25 to write the essay, so systematic logic and development are crucial. With more time, scoring is expected to be more precise and harsh.

Study Strategy

While you were able to 'make up' details in the original SAT, the Redesigned SAT requires a fact-based essay. Like the 2016 Redesigned Reading, it is very important to understand the author's main idea and argument and practice carrying out a fact-based argument.

D. Math Test

* The topic range and number of questions in each topic has been adjusted, so the overall difficulty of the math questions has been raised. Keep in mind that some question types and levels may match those of questions seen in AP math.

1. Focus on data analysis
– Similar to how Reading and Writing have put more focus on real-world questions
– Questions asking you about real-life situations

2. Questions using real-world context
   ex) showing you a scenario involving social science/history/science and asking you several
       questions about it

3. Pre-calculus questions added
– Trigonometry, complex number, radians, etc.

4. Some sections prohibit the use of a calculator
– No complicated calculation; limited to the level of calculating rational numbers
– 12 grid-in short answer questions

<Topic range>

Range	Number of questions	Percentage of total questions
Heart of Algebra (Creating, Solving, Interpreting Linear Expressions)	21	36%
Problem Solving and Data Analysis	16	27%
Passport to Advanced Math (Quadratic/Exponential Functions)	15	26%
Additional Topics (Area/Volume Calculation, Investigation of Lines, Angles, Triangles and Circles Using Theorem, Working with Trigonometric Functions	6	11%
Total	58	100%

<Classification by calculator use>

Classification	Question type	Exam length
Calculator	30 multiple choice 8 grid-ins	55minutes
NO calculator	15 multiple choice 5 grid-ins	25minutes
Total	**58 questions**	**80minutes**

Study Strategy

While you were able to 'make up' details in the original SAT, the Redesigned SAT requires a fact-based essay. Like the 2016 Redesigned Reading, it is very important to understand the author's main idea and argument and practice carrying out a fact-based argument.

Paul's New SAT Math 800

Diagnostic Test

Diagnostic Test

Q1

Which of the following numbers is NOT a solution to the inequality $2r-6\geq3r-4$?

A) 0

B) -2

C) -5

D) -6

Q2

$$x-3y=17$$
$$-6y-4x=22$$

What is the solution $(x,\ y)$ to the system of equations above?

A) $(-1,\ -6)$

B) $(5,\ -2)$

C) $(2,\ -5)$

D) $(-4,\ -3)$

Q3

Nikolai leased a car at $890.99 per month. There is a one−time commission fee of $55.49 and a tax of 5% on his monthly lease price. Which of the following represents Nikolai's total payment, in dollars, for leasing the car for x months?

A) $1.05(890.99x)+55.49$

B) $1.05(890.99x+55.49)$

C) $1.05x(890.99+55.49)$

D) $1.05(890.99x)+55.49x$

Q4

If $(px+1)(qx-4)=6x^2+rx-4$ for all values of x, and $p+q=5$, what are the two possible values of r?

A) 2 and 3

B) -5 and 3

C) -5 and -10

D) 3 and 4

Q5

If $2a-b=5$, what is the value of $\frac{16^a}{2^{2b}}$?

A) 4^4

B) 2^{10}

C) 512

D) Cannot be determined from the given information

Q6

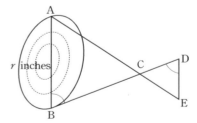

A geologist wants to determine the length r, in inches, of a tree stump in the forest as represented in the sketch above. The lengths represented by AC, CB, CD, and DE on the sketch were determined to be 40 inches, 30 inches, 15 inches, and 10 inches, respectively. Segments AE and BD intersect at C, and $\angle ABC$ and $\angle CDE$ have the same measure. What is the value of r?

Q7

A line in the $xy-$plane meets the $x-$axis at $(1, 0)$ and has a slope of -2. Which of the following points lies on the line?

A) $(0, -1)$
B) $(3, 0)$
C) $(0, 2)$
D) $(1, -2)$

Q8

In a right triangle, one angle measures $r°$, where $\cos r° = \dfrac{2}{5}$. What is $\sin(90° - r°)$?

Calculator

Q9

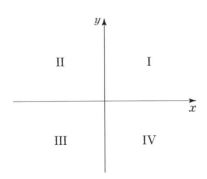

If the system of inequalities $y < -2x - 1$ and $y \le \dfrac{1}{2} - x + 1$ is graphed on the $xy-$plane above, which quadrant contains no solutions to the system?

A) Quadrant I
B) Quadrant II
C) Quadrant III
D) There are solutions in all four quadrants.

Q10

Height of Trees (in feet)				
1	8	8	8	8
9	10	10	10	10
11	11	11	12	12

The table above lists the height, to the nearest foot, of a random sample of 15 black willow trees. The outlier measurement of 1 foot is an error. Of the mean, median, and range of the values listed, which will change the most if the 1−foot measurement is removed from the data?

A) Mean
B) Median
C) Range
D) They will all change by the same amount.

Q11

	None	1 to 12	13 or more	Total
Group A	23	50	77	150
Group B	11	87	52	150
Total	34	137	129	300

The data in the table above were collected at a shooting range where people fired 20 shots on a fixed target. Group A consisted of 150 people who personally owned a gun, and Group B consisted of 150 people who did not personally own a gun. If a person is chosen at random from those who hit none to 12 shots on target, what is the probability that the person belonged in Group A?

A) $\dfrac{73}{100}$

B) $\dfrac{98}{100}$

C) $\dfrac{73}{171}$

D) $\dfrac{171}{300}$

Q12

If $y=x^2+x+1$, which of the following best shows this equation on a $xy-$coordinate plane?

A)

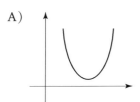

B)

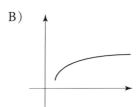

C)

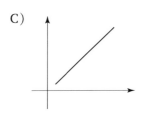

D)

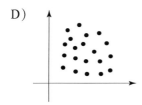

Q13

		Rockets	Mavericks	Spurs	Total
			Teams		
Texans	Male	38	35	57	130
	Female	47	54	39	140
	Total	85	89	96	270

Texan basketball fans responded to a survey that asked to choose one team they support out of the three basketball teams in Texas. The survey data were broken down as shown in the table above. Which of the following categories accounts for approximately 33 percent of all the survey respondents?

A) Male fans of the Rockets
B) Female fans of the Spurs
C) Male and female fans of the Mavericks
D) Male and female fans of the Spurs

Q14

On Friday, 4500 men and women attended a basketball game. The ratio of men to women was 2 to 3. How many men attended the basketball game?

A) 450
B) 900
C) 1800
D) 2700

Q15

In May, Sunny called s people every day for 10 days, and Khalim called k people every day for 5 days. Which of the following represents the total number of people called by Sunny and Khalim in May?

A) $10s+5k$
B) $10k+5s$
C) $50sk$
D) $15sk$

Q16

| 1 yard = 3 feet |
| 12 inches = 1 foot |

Tim wants to glue together 5 yardsticks in a straight line. However, all he has are 6−inch rulers. How many 6−inch rulers does Tim need to glue together in a straight line in order to reach the same length as that of 5 yardsticks?

A) 15
B) 30
C) 36
D) 180

Q17

Viktor owns a poultry farm with two types of hens. He noticed that Breed A hens lay 30 percent less eggs than Breed B hens do. Based on Viktor's observation, if Breed A hens laid 140 eggs, how many eggs did the Breed B hens lay?

A) 98
B) 140
C) 200
D) 245

Q18

$$f(x)=\frac{1}{(x-1)^2+6(x-1)+9}$$

For what value of x is the function f above undefined?

A) −2
B) −1
C) 0
D) 1

Q19

For what value of a is $|a-2|+3$ equal to 0?

A) −5
B) −1
C) 2
D) There is no such value of a.

Q20

For a polynomial $f(a)$, the value of $f(4)$ is 1. Which of the following must be true about $f(a)$?

A) The remainder when $f(a)$ is divided by $a-1$ is 4.

B) $a-1$ is a factor of $f(a)$.

C) $a+1$ is a factor of $f(a)$.

D) The remainder when $f(a)$ is divided by $a-4$ is 1.

Q21

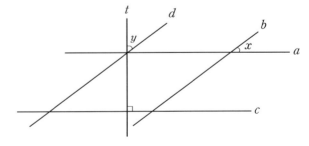

In the figure above, lines a and c are parallel, and lines b and d are parallel. If lines t and c are perpendicular and $\angle x$ is 43°, what is the measure of $\angle y$?

A) 43°
B) 47°
C) 86°

D) 90°

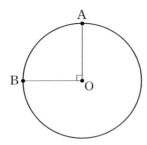

In the circle above, O is the center of the circle and Points A and B lie on the circumference of the circle.

If $\angle$ AOB is 90° and length of arc $\overset{\frown}{AB}$ is 3π, what is the area of the circle above?

A) 36π

B) 12π

C) 6π

D) 3π

Q23

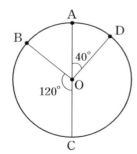

In the circle above, $\angle$ AOD is 40° and $\angle$ BOC is 120°. If the length of arc $\overset{\frown}{BC}$ is 6π, what is the length of arc $\overset{\frown}{AD}$?

A) 2π

B) 3π

C) 18π

D) 81π

Q24

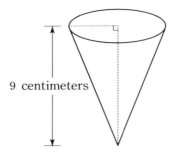

9 centimeters

The Jen and Berrie's ice cream store uses waffle cones in the shape of the cone above. If the volume of the waffle cone is 12π cubic centimeters, what is the circumference of the base of the cone, in centimeters?

A) 4π

B) 6π

C) $\dfrac{4}{\sqrt{3}}\pi$

D) Cannot be determined from the given information

Q25

Which of the following is the equation of a circle in the $xy-$plane with center $(1,\ 3)$ and a radius with endpoint $\left(\dfrac{7}{4},\ 4\right)$?

A) $(x-1)^2+(y-3)^2=\dfrac{25}{16}$

B) $(x+1)^2+(y+3)^2=\dfrac{25}{16}$

C) $(x-1)^2+(y-3)^2=\dfrac{5}{4}$

D) $(x+1)^2+(y+3)^2=\dfrac{5}{4}$

Diagnostic Test Answers

No Calculator

Q1. A
1–1. Linear Equations/Inequalities

Q2. C
1–2. Systems of Equations/Inequalities

Q3. A
1–3. Equations & Inequalities in Context

Q4. C
3–1. Factoring

Q5. B
3–5. Powers & Roots

Q6. 20
4–1. Triangles

Q7. C
1–4. Equations/Inequalities in the Coordinate Plane

Q8. 2/5
4–8. Trigonometry

Calculator

Q9. A
1–4. Relationships among Equations/Inequalities in the Coordinate Plane

Q10. C
2–1. Statistics

Q11. C
2–2. Probability

Q12. A
3–4. Functions

Q13. C
2–6. Percentages

Q14. C
2–4. Ratio

Q15. A
2–5. Rate

Q16. B
2–4. Ratio

Q17. C
2–6 Percentages

Q18. A
3–2. Equations

Q19. D
3–3. Absolute Value

Q20. D
3–2. Equations

Q21. B
4–2. Polygons

Q22. A
4–4. Circles

Q23. A
4–4.Circles

Q24. A
4–5. Solids

Q25. A
4–7. Circle Equation

Chapter 1

Heart of Algebra

Linear Equations/Inequalities

A. Single Variable Equation

$ax = b$

If $a \neq 0$, the solution is $x = \dfrac{b}{a}$

If $a = 0$, $b = 0$, the solution for x is every number.

If $a = 0$, $b \neq 0$, there is no solution for x.

a and b may not be integers.

They may be expressions:

ie. $(2y-1)x = 0$

For possible values of x to be all real numbers, $2y-1$ needs to equal 0.

$2y - 1 = 0$

$2y = 1$

$y = \dfrac{1}{2}$

Collecting the term means adding, subtracting, multiplying, or dividing both sides of the equation with the same number in order to cancel out constants so that the variable stands alone on one side of the equation.

$3x - 9 = 4x + 2$

"Collecting the term" means to put all the terms containing a variable on the left side, and all the constants on the right side

VARIABLE SIDE		CONSTANT SIDE
$3x - 4x$	$=$	$2 + 9$

Now just do the math.

$-x = 11$

$x = -11$

Now you can solve equations!

B. Basic Principles of Linear Equations/Inequalities

Steps to Solve

1) If there are fractions, eliminate the denominators and expand.

2) Collect the terms.

3) Divide by the coefficient of x to isolate x.

    *Be careful with inequalities — negative numbers flip the sign.

Eliminating Denominators

$$\frac{2}{x} = \frac{3}{x+1}$$

1) Multiply both sides by the denominators.

$$\frac{2}{x}(x)(x+1) = \frac{3}{x+1}(x)(x+1)$$

2) Cancel out.

$$\frac{2}{\cancel{x}}(\cancel{x})(x+1) = \frac{3}{\cancel{x+1}}(x)\cancel{(x+1)}$$

$$2(x+1) = 3x$$

3) Expand.

$$\overset{\frown}{2(x+1)} = 3x$$

$$2x+2 = 3x$$

Exercise

Let's solve the next equation:

$2x - 9 = 5$

First, collect the terms.

$2x = 5 + 9$

$\quad = 14$

Divide both sides of the equation by 2 in order to get the value of x.

$x = 7$

Let's try another, this time with fractions.

$$\frac{2}{x} = \frac{1}{2x+3}$$

$$\frac{2}{\cancel{x}} \times \cancel{x} \times (2x+3) = \frac{1}{\cancel{2x+3}} \times x \times \cancel{(2x+3)}$$

Do the math and cancel out the denominators, and get the next equation.

$2(2x+3)=x$

$4x+6=x$

Now, collect the terms.

$3x=-6$

$x=-2$

... And there you have it. Good Job!

Example Questions

1. If $4a+8=24$, what is the value of $8a-9$?

A) 4

B) 16

C) 23

D) 32

2. If $\dfrac{3}{a}=\dfrac{6}{a+15}$, what is the value of $\dfrac{a}{3}$?

A) 3

B) 5

C) 15

D) 45

3. If $\dfrac{5}{6}a-\dfrac{1}{6}a=\dfrac{1}{2}+\dfrac{1}{6}$, what is the value of a?

C. Inequalities

1) Properties

    (i) $a > b$

        $a + c > b + c$ You can add the same number to both sides

    (ii) $a > b$

        $ac > bc$ You can multiply both sides by a positive number.

    (iii) $a > b$

        $ac < bc, \ if \ c < 0$ BUT you must flip the sign's direction when multiplying by a negative number.

    (iv) If $a < b$ and $b < c$, then $a < c$

    (v) If $a < b$ and $x < y$, then $a + x < b + y$

2) Solving Multiple Inequalities

Be sure to do the same thing to these three sides.

$$c \leq ax + b \leq d$$
$$c - b \leq ax \leq d - b$$

If $a > 0$, $\dfrac{c - b}{a} \leq x \leq \dfrac{d - b}{a}$

If $a < 0$, $\dfrac{d - b}{a} \leq x \leq \dfrac{c - b}{a}$

Exercise

Let's solve an inequality.

$3x + 9 \leq 6$

Collect the terms.

$3x \leq -3$

Divide both sides of the inequality by 3.

$x \leq -1$

Pretty straight forward, right?

But here's a tricky one.

$3x + 9 \leq 4x + 6$

Both sides don't have a common denominator so let's just collect the terms.

$-x \le -3$

Now the tricky part is here.

When multiplying by a negative number to both sides of an inequality, the inequality sign ALWAYS TURNS THE OTHER WAY.

$x \ge 3$

Example Questions

1. If $4x-2 \ge 6$ what is the minimum possible value for $2x+3$?

A) 2

B) 4

C) 7

D) 8

2. If $2x+7+5(x-2) \ge 6x+7$, what is the minimum possible value of x?

A) 3

B) 7

C) 10

D) 11

3. If $3a-5 \le 2$, what is the maximum possible value for $6a-9$?

A) 3

B) 5

C) 7

D) 9

SAT Questions

1. If $\dfrac{2x-y}{2y}=\dfrac{2}{5}$, which of the following must also be true?

A) $\dfrac{y}{x}=\dfrac{9}{10}$

B) $\dfrac{x}{y}=\dfrac{9}{10}$

C) $\dfrac{2x+y}{y}=\dfrac{9}{10}$

D) $\dfrac{y}{x}=\dfrac{2}{5}$

2. If $\dfrac{a+2}{a-2}=5$, what is the value of a?

A) 3

B) 4

C) 5

D) 12

3. If $\dfrac{7}{r}=\dfrac{3}{r+12}$, what is the value of $\dfrac{r}{7}$?

A) -3

B) -21

C) 3

D) 7

4. If $6x-12\geq9$, what is the minimum possible value for $2x-9$?

A) -7

B) -2

C) 2

D) 5

5. $6y-(14-2y)=a(4y-7)$

   If the equation shown has infinitely many solutions and a is a constant, what is the value of a?

A) -1

B) 1

C) 2

D) 7

6. If $2(x-1)+2x=\frac{1}{4}(16x-20)+3$, what is the value of x?

A) $x=1$

B) $x=4$

C) There is no value of x for which the equation is true.

D) There are infinitely many values of x for which the equation is true.

7. If $\frac{n-5}{n+5}=6$, what is the value of n?

A) -7

B) -5

C) 3

D) 6

8. If there are infinitely many solutions for the inequality $6x+7\geq3(ax+2)$, what is the value of a?

A) -6

B) -2

C) 2

D) 6

9. If $\frac{1}{3}(3y)+4(y-2)=5(y-2)+7$, what is the value of y?

A) -8

B) -3

C) There is no value of y for which the equation is true.

D) There are infinitely many values of y for which the equation is true.

10. If $2(y+1)=\frac{x}{3}+2$, what is the value of $\frac{x}{y}$?

A) 2

B) 3

C) 6

D) It is impossible to determine the value in question because the information given is insufficient.

11. If $\frac{2(r+2)-7}{4}=\frac{14-(r+2)}{5}$, what is the value of r?

A) 2

B) 4.5

C) 6

D) 9

12. If $\frac{2x+7}{3}=\frac{3x+9}{4}$, what is the value of x?

A) 0

B) −1

C) 1

D) 55

13. If $x=ay$, where a is a constant, and $x=56$ when $y=4$, what is value of x when $y=3$?

A) 3

B) 14

C) 28

D) 42

14. If $3x+11-9(x+3)=5x-27$, what is the value of x?

A) 1

B) 5

C) 6

D) 11

15. If $\dfrac{3a+2}{5}=\dfrac{2a-8}{4}$, what is the value of a?

A) −48

B) −24

C) 12

D) 36

16. If $\dfrac{q}{3p}=7$, what is the value of $\dfrac{2q}{3p}$?

A) 7

B) 12

C) 14

D) 49

17. If $\dfrac{2k}{3r}=5$, what is the value of $\dfrac{15r}{2k}$?

A) 0

B) 1

C) 5

D) 6

18. If $9x-4\leq2x+11$, what is the maximum integer value of x?

A) -1

B) 2

C) 5

D) 8

Systems of Equations / Inequalities

A. Two Equations

1) A system of linear equations is a collection of linear equations involving the same set of variables.

2) n equations are needed to solve a system with n variables.

   Ex) two equations for two variables, three equations for three variables, etc.

3) Solve for y in terms of x:

   (i) Put y alone on left side.

   (ii) Put any other terms (that includes x and constants) on the right side.

B. Basic Principles of System of Equations/Inequalities

1) Solving for y in terms of x

   (i) Collect the terms, but put all the terms containing y on the left side.

   (ii) Divide by the coefficient of y to have the general form of the equation.

2) Plugging in

   (i) When plugging in, be sure to include parentheses first to avoid the common mistake of not distributing negative coefficients.

   ie. Plugging $y = -x + 3$ into $3x - y = 5$

$$3x - y = 5$$
$$3x - (-x + 3) = 5$$
$$3x + x - 3 = 5$$

Common Mistake! $\longrightarrow$

$3x - x + 3 = 5$

(wrong!)

You forgot to distribute the negative sign.

3) Subtracting Two Equations

   (i) Align the variables vertically and subtract terms by column.

$$
\begin{array}{r}
6x + 2y = 14 \\
-\ 4x + 2y = 6 \\
\hline
2x = 8
\end{array}
$$

4) Number of solutions

Given $y = m_1 x + b_1$

$\quad\quad y = m_2 x + b_2$

One Solution : if $m_1 \neq m_2$, $b_1 \neq b_2$

No Solution : if $m_1 = m_2$, $b_1 \neq b_2$

Infinitely many Solutions : if $m_1 = m_2$, $b_1 = b_2$

Exercise

The simplest kind of system equations involve two equations and two variables:

$4x + 2y = 6$

$3x + y = 7$

One method is called "Solve-and-Plug".

First, solve the top equation for y in terms of x:

$y = -2x + 3$

Now, plug this into the second equation as the y-value.

$3x + (-2x + 3) = 7$

The equation is now a single variable equation, and solving it will give the value of x.

$3x - 2x + 3 = 7$

$x = 4$

and also the value of y:

$y = -2x + 3 = -2 \times 4 + 3 = -5$

Another method is called "Align Variables".

Let's try with the same system of equations above and label them.

$4x+2y=6 \rightarrow$ ①

$3x+y=7 \rightarrow$ ②

Now align the coefficient of y by multiplying ② by 2.

②$\times 2$: $6x+2y=14$

since ②$\times 2$ and ① share the same coefficient for the variable y,

subtract the two equations to eliminate the variable y.

②$\times 2-$① :

$$
\begin{array}{r}
6x+2y=14 \\
-\underline{4x+2y=6} \\
2x=8
\end{array}
$$

Solving the equation will give us $x=4$.

Plug the $x-$value into equation ②.

$3\times 4+y=7$

$\quad 12+y=7$

$\qquad y=-5$

1. $2a+b=2$

    $4a-3b=19$

    Which of the following pairs of $(a,\ b)$ satisfies the system of equations above?

A) $(3,\ -2)$

B) $(2.5,\ -3)$

C) $(-2.5,\ 3)$

D) $(-3,\ -2)$

2. $45x-27=173+y$

   $\dfrac{y}{x}=9$

   In the system of equations above, what is the value of y?

3. $5p-rq=3$

   $3p-5q=7$

   In the system of equations above, r is a constant and p and q are variables. For what value of r will the system of equations have no solution?

   A) $\dfrac{5}{3}$

   B) $\dfrac{25}{3}$

   C) $\dfrac{3}{7}$

   D) 5

4. $5y-p=7y-11$

   $5z-q=7z-11$

   In the equations above, p and q are constants. If p is q minus 2, which of the following is true?

   A) y is z minus 1.

   B) z is y minus 1.

   C) z is y plus 1.

   D) z is y minus 2.

C. One Equation, One Inequality

Steps to Solve

1) Solve the equation.
2) Plug it into the equality.

▲ **Exercise**

Let's take this question with an equation and an inequality as an example.

> $x+2y=9$
> $x+y\leq6$
>
> According to the given information, what is the minimum possible value of y?

Since the question is asking for the minimum possible value of y,
we should manipulate the inequality to read in terms of y.
In order to do so, let's collect the terms on the given equation.
$x+2y=9$
$x=9-2y$
Now we have the $x-$value's relationship with y. So the next step would be ...?
Plugging it into the inequality. Good thinking!
$x+y\leq6$
Plug in the $x-$value:
$(9-2y)+y\leq6$
$9-y\leq6$
Collect the terms:
$9-6\leq y$
$\therefore 3\leq y$
Therefore, the minimum possible value of y would be 3.

Remember: — solve the equation
— plug it into the inequality
Not the other way around.
(i.e. do not solve the inequality first.)

1. $2x+4\leq3y$

   $y=\dfrac{1}{3}x$

   According to the given information, what is the maximum possible value of x?

A) -5

B) -4

C) -3

D) 0

2. $3x+5\geq4y$

   $\dfrac{1}{2}x=2y-7$

   According to the given information, what is the minimum possible integer value of x?

1. $kx+ry=13$

   $3x+7y=52$

   In the system of equations above, k and r are constants. If the system has infinitely many solutions, what is the value of $\dfrac{k}{r}$?

2. $3a-4b=-3$

   $4a-3b=-11$

   In the system of equations above, what is the value of $a+b$?

A) -8

B) -5

C) -3

D) 2

3. $\dfrac{z}{y}=9$

   $5(y+4)=z$

   In the system of equations above, what is the value of z?

A) 4

B) 5

C) 9

D) 45

4. $-2a+3b=9$

   $4a+2b=6$

   In the system of equations above, what is the value of a?

5. $5x+21=6y-4$

   $y+4=2x$

   In the system of equations above, what is the value of $y-x$?

A) 3

B) 7

C) 10

D) 14

6. $3r-a=5r-13$

   $3k-b=5k-13$

   In the equations above, a and b are constants. If b is a minus 6, which of the following is true?

A) r is k minus 1.

B) k is r plus 3.

C) k is r minus 3.

D) r is k plus 2.

7. $y=7x+5-2(x+1)$

$y=-\dfrac{1}{2}x$

If the system of equations above is satisfied by $(p,\ q)$, what is the value of $11(p+q)$?

A) $\dfrac{3}{11}$

B) $-\dfrac{3}{11}$

C) -3

D) 6

8. $5a+7=4b+2$

$2b=a+3$

In the system of equations above, what is the value of $6a$?

A) 1

B) 2

C) 4

D) 6

9. $3y+2=5z$

$2y=z+8$

In the system of equations above, what is the value of z?

A) 2

B) 4

C) 6

D) 8

10. $\dfrac{y}{x}=5$

$3(x+2)=y$

In the system of equations above, what is the value of y?

A) 3

B) 6

C) 15

D) 18

11. $4x+6=7y$

$8x-3=9y$

In the system of equations above, what is the value of x?

A) 3

B) 3.75

C) 6

D) 6.75

12. $2n+3m=4$

$3n+4m=5$

In the system of equations above, what is the value of $n+m$?

A) -1

B) 0

C) 1

D) 2

13. $5n-r=7n-9$

$3m-k=5m-9$

In the equations above, r and k are constants. If r is k minus 4, what is the value of $n-m$?

A) 2

B) 4

C) 5

D) 9

14. $6(x+3)-10=2(y+1)$

$y=\dfrac{1}{3}x$

In the system of equations above, what is the value of $8x$?

A) -9

B) $-\dfrac{9}{8}$

C) -6

D) 9

15. $6a+5b=26$

$2a-2b=5$

Which of the following pairs of $(a,\ b)$ satisfies the system of equations above?

A) $(3,\ -2)$

B) $(3.5,\ 1)$

C) $(3.5,\ -1)$

D) $(-3,\ -2)$

16. $4n - km = 9$

$5n - 4m = 12$

In the system of equations above, k is a constant and n and m are variables.
For what value of k will the system of equations have no solution?

A) 2.5

B) 3.2

C) 4

D) 5

17. $2r - 5 = 9k$

$r = 3k + 7$

In the system of equations above, what is the value of r?

A) 3

B) 7

C) 9

D) 16

18. $4y + a = 9y - 11$

$4z + b = 9z - 11$

In the equations above, a and b are constants. If b is a minus 5, what is the value of $y - z$?

A) -1

B) 0

C) 1

D) 4

19. $7a+9=5b$

$2a+4=b+7$

In the system of equations above, what is the value of $\frac{a+b}{3}$?

A) 7

B) 8

C) 13

D) 21

Equations & Inequalities in Context

In the Math section of the SAT there sometimes are questions that don't seem like math questions. Instead, there're a bunch of words giving you context and asking you to answer in numbers. Ridiculous!

These questions are designed to test your ability to pick out the mathematical implications in the given context. As you master these questions, they might actually help you in real life situations whether you're trying to figure out how much to pay after a meal with your friends or calculate how many days it takes you to eat a bag of candy. (For me, probably not even a minute.)

Frequently Used Terms

x less than y : $y-x$

x more than y : $y+x$

a times bigger than x : ax

a times smaller than x : $\dfrac{x}{a}$

Careful not to confuse these two!

$\longleftrightarrow$

x minus y : $x-y$

x plus y : $x+y$

a times x : ax

Exercise

> Schmidt has 23 more pairs of socks than Nick. If Schmidt and Nick have a total of 61 pairs of socks, how many pairs of socks does Nick have?

In this question, we want to know how many pairs of socks Nick has.
So, we set the number of Nick's pairs of socks as x.

Schmidt has 23 more pairs of socks than Nick, which means he has:
(Pairs of socks Nick has) $+23=x+23$

It is given that Nick and Schmidt combined have 61 pairs of socks.

$x+(x+23)=61$

$2x+23=61$

We now have officially established a linear equation using the context given in the question!

Now simply collect the terms.

$2x=61-23$

$2x=38$

$x=19$

Therefore, Nick has 19 pairs of socks.

A mystery is solved and the world is a much safer place now, thanks to you!

Sometimes questions require you to create a mathematical expression based on the given constants and variables.

Exercise

In May, Sunny called s people every day for 10 days, and Khalim called k people every day for 5 days. Which of the following represents the total number of people called by Sunny and Khalim in May?

Let's break down the question step by step:

Sunny called s people per day for 10 days.

$$\frac{s \text{ people}}{\text{day}} \times 10 \text{ day(s)} = 10s \text{ people}$$

Khalim called k people per day for 5 days.

$$\frac{k \text{ people}}{\text{day}} \times 5 \text{ day(s)} = 5k \text{ people}$$

$\therefore$ The total number of people called by Sunny and Khalim is: $10s+5k$

Exercise

Andy is a construction worker. Each day, he receives a pile of bricks to move. The number of bricks left to move at the end of the day can be estimated with the equation $B = 253 - 20h$, where B is the number of leftover bricks and h is the number of hours he has worked that day.
What does the number 20 signify in this question?

It is given in the question that B signifies the number of leftover bricks and h is the number of hours Andy has worked.
Since the equation solves for the amount of leftover bricks by subtracting $20h$ from 253, we can deduce that 253 is the initial workload of the day.

$20 \times h$ is subtracted from the initial workload to solve how many bricks are left over.

Since h is the number of hours that Andy worked, the logical deduction for the value 20 would be the number of bricks Andy moves in an hour.

Exercise

Here comes a tricky one.

> $g = 13.76 + 1.37m$
> $d = 10.01 + 2.12m$
> In the equations above, g and d represent the price per gallon, in dollars, of gasoline and diesel, respectively, m months after January 2014. What was the price per gallon of gasoline when it was equal to the price per gallon of diesel?

Since g and d each express the price per gallon of gasoline and diesel, when the price per gallon of gasoline and the price per gallon of diesel are equal to each other, $g = d$.
$13.76 + 1.37m = 10.01 + 2.12m$

Collect the terms.
$-0.75m = -3.75$
$m = \dfrac{3.75}{0.75} = 5$

Therefore, the price of gasoline and diesel equal each other after 5 months.

Oh, wait.

Double check what the question is asking you.

It's not the number of months, is it?

It's asking you to get the price of gasoline when the prices of gasoline and diesel are equal.

Plug $m=5$ into the equation for g.

$g=13.76+1.37m$

$g=13.76+1.37\times5$

  $13.76+6.85=20.61(\text{dollars})$

It's very important to know what the question is actually asking. Doing math is important, but in the New SAT you have to think more carefully.

SAT Questions

1. James has 45 more dollars than Jacob. If James and Jacob have 173 dollars combined, how much money, in dollars, does Jacob have?

A) 45
B) 64
C) 109
D) 128

2. At a coffee shop, a serving of iced tea has 50 more milliliters than a serving of coke. If 3 orders of coke and 4 orders of iced tea is a total of 4400 milliliters, how many milliliters is a serving of iced tea?

3. Elizabeth has 32 less marbles than Andy. If Andy and Elizabeth have 218 marbles combined, how many marbles does Andy have?

A) 32
B) 125
C) 173
D) 250

4. When 2 is subtracted from 5 times the number x, the result is 38. What number is the result when 9 is subtracted from 3 times the number x?

A) 5
B) 8
C) 15
D) 24

5. Troy and Abed each ordered tacos at a taco food truck. The price of Troy's tacos was a dollars, and the price of Abed's tacos was $2 less than the price of Troy's tacos. If Troy and Abed evenly divided the payment for their tacos and paid 15 percent sales taxes, which of the following expressions represents the amount, in dollars, each of them paid?

A) $0.15a - 0.15$
B) $1.15a - 1.15$
C) $2.3a - 1.15$
D) $2.3a - 2.3$

6. A toy racing car is scaled to $\frac{2}{7}$ the size of the actual car. If the length of the real-life car is 7 feet, what would be the length, in feet, of the toy car?

A) $\frac{49}{2}$

B) $\frac{2}{49}$

C) 2

D) 7

7. Jeff is x centimeters tall and he is $\frac{1}{5}x$ centimeters taller than Britta. If Britta's height is 156 centimeters, how tall, in centimeters, is Jeff?

A) 39

B) 139

C) 195

D) 203

8. For a rectangular box to be shipped through air at an international delivery service, the height and the perimeter of the bottom side of the box must together be equal to or less than 105 inches. If Pierce is trying to send a box that is 27 inches in height and 15 inches in length of its bottom face, what is the maximum possible width, in inches, of the bottom face of box?

A) 15

B) 20

C) 24

D) 48

9. Henry is participating in a triathlon where the participants must run, bike, and kayak a total of 40 miles. If Henry ran and biked at the speed of 6 miles per hour and 10 miles per hour, respectively, for two hours each, and finished the race in 5 hours, at what speed, in miles per hour, did Henry kayak at?

A) 4

B) 6.2

C) 8

D) 11

10. In Springdale, taxi fares are charged with a $5.00 initial fee, $1.00 per person, and $0.50 per mile. If Dean called a cab with four other friends and was charged a total of $65.50 dollars, how many miles did Dean and his friends travel?

11. For a musical's premiere, tickets that were pre—purchased online cost $15.00 each while tickets bought at the box office on premiere night cost $20.00 each. The total profit of the premiere night was the same as if every ticket purchased cost $18.00 each. If 200 tickets were pre-purchased, how many tickets were sold at the box office?

A) 200

B) 300

C) 350

D) 500

12. Sam and Jeremy collect stamps, and Jeremy has 21 less stamps than 4 times the amount of stamps that Sam has. If Sam and Jeremy have a total of 94 stamps, how many more stamps does Jeremy have than Sam?

A) 21

B) 23

C) 48

D) 71

13. At a gas station near a highway, three bags of beef jerky and two cokes cost $19.00 and five bags of beef jerky and five cokes cost $37.50. What is the difference between the price, in dollars, of one bag of beef jerky and one can of coke?

A) 0.50

B) 3.50

C) 4.00

D) 18.5

14. On Tuesday, Rameez and Cameron have $23.00 and $15.50, respectively, in their bank accounts. Starting from Tuesday, if Rameez adds $0.50 per day and Cameron adds $2.00 per day to their bank accounts, on what day will Rameez and Cameron have the same amount of money in their bank accounts? (Assuming the bank does not close on weekends.)

A) Friday

B) Saturday

C) Monday

D) Tuesday

15. In the children's section of a library, there is a total of 90 books in hardcover and paperback. If the amount of hardcovers is two times the amount of paperbacks minus nine, how many hardcover books are in the children's section?

A) 27
B) 33
C) 57
D) 66

16. A coffee shop has 21 tables that can seat a total of 71 people. If some of the tables can seat three people and the others seat four people, how many tables seat three people?

A) 5
B) 8
C) 13
D) 16

17. James is buying onions and garlic for $3.00 and $2.50, respectively, to prepare for Thanksgivings Day. If James spent a total of $72.50 from buying a total of 27 onions and garlic, how many onions did James buy?

A) 7
B) 10
C) 17
D) 20

18. In October, Turk ate t sandwiches every day for 13 days, and Carla ate c sandwiches every day for 3 days. Which of the following represents the total number of sandwiches eaten by Turk and Carla in October?

A) $13t+3c$

B) $3t+13c$

C) $16tc$

D) $39tc$

19. $a=3.24+0.35n$

$o=2.49+1.10n$

In the equations above, a and o represent the price per liter, in dollars, of apple juice and orange juice, respectively, n days after March 2015. What was the price per liter of apple juice when it was equal to the price per liter of orange juice?

A) $2.84

B) $3.24

C) $3.59

D) $4.34

20. Annie is buying 16GB and 32GB USBs that are priced at u and $2u$, respectively. If Annie bought 10 USBs and paid $17u$, how many 16GB USBs did Annie buy?

A) 2

B) 3

C) 4

D) 7

21. Archer bought 4 more sets of knives than sets of forks. There are 4 knives in each set of knives, and 5 forks in each set of forks. If the number of forks and knives Archer bought are the same, how many knives did Archer buy?

A) 16
B) 20
C) 80
D) 100

22. In a high school in Chapel Hill, there are four times as many football players as basketball players and twice as many basketball players as tennis players. If no student can play for two sports teams at the same time and there is a total of 66 athletes playing the three sports, how many students are football players?

23. On a two—section math test, the first section does not allow calculator use, and the other section allows calculators. The no—calculator questions are each worth 3 points, and have 20 questions. The calculator allowed questions are each worth 2 points and have 25 questions. A total score of 70 points is required to pass the test. If Fry got 8 questions wrong from the no—calculator section, what is the minimum amount of calculator allowed questions Fry must answer correctly in order to pass the test?

24. Lisa and Bart decide to open their piggy bank filled only with pennies. After dividing the pennies randomly, Lisa has 46 less pennies than Bart has. If Lisa and Bart have $13 in total, how many pennies does Bart have?   (1 dollar = 100 pennies)

A) 627
B) 673
C) 1253
D) 1346

25. Bailey bakes cookies at a bakery. Each day, she receives an order of cookies to make. The number of cookies left to bake at the end of the day can be estimated by the equation $C = 153 - 12h$, where C is the number of cookies left and h is the number of hours she has worked that day. What is the meaning of the value 153 in this equation?

A) Bailey will complete baking the cookies in 153 minutes.
B) Bailey bakes cookies at a rate of 153 per hour.
C) Bailey starts each day with 153 orders of cookies to bake.
D) Bailey bakes cookies at a rate of 47 per minute.

Equations/Inequalities in the Coordinate Plane

A. Basic Linear Equations on the Coordinate Plane

$y=ax+b$

a: slope of the line

b: y-intercept of the line

x-intercept : the intersection between the line and the x-axis (y-value is 0)

y-intercept : the intersection between the line and the y-axis (x-value is 0)

Exercise

A line in the xy-plane meets the x-axis at 1 and has a slope of -2.
Which of the following points lies on the line?

A) $(0, -1)$

B) $(3, 0)$

C) $(0, 2)$

D) $(1, -2)$

This question tests your knowledge on the nature of linear equations.
Using the information given by the question, establish a basic line equation.
Since the slope of the line is -2,

$y=-2x+b$

The x-intercept of the graph is 1. Therefore, plug in $(1, 0)$ to the equation above.

$0=-2\times1+b$

$0=-2+b$

Therefore, $b=2$.

Rewrite the line's equation.

$y=-2x+2$

Now, plug in the answer options to find what fits.

A) $-1=-2\times0+2$

$-1=2$

This option does not belong on the given line.

B) $0=-2\times3+2$

    $0=-6+2=-4$

This option does not belong on the given line.

C) $2=-2\times0+2$

    $2=2$

This option belongs on the given line.

D) $-2=-2\times1+2$

    $-2=-2+2=0$

This option does not belong on the given line.

B. Parallel and Perpendicular

If two lines are parallel to each other: slope is the same.

If two lines are perpendicular to each other: slopes are negative reciprocals of each other.

ex) $y=2x+3$ and $y=2x$ are parallel

    $y=2x+3$ is perpendicular to $y=-\dfrac{1}{2}x$

Exercise

In the xy-plane, lines $4x+2y=3$ and $ax+3y=3$ are parallel. What is the value of a?

Take the first equation and change it into a line equation form.

$2y=-4x+3$

$y=-2x+\dfrac{3}{2}$

Take the second equation and change it into a line equation form.

$3y=-ax+3$

$y=-\dfrac{a}{3}x+1$

Since the two equations are parallel, the slope is the same.

$-\dfrac{a}{3}=-2$

$\therefore a=6$

In the xy-plane, lines $4x+2y=3$ and $ax+3y=3$ are perpendicular. What is the value of a?

Take the first equation and change it into a line equation form.

$2y=-4x+3$

$y=-2x+\dfrac{3}{2}$

Take the second equation and change it into a line equation form.

$3y=-ax+3$

$y=-\dfrac{a}{3}x+1$

Since the two equations are perpendicular, the $-\dfrac{a}{3}$ is a negative reciprocal of -2.

$-\dfrac{a}{3}=\dfrac{1}{2}$

$\therefore a=-\dfrac{3}{2}$

C. Inequalities on the Coordinate Plane

$$y\leq 2x+5$$
$$y\leq -3x$$

In the xy-plane, if a point with coordinates $(p,\ q)$ lies in the solution set of the system of inequalities above, what is the maximum possible value of q?

The solution set of the inequalities will be the intersection of the areas below and including the boundary lines of $y=2x+5$ and $y=-3x$.

Drawing the two lines on the coordinate plane will form an 'X' shape since the slope of one equation is positive, and the other is negative.

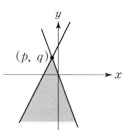

As you can see from the drawing, the greatest value of q will be at the point of intersection of the two lines.

Therefore, in order to get the greatest value of q, we must find the point where the two lines intersect.

$2x+5=-3x$
$5x=-5$
$x=-1$

Plug it into any of the inequalities.

$y\leq-3x$
$y\leq-3\times-1=3$

Therefore, the greatest value of q is 3.

Exercise

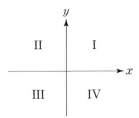

If the equation $6x+3y=9$ is drawn on the xy-plane above, which quadrant contains no solution to the line?

First we need to change the given equation to a line equation form.
Solve for y in terms of x.
$3y=-6x+9$
Divide both sides by 3.
$y=-2x+3$

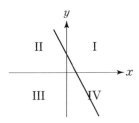

Above is the approximation of line $y=-2x+3$ graphed out on the coordinate plane. Therefore, Quadrant IV does not contain a solution for the equation.

SAT Questions

1.

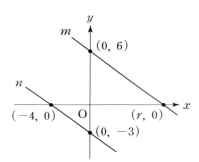

In the xy-plane above, line n is parallel to line m. What is the value of r?

A) 4
B) 6
C) 8
D) 11

2. The graph of a line in the xy-plane has slope -2 and contains the point $(1,\ 4)$. The graph of a second line passes through the points $(3,\ 0)$ and $(-3,\ -2)$. If the two lines intersect at $(p,\ q)$, what is the value of $p-q$?

A) 6
B) 4
C) 3
D) 0

3. $y \leq 25x - 450$

   $y \leq -5x$

   In the xy-plane, if a point with coordinates $(p,\ q)$ lies in the solution set of the system of inequalities above, what is the maximum possible value of q?

4.

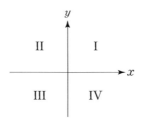

   If the system of inequalities $y \leq 2x + 6$ and $y > x$ is graphed on the xy-plane, which quadrant contains no solution to the system?

A) Quadrant I

B) Quadrant III

C) Quadrant IV

D) There are solutions for every quadrant.

5. If the slope of a line is $\dfrac{7}{3}$ and a point on the line is $(3,\ 15)$, which of the following is the y-intercept?

A) -8

B) -1

C) 8

D) 12

6.

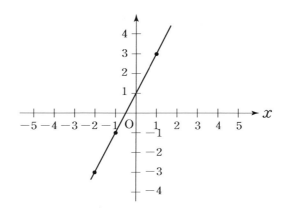

If the equation that represents the graph shown above is written in standard form $ax+by=c$, and $a=4$, what is the value of c?

7. In the xy-plane, lines $6x+2y=3$ and $9x+by=2$ are parallel. What is the value of b?

A) 1

B) 3

C) 4

D) 9

8.

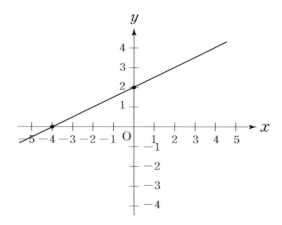

The graph of line l is drawn on the xy-plane above. Which of the following is the slope for a line that is perpendicular to line l ?

A) -2

B) -1

C) $\dfrac{1}{2}$

D) 2

9. If the slope of a line is -0.75 and a point on the line is $(16, \ 1)$, which of the following is the y-intercept?

A) -12

B) -1

C) $\ \ 4$

D) $\ \ 13$

10.

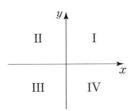

If the equation $2x+4y=3$ is drawn on the xy-plane above, which quadrant contains no solution to the line?

A) Quadrant I
B) Quadrant III
C) Quadrant IV
D) There are solutions for every quadrant.

11. A line on the xy-plane passes through the origin and has a slope of -2. Which of the following points lies on the line?

A) $(1, -2)$
B) $(1, 2)$
C) $(2, 4)$
D) $(4, 2)$

12. A line on the xy-plane passes through coordinates $(0, 2)$ and has a slope of $\frac{2}{3}$. Which of the following points DOES NOT lie on the line?

A) $(3, 4)$
B) $(-3, 0)$
C) $(-6, -2)$
D) $(2, 0)$

13. A line on the xy-plane meets the y-axis at 5 and has a slope of -3. Which of the following points lies on the line?

A) $(2, -1)$
B) $(-4, 3)$
C) $(5, 3)$
D) $(3, 0)$

14.

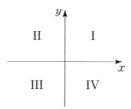

If the system of inequalities $y \leq -\frac{2}{3}x+6$ and $y>2x$ is graphed on the xy-plane, which quadrant contains no solution to the system?

A) Quadrant I
B) Quadrant III
C) Quadrant IV
D) There are solutions for every quadrant.

15.

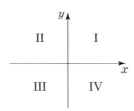

If the system of inequalities $y>2x-5$ and $y \leq -x$ is graphed on the xy-plane, which quadrant contains no solution to the system?

A) Quadrant I
B) Quadrant III
C) Quadrant IV
D) There are solutions for every quadrant.

16. $y \leq 4x-7$
$y \leq -2x+5$

In the xy-plane, if a point with coordinates (a, b) lies in the solution set of the system of inequalities above, what is the maximum possible value of b?

17.

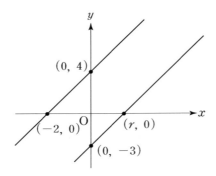

In the xy-plane above, the two lines are parallel. What is the value of r?

A) 1

B) 1.5

C) 2.5

D) 3

18.

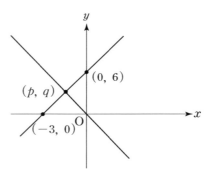

In the xy-plane above, the two lines are perpendicular and intersect at point (p, q). What is the value of q?

19. In the xy-plane, lines $4x+2y=1$ and $2x+by=2$ are parallel. What is the value of b?

A) 1

B) 1.5

C) 2

D) 4

20. In the xy-plane, lines $ax+3y=1$ and $7x+y=9$ are parallel. What is the value of a?

A) -21

B) -3

C) 7

D) 21

21. In the $xy-$plane, $ax+2y=7$ and $x+2y=6$ are perpendicular to each other. What is the value of a?

A) -4

B) -2

C) 2

D) 4

22. In the $xy-$plane, $2y\leq 4x+6$ and $3y\leq -6x+9$ meet at point $(p,\ q)$. What is the value of pq?

A) -3

B) 0

C) 2

D) 3

23.

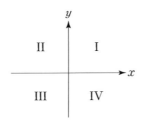

If the system of inequalities $y>3x-2$ and $2y\leq-4x$ is graphed on the xy-plane, which quadrant contains no solution to the system?

A) Quadrant I
B) Quadrant III
C) Quadrant IV
D) There are solutions for every quadrant.

24. The graph of a line on the xy-plane has slope -3 and contains the point $(1,\ 2)$. The graph of a second line passes through the points $(4,\ 0)$ and $(-4,\ -4)$. If the two lines intersect at $(r,\ k)$, what is the value of $r-k$?

A)   0
B)   1
C)   3
D)   7

25. $y\leq-11x+169$
    $y\leq2x$
    In the xy-plane, if a point with coordinates $(n,\ m)$ lies in the solution set of the system of inequalities above, what is the maximum possible value of m?

Chapter 2

Problem Solving and Data Analysis

Statistics

A. (Arithmetic) Mean : $\dfrac{\text{sum of values}}{\text{number of values}}$

B. Median : the middle number in a numerically ordered list of values

* When the number of values is even : find the arithmetic Mean of the two numbers in the middle.

*Increase the value of the numbers greater than the Median

*Decrease the value of the numbers smaller than the Median

$\longrightarrow$

Doesn't affect
the value of the Median

$\uparrow(\downarrow)$ all the numbers by $n \Rightarrow$ new Median = old Median $+(-)n$

C. Mode : the number that appears most frequently in a set of values

* Multiple Modes can exist.

ex) In Set $\{1,\ 2,\ 2,\ 3,\ 3,\ 4\}$, the Modes are $2,\ 3$.

D. Standard Deviation : a measure of how far the numbers are from the Mean

Standard Deviation of 0 means no spread at all

(ie. $\{2,\ 2,\ 2,\ 2,\ 2\}$ has a standard deviation of 0.

$\{2,\ 3,\ 4,\ 5,\ 6\}$ has a higher standard deviation.

$\{2,\ 12,\ 22,\ 32,\ 42\}$ has an even higher standard deviation)

E. Margins of Error & Confidence Intervals : a measure of precision of an estimate (i.e. how far from the actual value the estimates are likely to be)

ex) An average of 6 hours per week in the gym from the random sample of 300 college students has a margin of error of 1.5 hours at 95% confidence level. This means that in multiple random samples of size 300, the sample average will be within 1.5 hours of the population average in 95% of possible samples. In other words, you can be 95% confident that the interval from 4.5 hours to 7.5 hours includes the population average amount of time in the gym for all students at the college.

* When the confidence level is kept the same, the size of the margin of error is affected by two factors: sample size and the size of standard deviation

* Larger sample size → Smaller margin of error

  Smaller sample size → Larger margin of error

  Larger standard deviation → Larger margin of error

  Smaller standard deviation → Smaller margin of error

* Margin of error and confidence interval does not apply to the value of the variable for particular individuals. In the example, we are 95% confident that the interval from 4.5 hours to 7.5 hours includes the true average amount of time in the gym for all students at the college. It does not imply that 95% of the students spend between 4.5 hours and 7.5 hours in the gym.

Exercise

1. What is the mean of (20, 30, 50)?

2. What is the median of (2, 4, 9, 7, 10, 5)?

3. What is the mode of (1, 1, 1, 2, 2, 2, 3, 3)?

1. 60 is the median of a set of values $2T$, $6T$, $10T$. What is the value of T?

2. $\begin{cases} y=x+6 \\ z=y+3 \end{cases}$

   Based on the equations above, if x, y, z represent three numbers, what is the result when the average of the three numbers is subtracted from the median of the numbers?

   A) 0
   B) 0.5
   C) 1
   D) 1.5

3. Set X includes eight different numbers. All of the following can affect the value of the median EXCEPT

   A) Squaring each number
   B) Decreasing each number by 5
   C) Decreasing the largest number only
   D) Increasing the largest number only

4.

Exercising Hours per Week

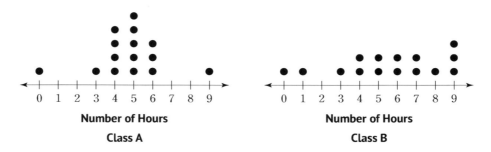

Number of Hours

Class A

Number of Hours

Class B

The dot plots above summarize the number of exercising hours of students in Class A and Class B. Which of the following correctly compares the standard deviation of the scores in each of the classes?

A) The standard deviation of the hours in Class A is smaller.

B) The standard deviation of the hours in Class B is smaller.

C) The standard deviations of the scores in Class A and Class B are the same.

D) The relationship cannot be determined from the information given.

5. A quality control manager at an M&M factory is investigating the number of chocolates in one bag of M&Ms. The manager selects 300 bags at random from the daily output of the M&Ms and finds that the average number of chocolates in one bag of M&M has a 95% confidence interval of 41 to 49 chocolates. Which of the following conclusions is the most reasonable based on the confidence interval?

A) 95% of all the M&M bags produced by the factory that day have between 41 and 49 chocolates inside.

B) 95% of all the M&M bags ever produced by the factory have between 41 and 49 chocolates inside.

C) It is plausible that the true average number of chocolates in one bag of M&M produced by the factory that day is between 41 and 49 chocolates.

D) It is plausible that the true average number of chocolates in one bag of M&M ever produced by the factory is between 41 and 49 chocolates.

Probability

A. Using Venn Diagram

1) Intersection $(A \cap B)$: the Set of Elements that are in both Set A and Set B

2) Union $(A \cup B)$: the Set of Elements in either Set A or Set B

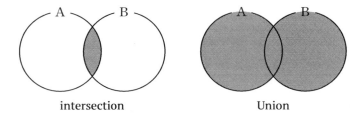

intersection   Union

3) # of Elements : # of Elements in $(A \cup B)$
   $= [(\text{# of Elements in } A) + (\text{# of Elements in } B) - \text{# of Elements in } (A \cap B)]$

B. Counting

1) Fundamental Counting Principle :

use when two INDEPENDENT cases occur at the same time.

When there are P different ways that case A can occur, and Q different ways that case B can occur $\Rightarrow P \times Q$ different ways, when cases A and B occur at the same time.

ex) There are 3 shirts and 4 jeans. How many different shirt—jean combinations are possible?

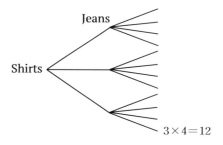

$3 \times 4 = 12$

2) Permutation and Combination

(ⅰ) Permutation : the number of ways in selecting r objects in a definite order from n objects

    * If order matters, when selecting r objects, Permutation is used.

    ex) (**Electing the President, then the Vice-President** vs. electing 2 Board Members)

$$\text{Permutation} = \frac{n}{(n-4)!} = {}_nP_r$$

(ⅱ) Combination : the number of ways in selecting r objects from n objects

    * As opposed to Permutation, the order of selecting r objects is not important.

    ex) (**Electing 2 Board Members** vs. electing the President then the Vice$-$President)

$$\text{Combination} = \frac{n!}{(n-4)!\,r!} = {}_nC_r \text{ (dividing by } r! \text{ eliminates repeating outcomes)}$$

3) Probability :

a measure of the likeliness that an event will occur, under the premise that all events are equally likely to occur

$$\frac{\text{The Number of Ways Event } A \text{ Can Occur}}{\text{Total Number of Outcomes}}$$

* Basic Properties

    1) Probability of an outcome A, or $P(A)$, is between 0 and 1, inclusively.

       That is, $0 \le P(A) \le 1$. (Impossible outcome if $P(A)=0$; outcome <u>certain</u> to happen if $P(A) = 1$)

    2) If we add together all probabilities of all outcomes, the answer is always 1.

       ex) Probability (of dice as $1+$ of dice as $2 + \cdots +$ of dice as 6) $=1$

    3) When two events, Event A and Event B, don't affect each other, Probability of A and B happening at the same time $=$ (probability of A) $\times$ (probability of B)

       That is, $P(A \cap B) = P(A) \times P(B)$, if A and B are independent.

* Geometric Probability In $2D$: compare the areas of two regions to calculate the Probability of an event.

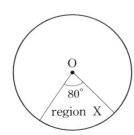

ex) The Probability that the spinner will land on region X?

    Solution : $\dfrac{\text{Area in Question}}{\text{Total Area}} = \dfrac{80}{360}$

1. There are 4 elements in set A, 6 elements in set B, and 2 elements in both. How many elements are in either set A or set B?

2. Suppose there are 4 types of shirts and 3 types of ties. How many different combinations of a shirt and a tie are possible?

3. What is the probability of rolling an odd number on a fair 6-sided die?

4. We want to select one president and one vice-president from five candidates. How many different combinations of one president and one vice-president are possible?

5. Now we want to select a committee of three. How many different ways can this committee be selected from the five candidates?

1. 8 students are in a room. If everyone shakes hands with everyone else in a room once and only once, how many handshakes will take place?

2. By using each of the digits 5, 6, 7 just once, different positive three-digit integers can be created. If the digits 5 and 6 must be adjacent, how many three-digit integers can be formed?

A) Two
B) Three
C) Four
D) Five

3. On a bookshelf, $\frac{1}{10}$ are non-fiction books, $\frac{1}{3}$ are fantasy books, and $\frac{1}{6}$ are science fiction books. If the 12 remaining books are romance, how many science fiction books are on the bookshelf?

A) 18
B) 30
C) 10
D) 5

4.

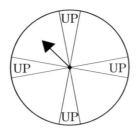

The spinner shown above is spun around its center and stops at a random position. The probability of a sector labeled 'up' ending up below the fixed arrow is $\frac{1}{9}$ (Assume that the arrow never points to any of the dividing lines). If the central angle of each sector labeled 'up' has the same degree measure x, what is the value of x?

A) 5
B) 7.5
C) 10
D) 30

5. A scoreboard contains two slots in which number cards ranging from 0 to 9 can be inserted. There are 12 cards available for each numeral. Assuming that each number card cannot be used more than once, how many scoreboards of consecutive scores, beginning with 01, can be formed?

A) 16
B) 17
C) 18
D) 20

6. Six students are sitting in a line in a classroom. If one student, A, never sits at either end, how many different sitting arrangements are possible?

7. In a certain game arcade, every 6th player is granted an extra life and every 8th player is given a gift token. A player is randomly selected from 100 consecutive players who will play at the arcade one day. What is the probability that the player will both gain an extra life and get a gift token?

A) $\dfrac{1}{100}$

B) $\dfrac{3}{100}$

C) $\dfrac{4}{100}$

D) $\dfrac{7}{100}$

Graphs and Data Analysis

A. Elements

1) <u>Unit</u> : a measurement of quantity. Indicates the size of the property

2) <u>Scaling</u> : the increments in which the data is represented

3) <u>Heading</u> : the title of the represented data

4) <u>Axes</u> : the variables (dependent or independent) involved in the data transformed into x and y axes; the x axis is horizontal, and the y axis is vertical

B. Tables

1) A <u>Table</u> is used to easily represent a list of data. Consisted of Columns and Rows. It will usually contain an independent variable and a dependent variable; a dependent variable changes due to the independent variable.

2) <u>Column</u> : the vertical arrangement of a Table

3) <u>Row</u> : the horizontal arrangement of a Table

* A Table may represent one independent variable, shared by two dependent variables.

ex) Table 1. Temperatures of Coffee and Green Tea at Various Hours

Time (h)	Temperature of Coffee (℃)	Temperature of Green Tea (℃)
0	34	38
1	32	30
2	29	29
3	28	27
4	24	26
5	25	24

1. Unit: How many minutes did it take for the coffee to cool to 28℃? (180 minutes)

2. Scaling: At which hour did the temperature of the green tea differ from the temperature of the coffee by 4℃ (0 hr)

C. Types of Graphs

1) <u>Bar Graph</u> : the most basic type of graph; shows how large each value is. May be horizontal or vertical. Usually derived from a Table of data with a single independent variable, with one or more dependent variables

    * In the case of multiple dependent variables, a Legend (key) will indicate which bar represents which variable.

    ex) Bar graph : Temperature vs. Time

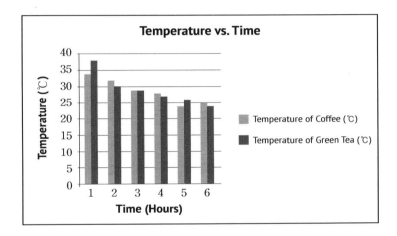

1. Unit: What temperature, in degrees Fahrenheit, is the coffee when the green tea reaches a temperature of 30 degrees Celsius? (degree Fahrenheit=1.80× degrees Celsius + 32.0; 89.6℉)

2. Scaling: What is the biggest temperature difference between the two drinks, and at which hour does this difference occur? (4℃; Hour 1)

3. Heading: What does the table represent? Explain in words. (The temperatures of coffee and green tea at various hours, from hour 1)

2) Scatter Plot : a graph of plotted points that shows the relationship between two sets of data.

     * Line of Best Fit : a line that best represents the trend of the data shown on the graph.

ex) Scatter plot : Y vs. X

Exercise

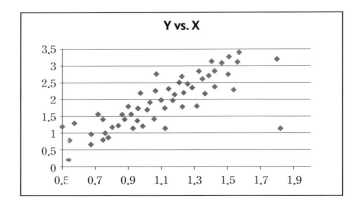

1. Heading : What could this graph be representing? (Various answers; situations in which the value of one variable increases with the other variable.)

2. Axes & Scaling : What is the coordinate of the point with the lowest x-value? $(0.5,\ 1.2)$

3. What type of equation would the line of best fit show for this graph? (Linear)

4. Looking at the graph, could you predict the next set of data? How? (Following the line of best fit would allow you to predict the next set of data.)

3) <u>Histogram</u> : a graph that is similar to the Bar Graph but groups its independent variable into ranges, showing how large each range of values is

ex) Histogram : Species A Survivability

Exercise

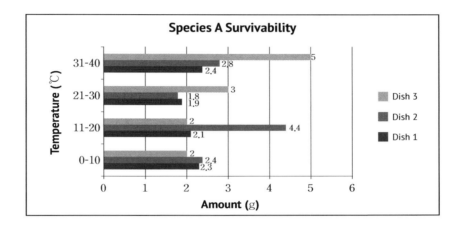

* Note that the graph is horizontal. However, the analytic method doesn't change.

1. Unit : If there was a total of 10 kg of species A in dish 2 at $11-20°C$, what percentage survived? (0.044%)

2. Scaling : Which temperature range is the most suitable for species A to survive, if they were to live in dish 3's environment? ($31-40°C$)

4) Line Graph : a graph that connects individual points of data by lines; shows how the data changes in value (as time passes, etc.)

ex) Line Graph : Company Values over Time

Exercise

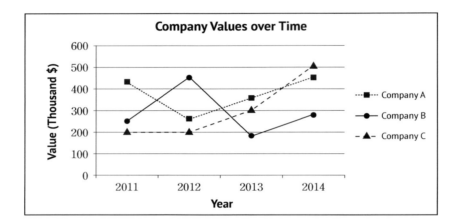

1. Unit : From 2011 to 2014, approximately how much did company C's value increase, in millions of dollars?
($0.3 Million)

5) Pie Chart : a type of graph, in the shape of a circle. Most commonly used to show the amount of portions in a whole

* As with a Bar Graph with multiple dependent variables, a Pie Chart will have a Legend to show what each part indicates.

ex) Pie Chart : Approval Rating: June 2014

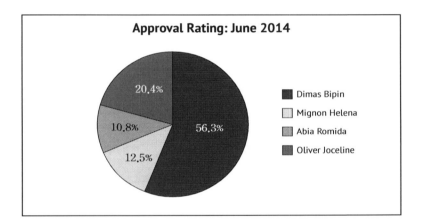

The following are the gas prices, for credit payment and for cash payment, per gallon.

	Regular	Plus	Premium
Credit	$2.11	$2.35	$2.47
Cash	$2.06	$2.29	$2.40

The following table shows the type of gas Tom and Barb purchased this year. Tom's car has a gas capacity of 18.5 gallons. Barb's car has a gas capacity of 17 gallons. Tom and Barb fill their tanks once a month, from zero gallons to the tank's full capacity.

Months	Tom	Barb
January - April	Plus	Premium
May - August	Regular	Plus
September - December	Regular	Regular

1. By how much is it more expensive to pay with credit? Round to the nearest hundredth percent.

A) Regular: 2.43% Plus: 2.62% Premium: 2.92%
B) Regular: 2.37% Plus: 2.55% Premium: 2.83%
C) Regular: 2.43% Plus: 2.18% Premium: 2.08%
D) Regular: 2.37% Plus: 2.13% Premium: 2.04%

2. If Tom fills his tank twice a month, by how much will his payments increase?

A) 100%, Tom originally only filled his tank once a month; if he filled his tank twice a month, he would spend double the original amount.
B) 50%, Tom only filled his tank twelve times this year.
C) 150%, Tom originally only filled his tank once a month; if he filled his tank twice a month, he would spend double the original amount.
D) 0%, nothing would change.

3. If Tom received $50,135 in wages this year and spent $474.34 on gas, what percent of his wage did he spend on gas, if he only paid in cash? Round to the nearest hundredth percent.

A) 9.5%
B) 0.95%
C) 0.97%
D) 9.7%

The following graph shows the number of students from the Class of 2014 and the majors they chose as they entered college.

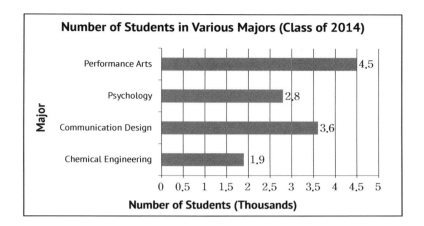

Number of Students in Various Majors (Class of 2014)

4. Of the students majoring in Chemical Engineering, about 23% change their major every year. For the Class of 2014, how many students changed their major from Chemical Engineering to something else at the end of their third year of college? Round to the nearest whole number.

A) 259

B) 867

C) 260

D) 337

Ratio

A. Direct Proportion:

When x increases by 2 or 3 times, y increases by 2 or 3 times.

e.g. 'x is directly proportional to y' can be expressed as:

$$x = ky \ (k \text{ is a constant})$$

B. Inverse Proportion:

When x increases by 2 or 3 times, y decreases by $\frac{1}{2}$ or $\frac{1}{3}$ times.

e.g. 'x is inversely proportional to y' can be expressed as:

$$x = k\frac{1}{y}$$

Exercise

1. If the ratio of A to B is $2 : 4$ and the ratio of B to C is $6 : 9$, what is the ratio of A to C?

2. If 4 pennies weigh 40 grams, what is the weight, in grams, of 80 pennies?

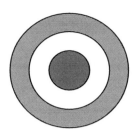

1. The three circles shown above are concentric and their radii are 2, 4, and 6, respectively. What is the ratio of the area of the small shaded circle to the area of the shaded ring?

A) 1 : 16

B) 1 : 9

C) 1 : 5

D) 1 : 4

2. The ratio of P to Q is 3 to 5 and the ratio of Q to R is 12 to 4. What is the ratio of R to P?

A) 5 to 4

B) 4 to 1

C) 5 to 9

D) 9 to 5

V　Rate

A. Motion Problem : Speed (Velocity) $\times$ Time $=$ Distance

$$\text{Average speed (velocity)} = \frac{\text{Total Distance}}{\text{Total Time}}$$

B. Work Problem : Rate of work $\times$ Time worked $=$ Amount of work done

---

Exercise

1. If a person travels 3 hours with an average speed of 25 miles per hour, what is the total distance of his / her trip in miles?

2. 6 workers can build a bridge in 10 days. How many days would it take for 2 workers to build the same bridge?

1. When chasing prey, a cheetah can run x miles in 5 minutes. When relaxed, it will only walk at $\frac{1}{5}$ of that speed. How many minutes will it take for a cheetah to walk to a pond $\frac{x}{2}$ miles away?

A) 10
B) 12.5
C) 20
D) 25

2. An elephant needs to eat 100 kg of food to be one-third full. How many kilograms of food does it need to eat to be completely full?

A) 200
B) 100
C) 300
D) 250

3. Jenny climbed up a climbing wall at an average speed of 0.5 feet per second and descended at an average speed of 3 feet per second. If her total time spent on the climbing wall was 7 minutes, how many minutes did it take Jenny to climb up the climbing wall?

A) 5
B) 5.5
C) 6
D) 6.5

Percentages

A. Percent : a number or ratio expressed as a fraction of 100

(If 5 people attended out of a pool of 20 people, $\dfrac{5}{20} \times 100 = 25\%$ attended)

B. Fraction, Decimal, Percent, Conversion, etc.

Fraction	$\dfrac{1}{10}$	$\dfrac{1}{8}$	$\dfrac{1}{6}$	$\dfrac{1}{5}$	$\dfrac{1}{4}$	$\dfrac{1}{3}$	$\dfrac{1}{2}$
Decimal	0.10	0.125	0.166⋯	0.20	0.25	0.33⋯	0.50
Percent	10%	12.5%	$16\dfrac{2}{3}\%$	20%	25%	$33\dfrac{1}{3}\%$	50%

C. Problem Types

1) x % of a number : $\dfrac{x}{100} \times \text{number} = \text{percent of that number}$

2) y % change : Percent change $= \dfrac{\text{amount of change}}{\text{original amount}} \times 100$

3) original amount :

① percent increase ($P\%$ Increase)

$$\text{original amount} = \dfrac{\text{new amount}}{1 + \dfrac{P}{100}}$$

② percent decrease ($P\%$ Decrease)

$$\text{original amount} = \dfrac{\text{new amount}}{1 - \dfrac{P}{100}}$$

1. What is $\frac{1}{8}$ in percentage?

2. What is 40% of 50?

3. midterm score: 70

   final score: 90

   What is the percent change from midterm to final?

4. If the price of a product, increased by 20%, is $60, what is its original price in dollars?

1. The percent increase from 8 to 14 is equal to the percent increase from 28 to x. What is the value of x?

A) 34

B) 42

C) 16

D) 49

2. A rise in the cost of corns caused the price of a bag of corn chips to increase by 20%. If the new price is $18, what was the original price of a bag of corn chips?

A) $3.6

B) $15

C) $14.4

D) $21.6

3. If a and b are positive numbers, what percent of $(2a+5)$ is b?

A) $\dfrac{1}{100b(2a+5)}\%$

B) $\dfrac{2a+5}{100b}\%$

C) $\dfrac{100b}{2a+5}\%$

D) $\left(\dfrac{100b}{2a+5}+1\right)\%$

Chapter 3

Passport to Advanced Math

Factoring

A. Factoring : method of writing numbers/polynomials as the product of their factors or divisors

Factor : a number/polynomial that divides another number/polynomial without remainders

B. Basic Laws

1) $ma+mb=m(a+b)$

2) $a^2\pm2ab+b^2=(a\pm b)^2$

3) $a^2-b^2=(a+b)(a-b)$

C. Technique

1) Factoring by Greatest Common Divisor :

$$15x^2+3x=(3x\times5x)+(3x\times1)$$
$$=3x(5x+1)$$

2) Factoring by Grouping :

$$(x^2-x-6)=x\times x+(2-3)x-2\times3$$
$$=(x-3)(x+2)$$

Exercise

Factor the following.

1. $9x^2+6x+3x^3$

2. $16x^2+32x+16$

3. $25x^2-4$

4. $21x^2-22x-8$

1.
$$ax^3+bx^2+cx+d=(5x+13)(3x^2+x-2)$$
If the above equation is true for all values of x, what is the value of b?

2. The equation $(3x-n)^2=9x^2-mx+16$ is true for all values of x. If $n>0$, what is the value of $m+n$?

A) 0

B) 4

C) 16

D) 28

3.

$$3\left(\frac{a}{b}+\frac{b}{a}\right)=k, \quad 4\left(\frac{a}{b}-\frac{b}{a}\right)=m$$

If $a\neq0, b\neq0$ in the equations above, which of the following is equal to k^2-m^2?

A) $\left(\frac{7a}{b}-\frac{b}{a}\right)\left(-\frac{a}{b}+\frac{7b}{a}\right)$

B) $\left(\frac{7a}{b}+\frac{b}{a}\right)\left(\frac{a}{b}+\frac{7b}{a}\right)$

C) $-\left(\frac{7a}{b}+\frac{b}{a}\right)\left(\frac{a}{b}+\frac{7b}{a}\right)$

D) $7\left(\frac{a}{b}-\frac{b}{a}\right)\left(-\frac{a}{b}+\frac{b}{a}\right)$

4. If $\dfrac{2x+4x+6x+8x+10x}{10x}=3$, what are all possible values of x?

A) All real numbers except 0

B) 0 only

C) 1 only

D) 3 only

Equations

A. Quadratic Equation : an equation whose highest variable degree is 2

1) Zero—Product Rule : if the product of two or more factors is zero, then at least one of the factors must be zero

   ex) $(x-2)(x+4)=0$ means $x=2$ or $x=-4$

2) Solving by Factoring : simplify the equation using factorization and apply the zero—product rule

3) Using the Quadratic Formula

   If $ax^2+bx+c=0$, then $x=\dfrac{-b\pm\sqrt{b^2-4ac}}{2a}$

   (i) Sum and Product of Two Roots

   If $ax^2+bx+c=0$ and the two roots of the equation are x_1 and x_2,

   then $x_1+x_2=-\dfrac{b}{a}$ and $x_1\times x_2=\dfrac{c}{a}$

   (ii) Discriminant: expression that appears under the radical sign in the quadratic formula (i.e.); reveals the nature and number of solutions of a quadratic equation

   If $b^2-4ac>0$, then the equation has two distinct real solutions

   If $b^2-4ac=0$, then the equation has one real solution

   If $b^2-4ac<0$, then the equation has no real solution, or two distinct complex solutions

B. Polynomial Equation : an equation whose highest variable degree is larger than 2

   ex) $3x^5+x^3+8x^2+1=0$ is a polynomial equation with a highest degree of 5

1) Dividing Polynomials by a Linear Expression : when dividing polynomials by a linear expression, there are two ways to find the remainder. One is to perform long division and the other is to use the function form of the polynomial. For example, to find the remainder when $2x^2-5x^2+x+9$ is divided by $x-3$:

   (i) Long Division

$$
\begin{array}{r}
3x\ +x+4 \\
x-3\ \overline{)\ 2x^3+5x^2+x+9} \\
\underline{2x^3-6x^2} \\
x^2\ +x \\
\underline{x^2-3x} \\
4x-\ 9 \\
\underline{4x-12} \\
21
\end{array}
$$

The remainder is 21.

(ii) Function form

    Let $P(x)=2x^3-5x^2+x+9$

    Since $x-3$ is the divisor, plug into $P(x)$ the solution to $x-3=0$ which is $x=3$.

    $P(x)=2(3)^3-5(3)^2+3+9=21$

    The remainder is 21.

As you can see, when trying to find the remainder of a polynomial divided by a linear expression, using the function form is the quickest method. On a related note, if a linear expression is a factor of a polynomial, let's say $Q(x)$, then the solution to $ax+b=0$, namely $x=-\dfrac{b}{a}$, will also be a solution to $Q(x)=0$.

In summary:

When polynomial $Q(x)$ is divided by $ax+b$, remainder is equal to $Q\left(-\dfrac{b}{a}\right)$.

If $ax+b$ is a factor of polynomial $Q(x)$, then $Q\left(-\dfrac{b}{a}\right)=0$.

C. Systems of Equations

In Chapter 1: Heart of Algebra, we learned to solve system of equations in which both equations were linear. In this section, we're going to look at systems of equations with two variables in which one equation is linear and the other is nonlinear.

D. Complex Equations in Context

Let's go back to Chapter 1: Heart of Algebra again. Remember those ridiculous questions that are filled with bunch of words but call themselves math questions? Well, here they are again except they're more complex than before. Ugh.

It's okay though. All the skills you learned until now are more than enough to get you through these tough−looking questions. In this section, you will be asked to manipulate equations to isolate a variable of interest, or use an equation regarding a context to figure out how one variable changes another variable, or even identify a new form of equation that will ultimately reveal new information about the context. Like before, these questions are designed to help you out in real life situations like figuring out how long it will take for your family to reach grandma's house during a holiday traffic jam. (Seems like never doesn't it?)

1. If $81-169x^2=0$, what are the possible values of x?

2. $2x^2-7x-10=0$

   What are the solutions to the equation above?

3. $(3x+4)(x+2)(x-5)=0$

   What are the zeroes of the given polynomial?

4. $k(x)=(3x-1)^5(x+7)^3(2x+5)^2(x-3)$

   The polynomial function k is defined above. How many distinct zeroes does k have?

5. What are the solution pairs $(x,\ y)$ to the system of equations shown below?

   $y=x^2-x-4$

   $y=-5x+8$

1. $(3x+7)(6-cx)=0$

   In the equation above, c is a constant. If the equation has the solutions $x=-\frac{7}{3}$ and $x=\frac{3}{2}$, what is the value of c?

2. $ty^2-6y=15$

   In the equation above, t is a constant. For what values of t does the equation have no real solution?

3. $x^3-9x^2-54x+216$

   The polynomial above has $(x-3)$ and $(x+6)$ as factors. What is the remaining factor?

4. $T(y)=(y-3)^3-7(y-3)^2+12(y-3)$

   The polynomial function T is defined above. What is the sum of the zeroes of T?

5. When $6x^3+x^2-29x+25$ is divided by $2x-3$, the result is $3x^2-5x-7+\frac{R}{2x-3}$, where R is a constant. What is the value of R?

6. What are the solution pairs (x, y) to the system of equations shown below?

$$y=-(x+5)^2+4$$

$$y=x+3$$

7. If (m, n) is a solution to the system of equations shown below and $m > 0$, what is the value of m?

$$7x^2=(y+8)(y-8)$$

$$2y=8x$$

8. Heather is selling homemade brownies for the school bake sale which happens every month. From her experience from last year, Heather predicts that for each $0.5 increase in brownie price, she will sell 10 less brownies. At the current price of $1.5 per brownie, an average of 80 brownies will be sold. Which of the following functions best models the amount of money that Heather expects to earn from the bake sale, y, based on an $$x$ increase in brownie price, assuming she only raises the price by units of $0.5?

A) $y=(1.5+x)\left(80-\dfrac{10x}{0.5}\right)$

B) $y=(1.5-x)\left(80+\dfrac{10x}{0.5}\right)$

C) $y=(1.5+x)\left(80-\dfrac{10}{x}\right)$

D) $y=(1.5+x)(80-10x)$

9. If an object of mass m is brought up to a height of h, the object's potential energy PE is given by the equation PE$=mgh$ where g is the gravitational constant. If the mass of the object is doubled and its height is halved, how does the potential energy change?

A) The potential energy is quartered (divided by 4).

B) The potential energy is halved.

C) The potential energy is unchanged.

D) The potential energy is doubled.

10. If an object starts moving in a straight line at an initial velocity v_0 and accelerates at a constant rate a for time t, the object's distance travelled s is given by the equation $s = v_0 t + \frac{1}{2} a t^2$. Which of the following correctly expresses a in terms of s, v_0, and t?

A) $a = \frac{2s}{t^2}$

B) $a = \frac{2v_0}{t}$

C) $a = \frac{2}{t^2}(s + v_0 t)$

D) $a = \frac{2}{t^2}(s - v_0 t)$

III Absolute Value

A. Absolute Value : the absolute value of x is written as $|x|$. It shows how far x is from 0 on the real number line

ex) If $|x|=3$, x is 3 units away from 0, without considering the direction, therefore $x=\pm 3$.

B. Absolute Value Equations : if $|expression\ with\ a\ variable|=a$, expression with a variable$=\pm a$

ex) If $|x-4|=8$, $x-4=\pm 8 \rightarrow x=12$, $x=-4$

C. Absolute Value Inequalities : the inequality $|x-a|<d$ means "the distance between x and a is less than d"

1) $|ax-b|<d \rightarrow -d<ax-b<d$

2) $|ax-b|>d \rightarrow ax-b<-d$ or $ax-b>d$

Exercise

Solve the following equation or inequality.

1. $|4x|=8$

2. $|3x+2|=11$

3. $|10x|<10$

4. $|5x-2|>8$

Functions

A. Terms

1) Function: a function relates an input variable, often expressed with x, to an output variable, often expressed with y

   ex) $y=f(x)$, where $f(x)=x^2+2$

2) Domain and Range

   (i) Domain : the set of all possible input values of a function

   (ii) Range : the set of all possible output values of a function

B. Types of Functions

1) Linear Function : expressed as $y=ax+b$, where a is the slope of the line, and b is the value of y where $x=0$ (y-intercept)

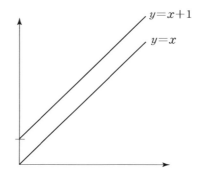

2) Absolute Value Function : expressed as $y=|x|$; has two parts : $y=x$ and $y=-x$

*y can only have positive values.

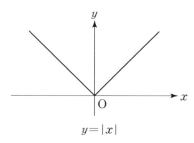

$y=|x|$

3) Quadratic Function : the graph of a quadratic function is a parabola whose axis of symmetry is parallel to the y-axis and goes through the vertex of the function. The graph is symmetric with respect to a line called the Axis of Symmetry

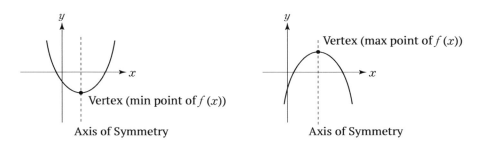

Vertex (max point of $f(x)$)

Vertex (min point of $f(x)$)

Axis of Symmetry   Axis of Symmetry

* A standard formula for a quadratic function is $f(x)=ax^2+bx+c$. If $a>0$, the graph is concave up ($\cup$-shaped), and y's minimum value is its vertex. If $a<0$, the graph is concave down ($\cap$-shaped), and y's maximum value is its vertex.

4) Exponential Function : denoted by $y=a^x$ (a is a constant, greater than 0)

Two cases exist : when a is $0<a<1$ and $a>1$

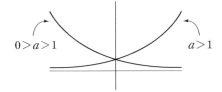

$0>a>1$ $a>1$

C. Transformations of Functions

1) Reflection

Action Taken in $y=f(x)$	Effect on Original Graph
Replace $f(x)=y$ with $-f(x)=y$	Reflects graph over the x axis
Replace x with $-x$	Reflects graph over the y axis

2) Shifting

Action taken in $y=f(x)$	Effect on Original Graph
Replace x with $x-(h)$	Shifts graph horizontally $|h|$ units If $h<0$, the shift is left If $h>0$, the shift is right
Add k to the function $y=f(x) \to y=f(x)+k$	Shifts graph vertically $|k|$ units If $k<0$, the shift is down If $k>0$, the shift is up

Exercise

1. Match each function with its graph.

(1) $y=ax+b$

(2) $y=|x|$

(3) $y=dx^2+ex+f$

(4) $y=g^x$

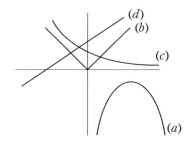

2. What happens to the graph of $f(x)$ if we replace x with $x-4$?

1. Function g is defined by $g(x)=\dfrac{3x-5}{2}$. For what value of x does $g(x)=5$?

2.

x	$f(x)$	$g(x)$
2	3	11
4	5	9
6	7	7
8	9	5
10	11	3

   Functions f and g are defined by the table above. What is the value of x that satisfies the equation $g(x)+5=f(x)-3$?

A) 4

B) 6

C) 8

D) 10

3.

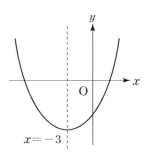

   The line of symmetry of the parabola shown on the graph above has the equation $x=-3$.
   The $x-$ intercepts of the parabola are $(-7,\ 0)$ and $(a,\ 0)$. What is the value of a?

A) 4

B) 5

C) 6

D) 1

4. The graph of the line $2x+5y-4=1$ on the xy-plane is reflected across the y-axis. What is the equation of the resulting reflection?

   A) $2x+5y=-5$
   B) $2x-5y=5$
   C) $-2x+5y=5$
   D) $-2x-5y=5$

5.

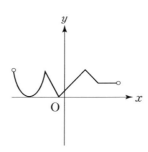

The complete graph of the function f is shown above. Function g is defined by $g(x)=-|f(x)|$. At how many points do the graphs of $f(x)$ and $g(x)$ intersect?

   A) None
   B) One
   C) Two
   D) Three

V   Powers & Roots

A. Power

1) Power : the value of a number or quantity raised to some exponent

2) Power Calculation Method

① $a^b \times a^c = a^{b+c}$

② $a^b \div a^c = a^{b-c}$

③ $(a^b)^c = a^{bc}$

④ $(a \cdot b)^c = a^c b^c$

⑤ $a^{-1} = \dfrac{1}{a}$

⑥ $a^0 = 1$

⑦ $a = (\sqrt[c]{a})^c$

B. Roots

1) Square Root : If A is multiplied by itself and results in B,

A is the Square Root of B

(± 3 is the square root of 9, ± 4 is the square root of 16, etc.)

* $\sqrt{\ }$ is used to represent square root of positive numbers. (ex. $\sqrt{9} = 3$, $\sqrt{16} = 4$)

2) Cube Root : If A is multiplied twice by itself and results in B,

A is the Cube Root of B

(-3 is the cube root of -27)

3) Operations of Square Roots

① $\sqrt{a} \times \sqrt{b} = \sqrt{ab}$

② $\dfrac{\sqrt{a}}{\sqrt{b}} = \sqrt{\dfrac{a}{b}}$

③ $(\sqrt{a})^2 = a$

④ $a\sqrt{b} + c\sqrt{b} = (a+c)\sqrt{b}$

⑤ $\dfrac{a}{\sqrt{b}} = \dfrac{a \times \sqrt{b}}{\sqrt{b} \times \sqrt{b}} = \dfrac{a}{b}\sqrt{b}$

Simplify the following.

1. $(5 \cdot 3)^2$

2. $(4^0)^3$

3. $\sqrt{25}$

4. $2\sqrt{3}+4\sqrt{3}$

5. $\dfrac{7}{\sqrt{8}}$

1. $(5 \times 10^k) + (3 \times 10^4) = (3.005 \times 10^4)$

    If the equation above is true, what is the value of k?

2. If $3^{t-2} = 27^2$, what is the value of t?

3. If $7x^3 = 56$, what is the value of $7x^6$?

4. If $m^2 = 3^{10}$, which of the following expressions represent 3^{11}?

    A) $6m^4$

    B) $9m^4$

    C) m^6

    D) $3m^2$

5. If a and x are real numbers for which $x^4 = -a$, which of the following could be true?

    I. $a > 0$

    II. $a = 0$

    III. $a < 0$

    A) I only

    B) III only

    C) I and II only

    D) II and III only

6. It is known that t is a positive integer. $5^t + 5^t$ is equal to which of the following?

A) $2 \cdot 5^t$

B) 5^{2t}

C) 10^t

D) 10^{2t}

7. If x is a non-negative integer, then all of the following can be unit digit of 7^x EXCEPT?

A) 9

B) 1

C) 3

D) 5

8. If $x = 3^3$, which of the following expressions is equal to 3^8?

A) $27x$

B) $243x$

C) x^3

D) $3x^2$

Chapter 4

Additional Topics

Triangles

A. Types

1) Isosceles Triangle : a triangle with two equal angles and two equal sides

2) Equilateral Triangle : a triangle with three equal sides (all three angles are $60°$)

3) Right Triangle : a triangle with one angle of $90°$

B. Pythagorean Theorem : $(opposite)^2 + (adjacent)^2 = (hypotenuse)^2$

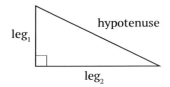

ex) $3^2 + 4^2 = 5^2$, $5^2 + 12^2 = 13^2$

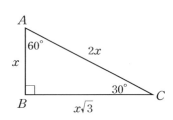 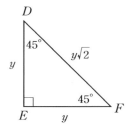

C. Special Triangles

1) $30° - 60° - 90°$
   $\overline{AB} : \overline{BC} : \overline{AC} = 1 : \sqrt{3} : 2$

2) $45° - 45° - 90°$
   $\overline{DE} : \overline{EF} : \overline{DF} = 1 : 1 : \sqrt{2}$

D. Triangle Inequality

Given that $a < b < c$,

1) One side of a triangle is longer than the difference between the other two sides.
$$a > c - b$$
$$b > c - a$$
$$c > b - a$$

2) One side of a triangle is shorter than the sum of both sides.
$$a + b > c$$
$$a + c > b$$
$$b + c > a$$

3) The longest side is at the opposite side of the greatest angle. The shortest side is at the opposite side of the smallest angle.

E. Similar Triangles

1) <u>Characteristics</u>
   (i) Three equal angles
   (ii) Same ratio of corresponding sides

2) <u>Similarity Rules</u> : at least one of the following must be satisfied for the triangles to be similar
   (i) Angle Angle : two pairs of the angles of the triangles are the same
   (ii) Side Angle Side : the ratio between one side of a triangle and the corresponding side of another triangle is equal to the ratio between another side of the first triangle and the corresponding side of the second triangle. The angle made between both these sides in both triangles must be the same
   (iii) Side Side Side : the ratio between all three corresponding sides of two triangles are equal

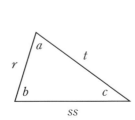 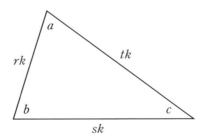

1. If △ABC is an equilateral triangle, find the ratio $x : y : z$.

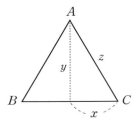

2. If □ABCD is a square, find the ratio $x : y : z$.

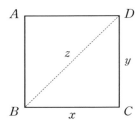

3. Find the length of $\overline{DF}$.

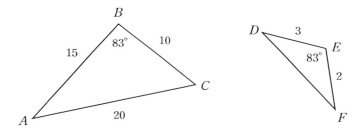

4. What are the values of x and y?

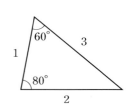
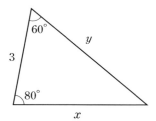

1. In the figure below, $z > 95$ and $x = y + 15$. If y is an integer, what is the greatest possible value of y?

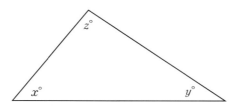

A) 70
B) 68
C) 35
D) 34

2. In the figure below, $\overline{CP} = \sqrt{3}$. What is the length of AB?

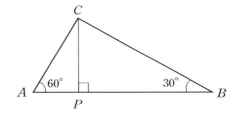

3. In the figure below, points O, A, B, C are equally spaced on line l and points O, P, Q, R are equally spaced on line m. If $\overline{OC} = 12$, $\overline{OR} = 15$, and $\overline{AP} = 3$, what is the perimeter of the quadrilateral BCRQ?

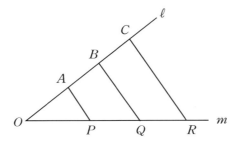

A) 23
B) 24
C) 26
D) 27

4. In the figure below, all of the following are isosceles triangles EXCEPT

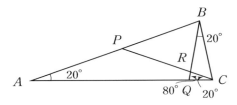

A) △APC
B) △CRQ
C) △ABC
D) △BPC

5. If the perimeter of the triangle below is 30, what is the length of the longest side?

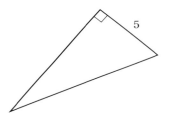

A) 12
B) $5\sqrt{3}$
C) 11
D) 13

6. In the figure below, $\triangle PQR$ is an isosceles triangle and $\triangle XYZ$ is an equilateral triangle. If $\angle PQR$ is 30 degrees and $\angle QXZ$ is 60 degrees, what is the degree measure of $\angle XYP$?

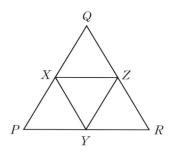

A) 30

B) 35

C) 45

D) 50

Polygons

Angles

1) <u>Sum of the Interior Angles</u> : $(n-2) \times 180$ where n is the number of sides.

2) <u>Sum of the Exterior Angles</u> : $360°$

3) <u>Regular Polygon</u> (regular $n-$polygon)

Each exterior angle $= \dfrac{360°}{n}$

Each interior angle $= 180° - \dfrac{360°}{n}$

A. Terms

1) <u>Acute</u> : any angles greater than $0°$ and smaller than $90°$

2) <u>Obtuse</u> : any angle greater than $90°$ and smaller than $180°$

3) <u>Right</u> : an angle of $90°$

4) <u>Adjacent Angles</u> : angles placed next to each other that share a common vertex/side, but do not overlap

B. Intersecting Lines

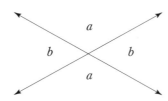

1) Opposite angles are equal in measure

2) The sum of Adjacent Angles is $180°$

C. Parallel Lines

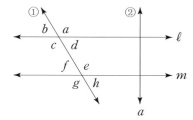

1) $\angle a = \angle c = \angle e = \angle g$
   $\angle b = \angle d = \angle f = \angle h$

2) When line n passes through either one of two parallel lines ℓ and m perpendicularly, then line n passes through the other line perpendicularly as well. (Since n and ℓ are vertical to each other, m and n are vertical as well.)

D. Exterior Angles

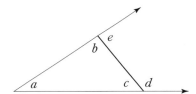

1) $\angle a + \angle b = 180 - \angle c = \angle d$

2) $\angle a + \angle c = 180 - \angle b = \angle e$

Special Types of Polygons

A. Parallelogram : a quadrilateral whose opposite sides are parallel

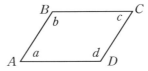

    * Properties : (i) AB=CD, BC=AD
                  (ii) $a=c$, $b=d$
                  (iii) $a+b=b+c=c+d=d+a$
                  (iv) each diagonal cuts the other diagonal in half

B. Rectangle : quadrilateral with four right angles

    * Properties : (i) a rectangle is a type of parallelogram, so it has the properties of a parallelogram
                  (ii) its two diagonals have the same length

C. Rhombus : a parallelogram with four equal sides

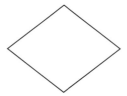

    *Properties : (i) has all the properties of a parallelogram
                 (ii) its two diagonals are perpendicular to each other

D. Square : a parallelogram with four equal sides and four right angles

* Properties : (i) has all the properties of a parallelogram

(ii) has all the properties of a rectangle and a rhombus

Exercise

1. Find the values of $a,b,c,d,$ and e if $\ell \parallel m$.

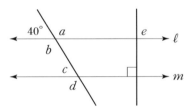

Questions 2 and 3 refer to the following regular polygon.

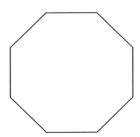

2. What is the sum of the interior angles of the given polygon?

3. What is the value of each exterior angle of the given polygon?

4. If □ABCD is a parallelogram, what is the value of $a+b$?

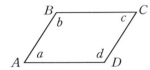

5. If □ABCD is a rhombus, what is the value of a?

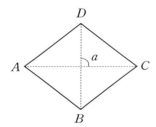

6. If □ABCD is a rectangle and the length of $\overline{AC}$ is 6, what is the length of $\overline{DE}$?

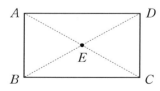

1. In the figure below, point O is the intersection of the line segments $\overline{AC}$ and $\overline{BE}$. If $\overline{OD}$ bisects $\angle EOC$ and $x=140$, what is the value of y?

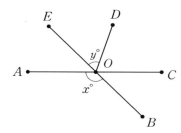

2. In the figure below, ℓ and m are parallel and $2b=e$. Which of the following is equal to c?

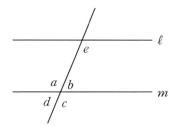

A) $a+b$
B) $a-b$
C) $3b-d$
D) $2b+d$

3. In the figure below, if $z=70$, what is the value of $3y-3x$?

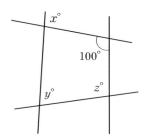

A) 0
B) 10
C) 15
D) 30

4. In the hexagon below, what is the sum of x, y, z, and w?

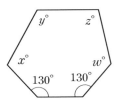

5. In the figure below, if □ABCD is a trapezoid and $h=2\sqrt{3}$, what is the length of $\overline{AB}$?

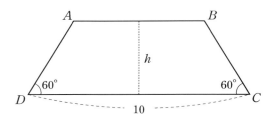

6. A large solid cube is made using identical small white cubes. All six faces of the large cube are painted yellow. If exactly 125 of the small cubes making up the large cube have no yellow paint on them, how many small cubes were used to make the large cube?

Perimeter and Area

A. Rectangle

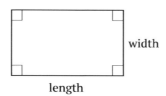

1) <u>Perimeter</u>$=2\times($length$+$width$)$

2) <u>Area</u>$=$length$\times$width

B. Parallelogram

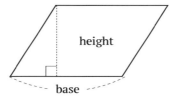

1) <u>Area</u>$=$base$\times$height

C. Rhombus

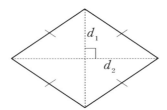

1) <u>Area</u>$=\dfrac{(\text{diagonal}_1\times\text{diagonal}_2)}{2}$

D. Square

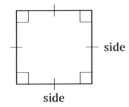

1) <u>Area</u> $= \text{side} \times \text{side} = \dfrac{(\text{diagonal})^2}{2}$

E. Triangle

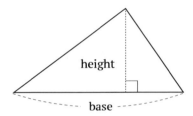

1) <u>Area</u> $= \dfrac{1}{2}(\text{height} \times \text{base})$

F. Trapezoid

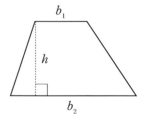

1) <u>Area</u> $= \text{height} \times \dfrac{b_1 + b_2}{2}$

1. If □ABCD is a rhombus, what is the area of □ABCD?

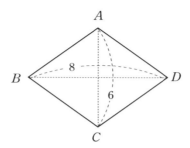

2. If □ABCD is a trapezoid, what is the area of □ABCD?

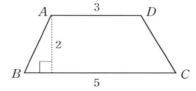

1. The area of the shaded region in the rectangle □ABCD is 160. What is the perimeter of △EFG?

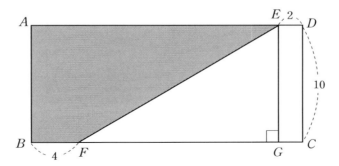

2. In the figure below, the base of the four regular hexagons lie alongside each other on a straight line. What is the distance between point A and point B?

A) 12

B) 21

C) 18

D) $10\sqrt{3}$

3. A piece of land is surrounded by a rectangular fence. If the length of the rectangle created by the fence is 60 m and the area of the land is 300 m^2, what is the total perimeter of the fence?

4. In the figure below, squares A, B, and C are constructed on each side of the right triangle. If the area of A and B are 25 and 144 each, what is the perimeter of the right triangle?

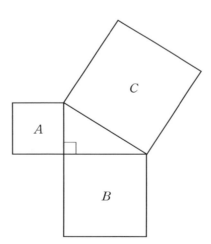

A) 17

B) 25

C) 30

D) 60

5. In the cone below, the radius of the circular base is 3 inches and the length of AB is 12 inches. If a piece of string is looped around the side of the cone as shown above from point B to point M, where M is the midpoint of AB, what is the length of the string?

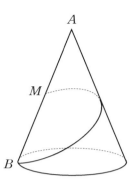

A) $3\sqrt{5}$

B) $6\sqrt{5}$

C) 18

D) 6π

Circles

A. Circles : the locus of all points that are at an equal distance (Radius) from the center

1) <u>Radius</u> : the distance from the center of a circle to its edge (or that line segment itself)

2) <u>Chord</u> : a line segment on the interior of a circle with both its endpoints lying on its edges

3) <u>Diameter</u> : a Chord that passes through the center of a circle

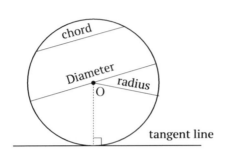 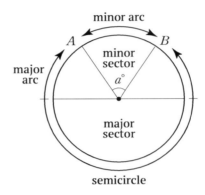

4) <u>Arc</u> : a part of the Circumference of a circle

5) <u>Sector</u> : a pie—shaped part of a circle bounded by an Arc and two Radii

6) <u>Tangent Line</u> : when a line is Tangent to a circle, that line touches the circle at exactly one point
(A line segment that connects the center of a circle and a tangential point is always perpendicular to a Tangent Line)

B. Circumference and Area

1) Circumference : $2\pi \times$ radius

2) Arc Length : $2\pi \times$ radius $\times \dfrac{\text{degree of arc}}{360}$

3) Area of a Circle : $\pi \times (\text{radius})^2$

4) Area of a Sector : $\pi \times (\text{radius})^2 \times \dfrac{\text{degree of arc}}{360}$

C. Circles with Polygons

1) <u>Inscribed Rectangles</u> : the diagonal of a rectangle becomes the diameter of a circle

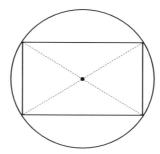

2) <u>Inscribed Circles</u> : the length of one side of a square = the diameter of a circle

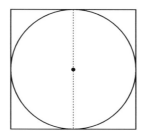

3) <u>Shaded Regions</u> : subtract the area of an unshaded part from the whole

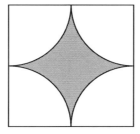

1. If the radius of the circle is 3, what is the area of the minor sector AOC? What is the length of the minor arc $\overgroup{AC}$?

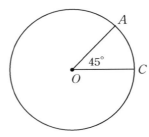

2. If the radius of the circle is 4, what is the length of the diagonal of the rectangle?

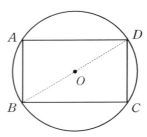

3. If □ABCD is a square and the length of its side is 10, what is the radius of the circle?

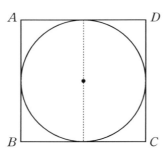

4. If □ABCD is a square whose side is 10, and a, b, c, d are midpoints of $\overline{AB}$, $\overline{BC}$, $\overline{CD}$, $\overline{AD}$, respectively, what is the area of the shaded region?

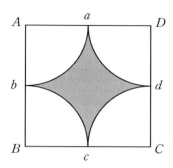

1. In the circle below, O is the center of the circle of radius 6. If M is the midpoint of $\overline{XY}$ and $\angle XOY = 120°$, what is the area of $\triangle MOX$?

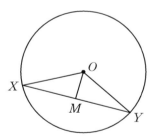

A) $\dfrac{9\sqrt{3}}{2}$

B) $9\sqrt{3}$

C) 9π

D) $\dfrac{9\pi}{2}$

2. Points $X, Y, Z,$ and W are the centers of identical circles with radii of r. What is the perimeter of the rectangle ▭ABCD in terms of r?

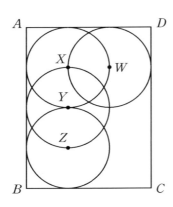

3. In the circle below, $\overline{AB}$, $\overline{CD}$, and $\overline{EF}$ are diameters. If the area of the shaded sector is $\frac{1}{10}$ of the area of the circle, what is the value of x?

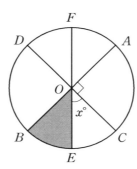

4. In the figure below, □ABCD is a square with a side length of 8. Semicircles are constructed by using the sides of the square as their diameters. If M and N are midpoints of $\overline{BC}$ and $\overline{AD}$, what is the total length of the darkened outline of the figure?

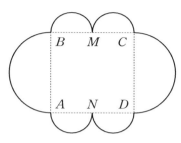

A) 12π

B) 14π

C) 16π

D) 18π

5. In the figure below, $\overarc{XY}$ is the arc of a circle with center O. If the length of arc $\overarc{XY}$ is 10π, what is the area of sector XOY?

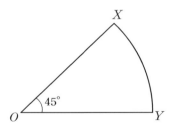

A) 144π

B) 169π

C) 196π

D) 200π

6. In the figure below, six small circles of equal radius are inside a large circle so that they are tangent to the large circle and three other small circles. A seventh circle with the same radius is tangent to each of the six small circles. If O is the center of the large circle, the area of the shaded region is how many times the area of one of the small circles?

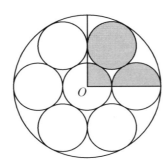

7. In the figure below, a square with side length 16 is divided into 16 squares. If each dot represents the center of the four corner squares, what is the area of the circle (not shown) that passes through the four dots?

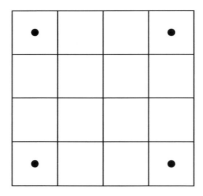

A) $36\sqrt{2}\,\pi$

B) 36π

C) 72π

D) $72\sqrt{2}\,\pi$

V

Solids

A. Rectangular Solid

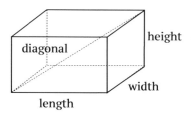

1) <u>Volume</u> = length × width × height

2) <u>Surface Area</u> = 2 × [(length × width) + (height × width) + (height × length)]

3) <u>Length of a Diagonal</u> = $\sqrt{(\text{length})^2 + (\text{width})^2 + (\text{height})^2}$

B. Cube

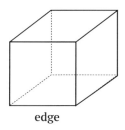

edge

1) <u>Volume</u> = (edge)^3

2) <u>Surface Area</u> = 6 × (edge)^2

C. Cylinder

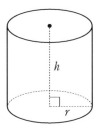

1) <u>Volume</u> = π × (radius)^2 × height

2) <u>Surface Area</u> = 2 × [π × (radius)^2] + [height × (2 × π × radius)]

D. Cone

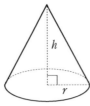

1) <u>Volume</u> $= \dfrac{1}{3} \times [\pi \times (\text{radius})^2 \times \text{height}]$

◢ Exercise

1. Find the length of the diagonal.

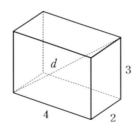

2. Find the volume and surface area of the cube.

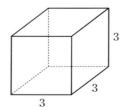

3. Find the volume and surface area of the cylinder.

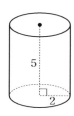

4. Find the volume of the cone.

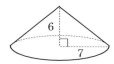

1. In the cube below, X and Y are the midpoints of two of the edges. If the length of each edge is 6, what is the length of the line segment $\overline{XY}$?

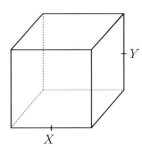

2. What is the surface area of a cube if its volume is 216 cubic inches?

VI

Coordinate Geometry

A. Basic Formulas

1) <u>Distance</u> : the Distance between (x_1, y_1) and (x_2, y_2) is $\sqrt{(x_2-x_1)^2+(y_2-y_1)^2}$

2) <u>Midpoint</u> : the Midpoint of a line that has (x_1, y_1) and (x_2, y_2) as endpoints is $\left(\dfrac{x_1+x_2}{2}, \dfrac{y_1+y_2}{2}\right)$

B. Finding the Slope of a Line

1) <u>Slope</u> : the change in y for a unit change in x along the line

2) <u>Slope Formula</u> : $\dfrac{y_2-y_1}{x_2-x_1}$ for the Slope of a line that passes through (x_1, y_1) and (x_2, y_2)

3) <u>Properties</u>

(i) Horizontal Line : Slope is zero

(ii) Vertical Line : Slope is not defined

(iii) "two different lines never intersect" = "the lines are parallel" = "they have the same slope and different y-intercepts"

(iv) Perpendicular Lines = product of their Slopes is -1

4) <u>Equation of a Line</u> : $y=mx+b$

(i) m is the slope, b is the y-intercept (value of y when $x=0$)

＊If you know the two points that a line passes through, or if you know one point and its slope, you can get the equation.

1. Find the distance between $(2, -1)$ and $(-3, 4)$.

2. If $A = (3, 2)$ and $B = (1, 0)$, find the midpoint of $\overline{AB}$.

3. Find the slope of a line that passes through $(3, 2)$ and $(5, 4)$.

4. Find the equation of a line that passes through $(4, 2)$ and $(10, 5)$.

SAT Questions

1. If the points $A(2, 6)$ and $B(-1, 6)$ and $C(2, 2)$ are vertices of a triangle, what is the area of the triangle?

2. In the figure below, OABC, ADEF, and DGHI are squares with sides of length 9, 3, and 6, respectively. What is the difference between the slopes of line segments $\overline{OI}$ and $\overline{OH}$?

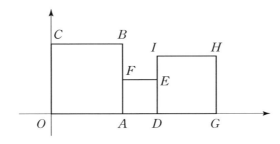

3. On the linear scales below, 20 and 120 on the X-scale corresponds to 80 and 140, respectively, on the Y-scale. Which of the following linear equations can be used to convert an X-scale value to a Y-scale value?

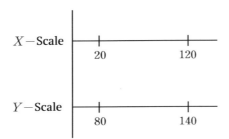

A) $Y=X+20$
B) $Y=1.2X+12$
C) $Y=0.6X+68$
D) $Y=X+60$

VII

Circle Equation

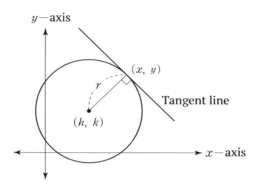

A. Equation

1) On a coordinate plane, the equation of a circle is :

$$(x-h)^2+(y-k)^2=r^2$$

2) Sometimes it is necessary to complete the square of a given expression in order to identify the equation of the circle.

$$\text{ex) } x^2+4x+y^2-6y-12=0$$
$$(x^2+4x)+(y^2-6y)-12=0$$
$$(x^2+4x+4)+(y^2-6y+9)-12-4-9=0$$
$$(x+2)^2+(y-3)^2-25=0$$
$$(x+2)^2+(y-3)^2=5^2$$

B. Intersection

1) If a line with known equation intersects a circle at any point, simply solve for x and y to identify the points of intersections.

C. Tangent

1) Perpendicular : a line segment drawn from the center of a circle to the point at which the tangent meets the circumference is Perpendicular to the tangent

2) Slopes : when two lines are Perpendicular to each other, the product of their Slopes is -1

1. What is the equation of a circle with center $(-2,\ 3)$ and radius 6?

2. A circle with its center at the origin has point A $(3,\ 4)$ on its circumference. What is the radius of the circle?

1. The slope of line l is tangent to a circle at point $(1,\ 5)$. Given that the slope of the line is $\frac{2}{5}$ and that the circle is centered at $(s,\ 2)$, find the value of s.

2. A circle with a known radius of 5 has a circumference that passes through the points $(1,-1)$. The y-coordinate of the center of the circle is 3. Given that the x-coordinate is positive, find the value of the center's x-coordinate.

3. The center of circle A lies on the x-axis where $x=-1$. A point on the circumference also lies on the x-axis where $x=3$. Given that a line is tangent to the circle at point $(1,\ p)$, at which point does the tangent intersect the x-axis?

A) $(4,\ 0)$

B) $\left(\dfrac{17}{4},\ 0\right)$

C) $(7,\ 0)$

D) $\left(\dfrac{19}{3},\ 0\right)$

4. A circle is known to have diameter $\overline{AB}$ with $A(7,-2)$ and $B(-1,\ 10)$ being points on the circumference. Rachel wants to construct an equation based on the coordinates $(a,\ b)$ also found on the circumference. Which of the following options shows the correct equation?

A) $(a-4)^2+(b-6)^2=208$

B) $(a-4)^2+(b+6)^2=104$

C) $(a-3)^2-(b-4)^2=104$

D) $(a-3)^2+(b-4)^2=52$

Trigonometry

A. Radians

1) The radian (θ) is a different way to measure the angle other than degrees $(^\circ)$.

2) <u>Formulas</u> : Arc length $(l) = r\theta$

$$\text{Area of sector} = \frac{1}{2}r^2\theta = \frac{1}{2}rl$$

3) <u>Conversion</u> : $180^\circ = \pi$ rad

$$360^\circ = 2\pi \text{ rad}$$

$$1 \text{ rad} = \frac{180^\circ}{\pi}$$

ex) In rad, $72^\circ = \dfrac{72^\circ}{180} \times \pi$ rad

$$= 1.257 \text{ rad}$$

B. Trigonometry

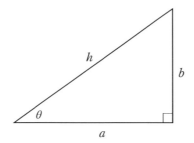

1) <u>Formulas</u> :

$$\sin \theta = \frac{b}{h}$$

$$\cos \theta = \frac{a}{h}$$

$$\tan \theta = \frac{b}{a}$$

2) <u>Special Angles</u> :

θ	Sine	Cosine	Tangent
0°	0	1	0
30°	$\dfrac{1}{2}$	$\dfrac{\sqrt{3}}{2}$	$\dfrac{1}{\sqrt{3}}$
45°	$\dfrac{1}{\sqrt{2}}$	$\dfrac{1}{\sqrt{2}}$	1
60°	$\dfrac{\sqrt{3}}{2}$	$\dfrac{1}{2}$	$\sqrt{3}$
90°	1	0	Not defined

3) <u>Other Angles</u>

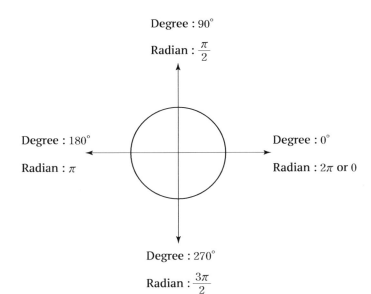

0° to 90° : all is positive

90° to 180° : sin x is positive, cos x and tan x are negative

180° to 270° : tan x is positive, sin x and cos x are negative

270° to 360° : cos x is positive, sin x and tan x are negative

4) Graphs

(ⅰ) Sine Graph ($y=\sin x$)

    Amplitude : 1

    Period : 2π

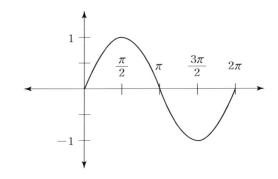

(ⅱ) Cosine Graph ($y=\cos x$)

    Amplitude : 1

    Period : 2π

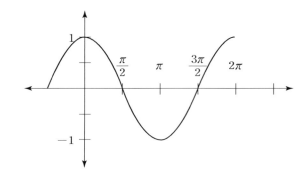

(ⅲ) Tangent Graph ($y=\tan x$)

    Amplitude : $-\infty$ to ∞

    Period : π

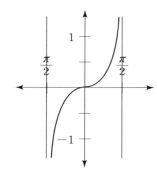

Exercise

1. What is $200°$ in radians?

2. In which quadrant are both $\cos x$ and $\sin x$ negative?

3. What is the period of $y = \sin x$?

SAT Questions

1. In a right triangle, an angle measures x, where $\sin x = \dfrac{5}{13}$. What is $\cos (90° - x)$?

2. An isosceles right triangle ABC has a hypotenuse of 5 with $\angle B = 90°$. If the area of the right triangle was doubled, what is the value of $\tan A$?

Complex Numbers

A. Complex Numbers : numbers that can be expressed in the form of $a+bi$, where a and b are Real Numbers, and i is the Imaginary Unit

1) Imaginary Unit i : number that satisfies $i^2=-1$

2) For all $a>0$, $\sqrt{-a}=\sqrt{a}\,i$
   Therefore, the square roots of $-a$ are $\pm\sqrt{-a}=\pm\sqrt{a}\,i$

3) Equality of Complex Numbers
   $a+bi=0 \iff a=0,\ b=0$
   $a+bi=c+di \iff a=c,\ b=d$ $(a, b, c,$ and d are Real Numbers$)$

4) Complex Number Operations

   If $a,\ b,\ c,$ and d are Real Numbers,

   A. If $a<0,\ b<0$, then $\sqrt{a}\cdot\sqrt{b}=-\sqrt{ab}$

   B. If $a>0,\ b<0$, then $\dfrac{\sqrt{a}}{\sqrt{b}}=-\sqrt{\dfrac{a}{b}}\,i$

   C. $(a+bi)+(c+di)=(a+c)+(b+d)i$

   D. $(a+bi)-(c+di)=(a-c)+(b-d)i$

   E. $(a+bi)(c+di)=(ac-bd)+(ad+bc)i$

   F. $\dfrac{a+bi}{c+di}=\dfrac{a+bi}{c+di}\cdot\dfrac{c-di}{c-di}=\dfrac{ac+bd}{c^2+d^2}+\dfrac{bc-ad}{c^2+d^2}\,i\ \ (c+di\neq0)$

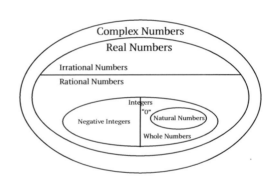

SAT Questions

1. What's the value of $(4+i)-(3-8i)$? $(i^2=-1)$

2. What's the value of $3+7i-(2-3i)\times i$? $(i^2=-1)$

3. What is the value of $(1+i)(2-i)(1+2i)$? $(i^2=-1)$

Extra Topics

A. Rewriting Expressions

There are several SAT questions that ask you to simply rewrite an existing expression. Skills involved in solving these problems include but are not limited to: expansion, grouping by common factors, equalizing denominators. The patterns involved with them aren't very varied so the more you solve them, the more you will get used to them.

B. Designing & Interpreting Experiments

1) Types of Studies
   (i) Observational Study: the investigator observes subjects and measures the possible changes in the variables without assigning treatments to the subjects

   (ii) Controlled Experiment: the investigator separates subjects into a control group that does not receive any treatment and an experimental group that receives a treatment and observes and measures the possible changes in the variables

   (iii) Sample Survey: the investigator uses methods such as a questionnaire or an interview to obtain data from a sample in order to estimate a population parameter of interest

2) Interpreting Data
   Back in Chapter 2, you learned basic skills involved with the analysis of tables and graphs. Those examples mostly asked you to estimate or calculate some characteristics of the sample or the population. However, another focus of gathering data from surveys and experiments is to investigate relationships between variables. Researchers use the data to draw conclusions about cause and effect. The credibility of the conclusion depends mainly on two factors: random sampling and random assignment.

   (i) Random Sampling: a group of subjects (a sample) is chosen randomly from a larger group (a population). Each individual has the same probability of being selected for the sample. Random sampling ensures that the result from the experiment can be appropriately generalized to the entire population.

   (ii) Random Assignment: individuals in the sample are randomly assigned to different treatments. Each treatment has the same probability of being assigned to an individual. Random assignment ensures that the treatment groups are relatively equivalent at the beginning of the experiment apart from the treatment they receive. Thus, it can be appropriate to draw conclusions about the cause and effect between the variables.

The following table summarizes the results of random sampling and assignment:

	Random Sampling	Non-random Sampling
Random Assignment	Result can be appropriately generalized to the population. Conclusion about cause and effect can be appropriately drawn.	Result cannot be appropriately generalized to the population. Conclusion about cause and effect can be appropriately drawn.
Non-random Assignment	Result can be appropriately generalized to the population. Conclusion about cause and effect cannot be appropriately drawn.	Result cannot be appropriately generalized to the population. Conclusion about cause and effect cannot be appropriately drawn.

SAT Questions

1. $(4mn^3)^2-(x-7)+\sqrt{49l^6}$

   Which of the following is equivalent to the expression above?

   A) $-(x-7)+(7l^3)+(4mn^6)$

   B) $-(x-7)+(7l^3)+(16m^2n^6)$

   C) $(16m^2n^6)-(7-x)+(7l^3)$

   D) $(7l^6)-(x-7)+(16m^2n^6)$

2. $\dfrac{3x}{5x+15}+\dfrac{x+4}{x^2+3x}$

   Which expression is equivalent to the above sum?

   A) $\dfrac{3x^2+5x+20}{5x^2+15x}$

   B) $\dfrac{3x^2+12x}{5x^3+30x^2+45x}$

   C) $\dfrac{4x+4}{x^2+8x+15}$

   D) $\dfrac{4x+4}{x+3}$

3. $\dfrac{45p^2q^4r^5+15p^5q^3r^6-25p^3q^5r^2}{5p^2q^3r^4}$

Which expressions is equivalent to the above for all $p>1$, $q>1$, and $r>1$?

A) $9pqr^3+3pr^2-5q$

B) $9q+3r^4-5p$

C) $\dfrac{9qr+3p^2r-5pq}{r^2}$

D) $\dfrac{9qr^3+3p^3r^4-5pq^2}{r^2}$

4. The expression $(x^2+t^2)^2$ can be written as $(1+a-b)x^4+2bx^2+ab$ where t, a, and b are constants. What is one possible value of a?

A) 1

B) t

C) t^2

D) t^4

5. The school swimming pool allows registered members to enter the pool one hour before opening time. The coach for the school swimming team found out that more than three quarters of the team was made up of students who were registered members of the swimming pool. Which of the following is an appropriate conclusion?

A) Registered members of the swimming pool perform better at athletics than non−registered students.

B) Registered members of the swimming pool are better at swimming than non−registered students.

C) Registering for the swimming pool was the cause of admission into the school swimming team.

D) No conclusion about cause and effect can be made regarding students in the school swimming team who registered for the swimming pool and their performance in the team.

6. A scientist wants to investigate the relationship between level of adrenaline in a mouse's body and the mouse's reaction time by randomly injecting small amount of adrenaline into some mouse and water into others and then observing how fast different treatment groups react to the sound of a cat's meow from behind them. Which of the following is the best description of the research design for this study?

A) Observational study
B) Sample survey
C) Controlled experiment
D) None of the above

7. A researcher conducted a survey to determine the average amount of time high school students in a certain large city spend playing computer games. The researcher asked 300 students who attended a local high school for boys, and 33 students refused to respond. Which of the following factors makes it least likely that a reliable conclusion can be drawn about the average time spent on computer games for all high school students in the city?

A) Sample size
B) Population size
C) The number of people who refused to respond
D) Where the survey was given

Question Answers & Explanations

1-1   Linear Equations/Inequalities

Example Questions 1

1. Linear Equations/Inequalities

$4a+8=24$

$4a=24-8=16$

$a=4$

$\therefore\ 8a-9=32-9=23$

Therefore, the answer is (C).

2. Linear Equations/Inequalities

$\dfrac{3}{a}=\dfrac{6}{a+15}$

$3(a+15)=6a$

$3a+45=6a$

$3a=45$

$\therefore\ a=15$

Therefore, $\dfrac{a}{3}=\dfrac{15}{3}=5$

Therefore, the answer is (B).

3. Linear Equations/Inequalities

$\left(\dfrac{5}{6}a-\dfrac{1}{6}a=\dfrac{1}{2}+\dfrac{1}{6}\right)\times 6$

$5a-a=3+1$

$4a=4$

$\therefore\ a=1$

Therefore, the answer is 1.

Example Questions 2

1. Linear Equations/Inequalities

$4x-2\geq 6\ \rightarrow\ ①$

$①\div 2:$

$2x-1\geq 3$

$\therefore\ 2x+3\geq 7$

Therefore, the answer is 7.

2. Linear Equations/Inequalities

$2x+7+5(x-2)\geq 6x+7$

$2x+7+5x-10\geq 6x+7$

$7x-3\geq 6x+7$

$\therefore\ x\geq 10$

Therefore, the answer is (C).

3. Linear Equations/Inequalities

$3a-5\leq 2$

$3a\leq 7$

$6a\leq 14$

$\therefore\ 6a-9\leq 5$

Therefore, the answer is (B).

SAT Questions

1. Linear Equations/Inequalities

$\dfrac{2x-y}{2y}=\dfrac{2}{5}$

$5(2x-y)=4y$

$10x-5y=4y$

$10x=9y$

$\therefore\ \dfrac{x}{y}=\dfrac{9}{10}$

Therefore, the answer is (B).

2. Linear Equations/Inequalities

$\dfrac{a+2}{a-2}=5$

$a+2=5(a-2)$

$a+2=5a-10$

$4a=12$

$\therefore\ a=3$

Therefore the answer is (A).

3. Linear Equations/Inequalities

$$\frac{7}{r} = \frac{3}{r+12}$$

$$7(r+12) = 3r$$

$$7r + 84 = 3r$$

$$4r = -84$$

$$\therefore \ r = -21$$

$$\frac{r}{7} = -3$$

Therefore, the answer is (A).

4. Linear Equations/Inequalities

$$6x - 12 \geq 9$$

$$6x \geq 21$$

$$2x \geq 7$$

$$\therefore \ 2x - 9 \geq -2$$

Therefore, the answer is (B).

5. Linear Equations/Inequalities

$$6y - (14 - 2y) = a(4y - 7)$$

$$6y - 14 + 2y = 4ay - 7a$$

$$(8 - 4a)y = 14 - 7a$$

For the equation to have infinitely many solutions,
$8 - 4a$ and $14 - 7a$ must be 0.
Both $8 - 4a$ and $14 - 7a$ is 0 when $a = 2$.
Therefore, the answer is (C)

6. Linear Equations/Inequalities

$$2(x-1) + 2x = \frac{1}{4}(16x - 20) + 3$$

$$2x - 2 + 2x = 4x - 5 + 3$$

$$4x - 2 = 4x - 2$$

$$\therefore \ x = x$$

which means there are infinitely many values for this equation.

Therefore, the answer is (D).

7. Linear Equations/Inequalities

$$\frac{n-5}{n+5} = 6$$

$$n - 5 = 6(n+5)$$

$$n - 5 = 6n + 30$$

$$5n = -35$$

$$\therefore \ n = -7$$

Therefore, the answer is (A).

8. Linear Equations/Inequalities

$$6x + 7 \geq 3(ax + 2)$$

$$6x + 7 \geq 3ax + 6$$

$$(6 - 3a)x \geq -1$$

In order for there to be infinitely many solutions to the inequality above,

$$6 - 3a = 0$$

$$\therefore \ a = 2$$

Therefore, the answer is (C).

9. Linear Equations/Inequalities

$$\frac{1}{3}(3y) + 4(y - 2) = 5(y - 2) + 7$$

$$y + 4y - 8 = 5y - 10 + 7$$

$$5y - 8 = 5y - 3$$

$$5y - 5y = 5$$

$$\therefore \ 0 \times y = 5$$

Therefore, there is no value of y where this equation is true.

Therefore, the answer is (C).

10. Linear Equations/Inequalities

$$2(y + 1) = \frac{x}{3} + 2$$

$$2y + 2 = \frac{x}{3} + 2$$

$$2y = \frac{x}{3}$$

$$\therefore \ \frac{x}{y} = 6$$

Therefore, the answer is (C).

11. Linear Equations/Inequalities

$$\frac{2(r+2)-7}{4}=\frac{14-(r+2)}{5}$$

$$\frac{2r+4-7}{4}=\frac{14-r-2}{5}$$

$$\frac{2r-3}{4}=\frac{12-r}{5}$$

$$5(2r-3)=4(12-r)$$

$$10r-15=48-4r$$

$$14r=63$$

$$\therefore\ r=\frac{9}{2}\,(=4.5)$$

Therefore, the answer is (B).

12. Linear Equations/Inequalities

$$\frac{2x+7}{3}=\frac{3x+9}{4}$$

$$4(2x+7)=3(3x+9)$$

$$8x+28=9x+27$$

$$\therefore\ x=1$$

Therefore, the answer is (C).

13. Linear Equations/Inequalities

In the given equation $x=ay$, $x=56$ when $y=4$.

$$56=4a$$

$$a=14$$

$$\therefore\ x=14y$$

Therefore, when $y=3$,

$$x=14\times3=42$$

Therefore, the answer is (D).

14. Linear Equations/Inequalities

$$3x+11-9(x+3)=5x-27$$

$$3x+11-9x-27=5x-27$$

$$-6x+11=5x$$

$$11x=11$$

$$\therefore\ x=1$$

Therefore, the answer is (A).

15. Linear Equations/Inequalities

$$\frac{3a+2}{5}=\frac{2a-8}{4}$$

$$4(3a+2)=5(2a-8)$$

$$12a+8=10a-40$$

$$2a=-48$$

$$\therefore\ a=-24$$

Therefore, the answer is (B).

16. Linear Equations/Inequalities

$$\frac{q}{3p}=7$$

$$q=21p$$

$$\therefore\ \frac{2q}{3p}=\frac{2(21p)}{3p}=14$$

Therefore, the answer is (C).

17. Linear Equations/Inequalities

$$\frac{2k}{3r}=5$$

$$2k=15r$$

$$\therefore\ \frac{15r}{2k}=\frac{15r}{15r}=1$$

Therefore, the answer is (B).

18. Linear Equations/Inequalities

$$9x-4\leq2x+11$$

$$7x\leq15$$

$$x\leq\frac{15}{7}\approx2.14$$

Therefore, the answer is (B).

1-2　System of Equations/Inequalities

Example Questions 1

1. System of Equations/Inequalities

$2a+b=2 \rightarrow$ ①

$4a-3b=19 \rightarrow$ ②

②$-$①$\times 2$:

$-5b=15$

$b=-3$

Plug $b=-3$ into ①

$2a-3=2$

$2a=5$

$a=\dfrac{5}{2}=2.5$

$\therefore (a, b)=(2.5, -3)$

Therefore, the answer is (B).

2. System of Equations/Inequalities

From the second equation, $y=9x$

Substitute into the first equation,

$45x-27=173+9x$

$36x=200$

$9x=50$

$\therefore y=50$

Therefore, the answer is 50.

3. System of Equations/Inequalities

$5p-rq=3 \rightarrow$ ①

$3p-5q=7 \rightarrow$ ②

①$\times 3$: $15p-3rq=9$

②$\times 5$: $15p-25q=35$

①$\times 3-$②$\times 5$: $(3-r+25)q=-26$

For the system of equations to have no solution,

$-3r+25=0$

$3r=25$

$\therefore r=\dfrac{25}{3}$

Therefore, the answer is (B).

4. System of Equations/Inequalities

$5y-p=7y-11 \Rightarrow -2y-p=-11$

$5z-q=7z-11 \Rightarrow -2z-q=-11$

$\therefore -2y-p=-2z-q$

Since it is given that $p=q-2$

$-2y-(q-2)=-2z-q$

$-2y-q+2=-2z-q$

$-2y+2=-2z$

$\therefore y-1=z$

Therefore, the answer is (B).

Example Questions 2

1. System of Equations/Inequalities

Plug the second equation, $y=\dfrac{1}{3}x$, into the first inequality.

$2x+4\leq 3\left(\dfrac{1}{3}x\right)$

$2x+4\leq x$

$\therefore x\leq -4$

Therefore, the answer is (B).

2. System of Equations/Inequalities

If we solve the equation for y,

$2y=\dfrac{1}{2}x+7$

Plug $2y$ into the inequality.

$3x+5\geq 2\left(\dfrac{1}{2}x+7\right)$

$3x+5\geq x+14$

$2x\geq 9$

$x\geq\dfrac{9}{2}=4.5$

$\therefore$ The minimum possible integer value of x is 5.

Therefore, the answer is 5.

1. System of Equations/Inequalities

$kx+ry=13 \rightarrow ①$

$3x+7y=52$

$①×4 : 4kx+4ry=52$

For this system of equation to have infinitely many solutions, the coefficients of the two equations must match.

$4k=3, \ 4r=7$

$\therefore \ \dfrac{4k}{4r}=\dfrac{k}{r}=\dfrac{3}{7}$

Therefore, the answer is $\dfrac{3}{7}$.

2. System of Equations/Inequalities

$3a-4b=-3 \rightarrow ①$

$4a-3b=-11 \rightarrow ②$

$①×3 : 9a-12b=-9$

$②×4 : 16a-12b=-44$

$①×3-②×4 :$

$-7a=35$

$\therefore \ a=-5$

Plug $a=-5$ into $①$

$-15-4b=-3$

$4b=-12$

$\therefore \ b=-3$

Therefore, $a+b=-5-3=-8$

Therefore, the answer is (A).

3. System of Equations/Inequalities

$\dfrac{z}{y}=9$

$z=9y \rightarrow ①$

$5(y+4)=z$

$5y+20=z \rightarrow ②$

$\therefore 5y+20=9y$

$4y=20$

$y=5$

From $②$,

$\therefore \ z=9×5=45$

Therefore, the answer is (D).

4. System of Equations/Inequalities

$-2a+3b=9 \rightarrow ①$

$4a+2b=6 \rightarrow ②$

$①×2 : -4a+6b=18$

$②+①×2 :$

$8b=24$

$b=3$

Plug $b=3$ into $①$

$-2a+9=9$

$\therefore \ a=0$

Therefore, the answer is 0.

5. System of Equations/Inequalities

$y+4=2x$

$y=2x-4$

Plug y into the first equation

$5x+21=6(2x-4)-4$

$5x+21=12x-24-4$

$5x+21=12x-28$

$7x=49$

$x=7$

$y=2×7-4=10$

$\therefore \ y-x=10-7=3$

Therefore, the answer is (A).

6. System of Equations/Inequalities

$3r-a=5r-13 \Rightarrow -2r-a=-13$

$3k-b=5k-13 \Rightarrow -2k-b=-13$

$\therefore \ -2r-a=-2k-b$

Since it is given that $b=a-6$,

$-2r-a=-2k-(a-6)$

$-2r-a=-2k-a+6$

$-2r=-2k+6$

$2k-2r=6$

$k-r=3$

$\therefore \ k=r+3$

Therefore, the answer is (B).

7. System of Equations/Inequalities

$y = 7x + 5 - 2(x+1)$

$\quad = 7x + 5 - 2x - 2$

$\quad = 5x + 3 \quad \rightarrow \quad ①$

$y = -\dfrac{1}{2}x \quad \rightarrow \quad ②$

To solve for (p, q)

$5x + 3 = -\dfrac{1}{2}x$

$10x + 6 = -x$

$11x = -6$

$x = p = -\dfrac{6}{11}$

$q = -\dfrac{1}{2} \times -\dfrac{6}{11} = \dfrac{3}{11}$

From ②,

$\therefore \ 11(p+q) = 11\left(-\dfrac{6}{11} + \dfrac{3}{11}\right) = -3$

Therefore, the answer is (C).

8. System of Equations/Inequalities

$2b = a + 3$

Plug $2b$ into the first equation.

$5a + 7 = 2(2b) + 2$

$5a + 7 = 2(a+3) + 2$

$5a + 7 = 2a + 6 + 2$

$3a = 1$

$\therefore \ 6a = 2$

Therefore, the answer is (B).

9. System of Equations/Inequalities

$2y = z + 8$

$2y - 8 = z \quad \rightarrow \quad ②$

Plug z into the first equation.

$3y + 2 = 5(2y - 8)$

$3y + 2 = 10y - 40$

$7y = 42$

$y = 6$

From ②

$\therefore \ z = 2 \times 6 - 8 = 4$

Therefore, the answer is (B).

10. System of Equations/Inequalities

From the first equation, $y = 5x$

Substitute into the first equation,

$3(x+2) = 5x$

$3x + 6 = 5x$

$2x = 6$

$x = 3$

$\therefore \ y = 5 \times 3 = 15$

Therefore, the answer is (C).

11. System of Equations/Inequalities

$4x + 6 = 7y \quad \rightarrow \quad ①$

$8x - 3 = 9y \quad \rightarrow \quad ②$

$① \times 2 : 8x + 12 = 14y$

$① \times 2 - ② :$

$5y = 15$

$y = 3$

Plug $y = 3$ into ①

$4x + 6 = 21$

$4x = 15$

$\therefore \ x = \dfrac{15}{4} = 3.75$

Therefore, the answer is (B).

12. System of Equations/Inequalities

$2n + 3m = 4 \quad \rightarrow \quad ①$

$3n + 4m = 5 \quad \rightarrow \quad ②$

$① \times 3 : 6n + 9m = 12$

$② \times 2 : 6n + 8m = 10$

$① \times 3 - ② \times 2$

$m = 2$

Substitute into ①,

$2n + 3 \times 2 = 4$

$2n = -2$

$n = -1$

$\therefore \ n + m = -1 + 2 = 1$

Therefore, the answer is (C).

13. System of Equations/Inequalities

$5n-r=7n-9 \Rightarrow -2n-r=-9$

$3m-k=5m-9 \Rightarrow -2m-k=-9$

$\therefore -2n-r=-2m-k$

Since it is given that $r=k-4$,

$-2n-(k-4)=-2m-k$

$-2n-k+4=-2m-k$

$-2n+4=-2m$

$4=2n-2m$

$\therefore n-m=2$

Therefore, the answer is (A).

14. System of Equations/Inequalities

Plug $y=\frac{1}{3}x$ into the first equation,

$6(x+3)-10=2\left(\frac{1}{3}x+1\right)$

$6x+8=\frac{2}{3}x+2$

$\frac{16}{3}x=-6$

$x=-6\times\frac{3}{16}=-\frac{9}{8}$

$\therefore 8x=-9$

Therefore, the answer is (A).

15. System of Equations/Inequalities

$6a+5b=26 \rightarrow ①$

$2a-2b=5 \rightarrow ②$

$②\times 3 : 6a-6b=15$

$①-②\times 3 :$

$11b=11$

$b=1$

Plug into ②,

$2a-2=5$

$a=\frac{7}{2}=3.5$

$\therefore (a, b)=(3.5, 1)$

Therefore, the answer is (B).

16. System of Equations/Inequalities

$4n-km=9 \rightarrow ①$

$5n-4m=12 \rightarrow ②$

$①\times 5 : 20n-5km=45$

$②\times 4 : 20n-16m=48$

$①\times 5-②\times 4 :$

$(-5k+16)m=-3$

For this system of equation to have no solution,

$-5k+16=0$

$5k=16$

$\therefore k=\frac{16}{5}=3.2$

Therefore, the answer is (B).

17. System of Equations/Inequalities

Plug the second equation $r=3k+7$ into the first equation.

$2(3k+7)-5=9k$

$6k+14-5=9k$

$3k=9$

$k=3$

$r=3\times 3+7$

$\therefore r=16$

Therefore, the answer is (D).

18. System of Equations/Inequalities

$4y+a=9y-11 \Rightarrow 5y=11+a \rightarrow ①$

$4z+b=9z-11 \Rightarrow 5z=11+b \rightarrow ②$

Since it is given that $b=a-5$, plug into ②,

$5z=11+(a-5)$

$5z+5=11+a=5y$ (From ①)

$\therefore 5y=5z+5$

$5(y-z)=5$

$\therefore y-z=1$

Therefore, the answer is (C).

19. System of Equations/Inequalities

If we solve the second equation for b,

$b = 2a - 3$

Plug $b = 2a - 3$ into the first equation.

$7a + 9 = 5(2a - 3)$

$7a + 9 = 10a - 15$

$3a = 24$

$a = 8$

$b = 2 \times 8 - 3 = 13$

$\therefore \ \dfrac{a+b}{3} = \dfrac{21}{3} = 7$

Therefore, the answer is (A).

1-3   Equations/Inequalities in Context

1. Equalities/Inequalities in Context

If the amount of money Jacob has is x, James has $x + 45$ dollars.

Since Jacob and James have a combined amount of 173 dollars,

$x + (x + 45) = 173$

$2x + 45 = 173$

$2x = 128$

$\therefore \ x = 64$

Therefore, the answer is (B).

2. Equalities/Inequalities in Context

If one serving of Coke is x milliliters, one serving of Iced Tea is $x + 50$ milliliters.

Since 3 Cokes and 4 Iced Teas are 4400 milliliters,

$3x + 4(x + 50) = 4400$

$7x + 200 = 4400$

$7x = 4200$

$x = 600$

$\therefore$ One serving of Iced Tea $= x + 50 = 650$ milliliters.

Therefore, the answer is 650.

3. Equalities/Inequalities in Context

If the number of marbles Andy has is x, the number of marbles Elizabeth has is $x - 32$.

Since Andy and Elizabeth have a combined number of 218 marbles,

$x + (x - 32) = 218$

$2x = 250$

$\therefore \ x = 125$

Therefore, the answer is (B).

4. Equalities/Inequalities in Context

$5x - 2 = 38$

$5x = 40$

$x = 8$

$\therefore \ 3x - 9 = 24 - 9 = 15$

Therefore, the answer is (C).

5. Equalities/Inequalities in Context

Troy's tacos: a dollars

Abed's tacos: $a - 2$ dollars

Total payment:

$(a + (a - 2))(1.15) = (2a - 2)(1.15) = 2.30a - 2.30$

Since Troy and Abed evenly divided the bill in two,

$\dfrac{2.30a - 2.30}{2} = 1.15a - 1.15$

Therefore, the answer is (B).

6. Equalities/Inequalities in Context

If the real-life car's length is x, the length of the toy car is $\dfrac{2}{7}x$.

Since it is given that $x = 7$

$7 \times \dfrac{2}{7} = 2$

Therefore, the answer is (C).

7. Equalities/Inequalities in Context

If Jeff is x centimeters tall, Britta is $x - \frac{1}{5}x$

centimeters tall.

Britta's height is 156 centimeters.

$x - \frac{1}{5}x = 156$

$\frac{4}{5}x = 156$

$\therefore \ x = 195$

Therefore, the answer is (C).

8. Equalities/Inequalities in Context

Height of the box is 27 inches, and the perimeter of the bottom side of the box consists of the width, w, and length, 15 inches.

$27 + 2(w + 15) \leq 105$

$27 + 2w + 30 \leq 105$

$2w \leq 48$

$\therefore \ w \leq 24$

Therefore, the answer is (C).

9. Equalities/Inequalities in Context

Henry finished the race in 5 hours, in which he ran and biked a total of 4 hours.

Therefore, he kayaked for 1 hour.

If Henry kayaked in x miles per hour,

$(6 \times 2) + (10 \times 2) + (x \times 1) = 40$

$12 + 20 + x = 40$

$\therefore \ x = 8$

Therefore, the answer is (C).

10. Equalities/Inequalities in Context

Number of miles Dean and friends traveled: x

Total number of people riding cab is 5.

$5 + 1 \times 5 + 0.5x = 65.50$

$0.5x = 55.50$

$\therefore \ x = 111$

Therefore, the answer is 111.

11. Equalities/Inequalities in Context

Number of tickets sold at box office : x

Number of pre−purchased tickets: 200

$15 \times 200 + 20x = 18(200 + x)$

$3000 + 20x = 3600 + 18x$

$2x = 600$

$\therefore \ x = 300$

Therefore, the answer is (B).

12. Equalities/Inequalities in Context

Number of Sam's stamps: x

Number of Jeremy's stamps: $4x - 21$

$x + (4x - 21) = 94$

$5x = 115$

$x = 23$

$\therefore \ (4x - 21) - x = 3x - 21 = 3 \times 23 - 21 = 48$

Therefore, the answer is (C).

13. Equalities/Inequalities in Context

Bags of beef jerky : j

Number of cokes : c

$3j + 2c = 19 \ \rightarrow \ ①$

$5j + 5c = 37.5 \ \rightarrow \ ②$

$① \times 2 : \ 6j + 4c = 38$

$① \times 2 - ②$

$j - c = 0.50$

Therefore, the answer is (A).

14. Equalities/Inequalities in Context

Rameez: $23 + 0.50d$

Cameron: $15.50 + 2d$

$23 + 0.50d = 15.50 + 2d$

$1.5d = 7.5$

$\therefore \ d = 5$

Therefore, 5 days after Tuesday (including Tuesday) is Saturday.

Therefore, the answer is (B).

15. Equalities/Inequalities in Context

Paperback books: x

Hardcover books: $2x-9$

$x+(2x-9)=90$

$3x=99$

$x=33$

$\therefore\ 2x-9=66-9=57$

Therefore, the answer is (C).

16. Equalities/Inequalities in Context

3-people table: x

4-people table: y

$x+y=21\ \rightarrow\ ①$

$3x+4y=71\ \rightarrow\ ②$

$①\times3:\ 3x+3y=63$

$②-①\times3$

$y=8$

$\therefore\ x=21-8=13$

Therefore, the answer is (C).

17. Equalities/Inequalities in Context

Onions: x

Garlic: $27-x$

$3x+2.5(27-x)=72.50$

$0.5x+67.5=72.50$

$0.5x=5$

$x=10$

Therefore, the answer is (B).

18. Equalities/Inequalities in Context

Turk ate t sandwiches per day for 13 days: $13t$

Carla ate c sandwiches per day for 3 days: $3c$

Total number of sandwiches eaten by Turk and Carla during the month: $13t+3c$

Therefore, the answer is (A).

19. Equalities/Inequalities in Context

When the price per liter of apple juice and orange juice is the same,

$3.24+0.35n=2.49+1.10n$

$0.75n=0.75$

$\therefore\ n=1$

The price per liter of apple juice when $n=1$,

$\therefore\ 3.24+0.35=3.59$

Therefore, the answer is (C).

20. Equalities/Inequalities in Context

If the number of 16GB USBs and 32GB USBs is a and b respectively,

$a+b=10$

Plug in $b=10-a$ into the second equation.

$ua+2u(10-a)=17u$

$a+20-2a=17$

$\therefore\ a=3$

Therefore, the answer is (B).

21. Equalities/Inequalities in Context

Sets of forks: x

Sets of knives: $x+4$

$5x=4(x+4)$

$5x=4x+16$

$x=16$

$\therefore\ 4(x+4)=4(16+4)=80$

Therefore, the answer is (C).

22. Equalities/Inequalities in Context

Basketball players: x

Football players: $4x$

Tennis players: $\frac{1}{2}x$

$4x+x+\frac{1}{2}x=66$

$5.5x=66$

$x=12$

$\therefore$ Number of football players $=4x=48$

Therefore, the answer is 48.

23. Equalities/Inequalities in Context

No-Calculator questions are worth 3 points and Calculator using questions are worth 2 points.

Fry got 12 No-Calculator questions right.

If we set the number of Calculator-allowed questions that Fry answered correctly as x,

$12 \times 3 + 2x \geq 70$

$36 + 2x \geq 70$

$2x \geq 34$

$\therefore x \geq 17$

Therefore, the answer is 17.

24. Equalities/Inequalities in Context

Pennies Bart has: b

Pennies Lisa has: $b - 46$

13 dollars = 1300 pennies

$b + (b - 46) = 1300$

$2b = 1346$

$\therefore b = 673$

Therefore, the answer is (B).

25. Equalities/Inequalities in Context

In the given equation $C = 153 - 12h$,

C represents the number of cookies left to bake, and h is the number of hours Bailey has worked.

Therefore, the number 12 represents the number of cookies Bailey bakes in an hour.

From the information above, we can infer that the number 153 represents the initial number of cookies to bake daily.

Therefore, the answer is (C).

1-4   Equations/Inequalities on the Coordinate Plane

SAT Question

1. Equations/Inequalities in the Coordinate Plane

Slope of line n:

$\dfrac{-3-0}{0-(-4)} = -\dfrac{3}{4}$

y-intercept of line n is -3.

$\therefore$ Equation of line n is $y = -\dfrac{3}{4}x - 3$

Since line m is parallel to line n and has a y-intercept of 6,

Equation of line m is $y = -\dfrac{3}{4}x + 6$

r is the x value of line m when the y value is 0.

$0 = -\dfrac{3}{4}r + 6$

$\dfrac{3}{4}r = 6$

$\therefore r = 8$

Therefore, the answer is (C).

2. Equations/Inequalities in the Coordinate Plane

The equation for the line with slope -2 and point (1, 4) is,

$y = -2x + a$

$4 = -2 + a$

$a = 6$

$\therefore y = -2x + 6$

The equation for the line with points (3, 0), (−3, −2) is,

slope: $\dfrac{0-(-2)}{3-(-3)} = \dfrac{2}{6} = \dfrac{1}{3}$

$y = \dfrac{1}{3}x + b$

$0 = \dfrac{1}{3} \times 3 + b$

$b = -1$

$\therefore y = \dfrac{1}{3}x - 1$

The two lines intersect at point (p, q), therefore,

$\dfrac{1}{3}x - 1 = -2x + 6$

$$\frac{7}{3}x=7$$

$p=3,\ q=0$

$\therefore\ p-q=3$

Therefore, the answer is (C).

3. Equations/Inequalities in the Coordinate Plane

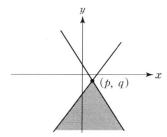

The solution set of the inequalities will be the intersection of the areas below and including the boundary lines $y=25x-450$ and $y=-5x$. Because the slope of one equation is positive (25) and the other is negative (-5), the graph will look like an 'X'. The greatest value of q will be the point of intersection of the two lines.

$25x-450=-5x$

$30x=450$

$x=15$

$\therefore\ y=-5\times15=-75$

Therefore, the answer is -75.

4. Equations/Inequalities in the Coordinate Plane

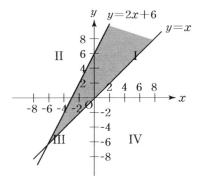

Above is the given system of inequalities drawn on the xy-plane. The colored area shows the solution set to the system of inequalities. There are no solutions in Quadrant IV.

Therefore, the answer is (C).

5. Equations/Inequalities in the Coordinate Plane

If we set the y-intercept of the line as b,

$$y=\frac{7}{3}x+b$$

Since the line passes through point $(3,\ 15)$,

$$15=\frac{7}{3}\times3+b$$

$\therefore\ b=15-7=8$

Therefore, the answer is (C).

6. Equations/Inequalities in the Coordinate Plane

If we write the equation of the line from the given figure, $y=2x+1$.

$ax+by=c$

$by=-ax+c$

$$y=-\frac{a}{b}x+\frac{c}{b}=2x+1$$

It is given that $a=4$,

$$-\frac{4}{b}=2$$

$b=-2$

$$\frac{c}{b}=\frac{c}{(-2)}=1$$

$\therefore\ c=-2$

Therefore, the answer is -2.

7. Equations/Inequalities in the Coordinate Plane

Rewrite the given equations to a standard line equation.

$6x+2y=3$

$2y=-6x+3$

$$y=-3x+\frac{3}{2}$$

$9x+by=2$

$by=-9x+2$

$$y=-\frac{9}{b}x+\frac{2}{b}$$

Since the two lines are parallel to each other, they share the same slope.

$$-3=-\frac{9}{b}$$

$\therefore\ b=3$

Therefore, the answer is (B).

8. Equations/Inequalities in the Coordinate Plane

From the given graph, it is shown that the graph passes points $(-4, 0)$ and $(0, 2)$.

Therefore, the slope of line l:

$$\frac{2-0}{0-(-4)} = \frac{1}{2}$$

The slope of a perpendicular line is the negative reciprocal of given line.

$\therefore$ slope of line perpendicular to line $l = -2$

Therefore, the answer is (A).

9. Equations/Inequalities in the Coordinate Plane

Create a standard line equation based on the given information.

$y = -0.75x + b$

Since the line passes point $(16, 1)$,

$$1 = -\frac{3}{4} \times 16 + b$$

$$1 = -12 + b$$

$\therefore b = 13$

Therefore, the answer is (D).

10. Equations/Inequalities in the Coordinate Plane

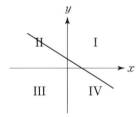

Rewrite $2x + 4y = 3$ as a line equation.

$4y = -2x + 3$

$\therefore t = -\frac{1}{2}x + \frac{3}{4}$

When the equation above is graphed on the xy-plane, it does not pass through quadrant III.

Therefore, the answer is (B).

11. Equations/Inequalities in the Coordinate Plane

A line that passes through the origin and has a slope of -2 is,

$y = -2x$

If every answer option is plugged into the equation, the only point that fits is $(1, -2)$.

Therefore, the answer is (A).

12. Equations/Inequalities in the Coordinate Plane

A line that passes through the point $(0,2)$ and has a slope of $\frac{2}{3}$ is,

$$y = \frac{2}{3}x + 2$$

If every answer option is plugged into the equation, the only point that does not fit is $(2,0)$.

Therefore, the answer is (D).

13. Equations/Inequalities in the Coordinate Plane

A line that meets the y-axis at $+5$ and has a slope of -3 is,

$y = -3x + 5$

If every answer option is plugged into the equation, the only point that fits is $(2, -1)$.

Therefore, the answer is (A).

14. Equations/Inequalities in the Coordinate Plane

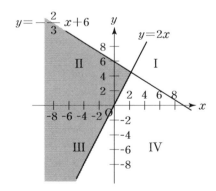

Above is the given system of inequalities drawn on the xy-plane. The colored area shows the solution set to the system of inequalities. There are no solutions in Quadrant IV.

Therefore, the answer is (C).

15. Equations/Inequalities in the Coordinate Plane

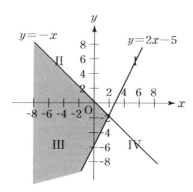

Above is the given system of inequalities drawn on the xy-plane. The colored area shows the solution set to the system of inequalities. There are no solutions in Quadrant I.

Therefore, the answer is (A).

16. Equations/Inequalities in the Coordinate Plane

The solution set of the inequalities will be the intersection of the areas below and including the boundary lines $y=4x-7$ and $y=-2x+5$.

The greatest value of $(a,\ b)$ will be the point of intersection of the two lines.

$4x-7=-2x+5$

$6x=12$

$x=2$

$\therefore\ y=4\times2-7=1$

Therefore, the answer is 1.

17. Equations/Inequalities in the Coordinate Plane

Slope of line with points $(0,\ 4)$ and $(-2,\ 0)$:

$$\frac{4-0}{0-(-2)}=2$$

y-intercept of this line is 4.

$\therefore$ Equation of this line is $y=2x+4$

Since the two lines are parallel and the line below has a y-intercept of -3,

Equation of the line below is $y=2x-3$

r is the x value of the line below when the y value is 0.

$0=2x-3$

$2x=3$

$\therefore\ x=\frac{3}{2}=1.5$

Therefore, the answer is (B).

18. Equations/Inequalities in the Coordinate Plane

Let's set the line with points $(0,\ 6)$ and $(-3,\ 0)$ as line 1 and the other as line 2.

Slope of line 1:

$$\frac{6-0}{0-(-3)}=2$$

y-intercept of line 1 is 6.

$\therefore$ Equation of line 1 is $y=2x+6$

Since the two lines are perpendicular and line 2 passes through the origin,

Equation of line 2 is $y=-\frac{1}{2}x$

Point $(p,\ q)$ is where the two lines intersect.

$2x+6=-\frac{1}{2}x$

$\frac{5}{2}x=-6$

$x=-\frac{12}{5}$

$y=-\frac{12}{5}\times-\frac{1}{2}=\frac{6}{5}=1.2$

Therefore, the answer is 1.2.

19. Equations/Inequalities in the Coordinate Plane

Rewrite the given equations to a standard line equation.

$4x+2y=1$

$2y=-4x+1$

$y=-2x+\frac{1}{2}$

$2x+by=2$

$by=-2x+2$

$y=-\frac{2}{b}x+\frac{2}{b}$

Since the two lines are parallel to each other, they share the same slope.

$$-2=-\frac{2}{b}$$

$\therefore\ b=1$

Therefore, the answer is (A).

20. Equations/Inequalities in the Coordinate Plane

Rewrite the given equations to a standard line equation.

$7x+y=9$

$y=-7x+9$

$ax+3y=1$

$3y=-ax+1$

$y=-\frac{a}{3}x+\frac{1}{3}$

Since the two lines are parallel to each other, they share the same slope.

$$-7=-\frac{a}{3}$$

$\therefore\ a=21$

Therefore, the answer is (D).

21. Equations/Inequalities in the Coordinate Plane

Rewrite the given equations to a standard line equation.

$x+2y=6$

$2y=-x+6$

$y=-\frac{1}{2}x+3$

$ax+2y=7$

$2y=-ax+7$

$y=-\frac{a}{2}x+\frac{7}{2}$

Since the two lines are perpendicular to each other,

$-\frac{a}{2}$ would be the negative reciprocal of $-\frac{1}{2}$.

$$2=-\frac{a}{2}$$

$\therefore\ a=-4$

Therefore, the answer is (A).

22. Equations/Inequalities in the Coordinate Plane

The solution set of the inequalities will be the intersection of the areas below and including the boundary lines $2y=4x+6$ and $3y=-6x+9$.

The greatest value of $(p,\ q)$ will be the point of intersection of the two lines.

Rewrite the equations as: $y=2x+3$ and $y=-2x+3$

$2x+3=-2x+3$

$4x=0$

$x=0$

$y=2\times0+3=3$

$\therefore\ pq=3\times0=0$

Therefore, the answer is (B).

23. Equations/Inequalities in the Coordinate Plane

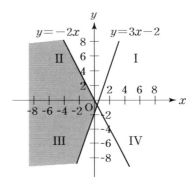

$2y\le-4x$ can be rewritten into $y\le-2x$

Above is the given system of inequalities drawn on the xy-plane. The colored area shows the solution set to the system of inequalities. There are no solutions in Quadrant I.

Therefore, the answer is (A).

24. Equations/Inequalities in the Coordinate Plane

Let's set the line with the slope of -3 and point $(1,\ 2)$ line 1 and the other as line 2.

$y=-3x+b$

Line 1 passes the point $(1,\ 2)$ so,

$2=-3\times1+b$

$b=5$

$\therefore$ Equation of line 1 is $y=-3x+5$

Line 2 passes the point $(4, 0)$ and $(-4, -4)$.

Slope of line 2:

$$\frac{0-(-4)}{4-(-4)} = \frac{4}{8} = \frac{1}{2}$$

$$y = \frac{1}{2}x + c$$

$$0 = \frac{1}{2} \times 4 + c$$

$$c = -2$$

$\therefore$ Equation of line 2 is $y = \frac{1}{2}x - 2$

Point (r, k) is where the two lines intersect.

$$-3x + 5 = \frac{1}{2}x - 2$$

$$\frac{7}{2}x = 7$$

$\therefore x = r = 2$

$$k = \frac{1}{2} \times 2 - 2 = -1$$

$\therefore r - k = 2 - (-1) = 3$

Therefore, the answer is (C).

25. Equations/Inequalities in the Coordinate Plane

The solution set of the inequalities will be the intersection of the areas below and including the boundary lines $y = 2x$ and $y = -11x + 169$.

The greatest value of (n, m) will be the point of intersection of the two lines.

$$2x = -11x + 169$$

$$13x = 169$$

$$x = 13$$

$\therefore y = 2 \times 13 = 26$

Therefore, the answer is 26.

I. Statistics

Exercise

1. $\dfrac{20+30+50}{3}=\dfrac{100}{3}$

2. $\{2,\ 4,\ 5,\ 7,\ 9,\ 10\}\Rightarrow$ median
$$=\dfrac{5+7}{2}=6$$

3. 1, 2

SAT Question

1. $60=6T$
$T=10$
The answer is 10.

2. $x<y<z$
$x<x+6<x+9\Rightarrow$ median$=x+6$
average$=\dfrac{x+(x+6)+(x+9)}{3}$
$$=\dfrac{3x+15}{3}=x+5$$
$x+6-(x+5)=1$
Therefore, the answer is (C).

3. (A), (B), (C) all change the median. However, even if the biggest number in Set X gets bigger, the increase has no impact on the median.
Therefore, the answer is (D).

4. The dots in the plot on the left (Class A) are more concentrated towards a specific number, around 5.
Therefore, the answer is (A).

5. In this question, a 95% confidence interval of 41 to 49 chocolates means that when multiple samples of 300 bags of M&Ms are investigated for the average number of chocolates inside them, 95% of them will be between 41 and 49. It does not mean 95% of the bags produced have between 41 and 49 chocolates inside. Also, be careful not to confuse the answer for (D) as this result applies to only the particular day that the investigation was carried out and not for all the M&Ms the factory produced.
Therefore, the answer is (C).

II. Probability

Exercise

1. $4+6-2=8$

2. $4\times3=12$

3. $\dfrac{3}{6}=\dfrac{1}{2}$

4. $\dfrac{5!}{(5-2)!}=20$

5. $\dfrac{5!}{(5-2)!2!}=\dfrac{5\cdot4\cdot3}{3\cdot2}=10$

1. # of handshakes the 1st person has:

once with 7 other people → 7 handshakes

# of handshakes the 2nd person has:

once with 6 remaining people → 6 handshakes

$\vdots$

# of handshakes the 7th person has:

once with 1 remaining person → 1 handshake

total $= 7+6+5+4+3+2+1 = 28$ handshakes

Therefore, the answer is 28.

2. $5+6+7$

$7+5+6$

$6+5+7$

$7+6+5$

Therefore, the answer is (C).

3. $x =$ fraction of romance books

$$\frac{3}{30} + \frac{10}{30} + \frac{5}{30} + x = 1$$

$$x = \frac{2}{5}$$

12 romance books $= \frac{2}{5} \times$ total number of books

Total number of books $= 30$

SF books $= 30 \times \frac{1}{6} = 5$ books.

Therefore, the answer is (D).

4. $4x = \frac{1}{9} \times 360$

$4 = 40$

$x = 10$

Therefore, the answer is (C).

5. 12 cards for each numeral ranging from 0 to 9

01	✔	11 ✔	→ 1 is used two times.
02		12 ✔	
03		13 ✔	
04		14 ✔	
05		15 ✔	
06		16 ✔	
07		17 ✔	
08		18 ✔	
09		19 ✔	→ 1 is used 12 times up to here.
10	✔	20	

Therefore, the answer is (D).

6. $6 \times 5 \times 4 \times 3 \times 2 \times 1 = 720$

$5 \times 4 \times 3 \times 2 \times 1 = 120$

(2 exists at the beginning and at the end)

$720 - (2 \times 120) = 480$

Therefore, the answer is 480.

7. LCM of 6 and $8 = 24$

$$\frac{100}{24} = 4 \text{(remainder 2)}$$

Probability $= \frac{4}{100}$

Therefore, the answer is (C).

III. Graphs and Data Analysis

1. Credit vs. cash for regular:

$\frac{2.11}{2.06} = 1.02427 = 102.43\%$

which means that credit is 2.43% more expensive

Credit vs. cash for plus:

$\frac{2.35}{2.29} = 1.0262 = 102.62\%$

credit is 2.62% more expensive

$\frac{2.47}{2.40} = 1.02917 = 102.917\%$

Credit vs. cash for premium:

credit is 2.92% more expensive

Therefore, the answer is (A).

2. If Tom fills his tank twice a month, he will have to pay for twice the number of gallons. Thus, his gas payments will increase by 100%.
Therefore, the answer is (A).

3. $\frac{474.34}{50,135} = 0.00946 \approx 0.95\%$
Therefore, the answer is (B).

4. To begin with there were $1,900$ Chemical Engineering students.

The number of students who stayed in Chemical Engineering until the beginning of their third year
$= 1,900 \times 0.77 \times 0.77$
The number of students who changed from Chemical Engineering to something else at the end of their third year
$= 1,900 \times 0.77 \times 0.77 \times 0.23 = 259.0973$
Therefore, the answer is (A).

IV. Ratio

1. $6 : 12 : 18 = A : B : C \rightarrow A : C = 1 : 3$

2. $4 : 40 = 80 : x \rightarrow 4x = 3200 \rightarrow x = 800$

1. small circle's area: 4π
largest circle's area: 36π
middle circle's area: 16π
outer ring's area: $36\pi - 16\pi = 20\pi$
small circle's area : outer ring's area $= 4\pi : 20\pi = 1 : 5$
Therefore, the answer is (C).

2. $P : Q = 3 : 5 \qquad Q : R = 12 : 4$
$\quad P : Q = 36 : 60 \qquad Q : R = 60 : 20$
$\quad R : P = 20 : 36 = 5 : 9$
Therefore, the answer is (C).

V. Rate

1. $25 \times 3 = 75$

2. If it takes 10 days for 6 workers to build one bridge, it will take 60 days for one worker to build one bridge. Since there are two workers, it will take 30 days to build one bridge.

1. 1) When the cheetah runs: travels x miles in 5

minutes $\rightarrow$ $\dfrac{x}{5}$ miles per minute

2) When the cheetah walks: travels at $\dfrac{1}{5}$ of its

running speed $\rightarrow$ $\dfrac{x}{25}$ miles per minute

$\dfrac{x}{2} \div \dfrac{x}{25} = 12.5$ miles

Therefore, the answer is (B).

2. $\dfrac{1}{3} : 100 = 1 : x$

$100 = \dfrac{1}{3}x$

$300 = x$

Therefore, the answer is (C).

3. $A \rightarrow B$ $(0.5f/\min) | A \leftarrow B$ $(3f/\min)$

$\text{time} = \dfrac{\text{distance}}{\text{speed}}$

$\dfrac{x}{0.5} + \dfrac{x}{3} = 7$

$\dfrac{6x}{3} + \dfrac{x}{3} = 7$

$\dfrac{7x}{3} = 7$

$7x = 21$

$x = 3$ (Be careful! $x=$distance)

$\dfrac{3}{0.5} = 6$ min.

Therefore, the answer is (C).

VI. Percentages

1. $\dfrac{1}{8} \times 100(\%) = 12.5(\%)$

2. $50 \times \dfrac{40}{100} = 20$

3. $\dfrac{90-70}{70} \times 100(\%) = \dfrac{20}{70} \times 100(\%)$

$= 28.571... \approx 28.6(\%)$

4. $x \times \dfrac{120}{100} = 60$

$x = 60 \times \dfrac{120}{100} = 50$

1. $\dfrac{14-8}{8} \times 100 = 75\%$

$\dfrac{x-28}{28} = 0.75$

$x = 49$

Therefore, the answer is (D).

2. $1.2x = 18$

$x = 15$

Therefore, the answer is (B).

3. 1) Let the percentage be k $\rightarrow$ $\dfrac{k}{100} \times (2a+5) = b$

$\dfrac{k}{100} = \dfrac{b}{2a+5}$ $\rightarrow$ $k = \left(\dfrac{b}{2a+5}\right) \times 100$

$\therefore$ $\dfrac{100b}{2a+5}\%$

2) Simply put, what percentage of 10 is 1?

It's $\dfrac{1}{10} \times 100\%$.

Likewise, just substitute with $(2a+5)$ and b.

$\dfrac{b}{2a+5} \times 100\%$

$\therefore$ $\dfrac{100b}{2a+5}\%$

Therefore, the answer is (C).

I. Factoring

1. $3x(x+2)(x+1)$

2. $16(x+1)^2$

3. $(5x+2)(5x-2)$

4. $(7x+2)(3x-4)$

1. $15x^3+44x^2+3x-26$

$b=44$

Therefore, the answer is 44.

2. $9x^2-6nx+n^2=9x^2-mx+16$

$n=4, \ m=24$

$n+m=28$

Therefore, the answer is (D).

3. $k^2-m^2=(k+m)(k-m)$

$$=\left[3\left(\frac{a}{b}+\frac{b}{a}\right)+4\left(\frac{a}{b}-\frac{b}{a}\right)\right]$$

$$\times\left[3\left(\frac{a}{b}+\frac{b}{a}\right)-4\left(\frac{a}{b}-\frac{b}{a}\right)\right]$$

$$=\left(\frac{3a}{b}+\frac{3b}{a}+\frac{4a}{b}-\frac{4b}{a}\right)$$

$$\times\left(\frac{3a}{b}+\frac{3b}{a}-\frac{4a}{b}+\frac{4b}{a}\right)$$

$$=\left(\frac{7a}{b}+\frac{-b}{a}\right)\times\left(\frac{-a}{b}+\frac{7b}{a}\right)$$

Therefore, the answer is (A).

4. $\dfrac{2x+4x+6x+8x+10x}{10x}=\dfrac{30x}{10x}=3 \ (x\in R)$

But! Denominator must not be 0.

Thus, $x\neq 0$

Therefore, the answer is (A).

II. Equations

1. $81-169x^2=0$

$(9+13x)(9-13x)=0$

$x=-\dfrac{9}{13}$ or $\dfrac{9}{13}$

2. $2x^2-7x-10=0$

$$x=\frac{7\pm\sqrt{(-7)^2-4(2)(-10)}}{2(2)}$$

$$=\frac{7\pm\sqrt{49+80}}{4}$$

$$=\frac{7\pm\sqrt{129}}{4}$$

$x=\dfrac{7}{4}+\dfrac{\sqrt{129}}{4}$ or $\dfrac{7}{4}-\dfrac{\sqrt{129}}{4}$

3. $\left\{-\dfrac{4}{3}, \ -2.5\right\}$

4. 4

5. $y=x^2-x-4$

$y=-5x+8$

$x^2-x-4=-5x+8$

$x^2+4x-12=0$

$(x-2)(x+6)=0$

$x=2, \ y=-2$ or $x=-6, \ y=38$

$(2, \ -2)$ and $(-6, \ 38)$

1. Solution to $+-cx=0$ is $x=\dfrac{3}{2}$.

$6-\dfrac{3}{2}c=0$

$6=\dfrac{3}{2}c$

$c=4$

Therefore, the answer is 4.

2. $ty^2-6y=15$

In order for the equation to have no real solution, the determinant has to be less than zero.

$ty^2-6y-15=0$

Determinant $=(-6)^2-4t(-15)$

$\qquad\qquad =36+60t<0$

$t<-\dfrac{36}{60}\left(=-\dfrac{3}{5}\right)$

Therefore, the answer is $t<-\dfrac{3}{5}$.

3. Here, the constant of the polynomial is the negative product of all the zeroes of the polynomial. Since $(x-3)$ and $(x+6)$ are two of the factors, 3 and -6 are two of the zeroes.

If the remaining zero is k, then:

$3\times(-6)\times k=-18 \quad k=-216$

$k=12$

Therefore, the answer is $(x-12)$.

4. $T(y)=(y-3)^3-7(y-3)^2+12(y-3)$

$T(y)=(y-3)[(y-3)^2-7(y-3)+12]$

$\qquad =(y-3)\{[(y-3)-3][(y-3)-4]\}$

$\qquad =(y-3)(y-6)(y-7)$

$3+6+7=16$

Therefore, the answer is 16.

5. Let $P(x)=6x^3+x^2-29x+25$.

$P\left(\dfrac{3}{2}\right)=6\left(\dfrac{3}{2}\right)^3+\left(\dfrac{3}{2}\right)^2-29\left(\dfrac{3}{2}\right)+25$

$\qquad\quad =\dfrac{81}{4}+\dfrac{9}{4}-\dfrac{87}{2}+25$

$\qquad\quad =4$

Therefore, the answer is 4.

6. $x+3=-(x+5)^2+4$

$x+3=-x^2-10x-25+4$

$x^2+11x+24=0$

$(x+3)(x+8)=0$

$x=-3,\ y=0$ or $x=-8,\ y=-5$

Therefore, the answer is $(-8,\ -5)$ and $(-3,\ 0)$.

7. $7x^2=(y+8)(y-8)$

$y=4x$

$7x^2=(4x+8)(4x-8)$

$7x^2=16x^2-64$

$9x^2-64=0$

$(3x+8)(3x-8)=0$

$x=\dfrac{8}{3}$ or $-\dfrac{8}{3}$

Since $m>0,\ m=\dfrac{8}{3}$

Therefore, the answer is $\dfrac{8}{3}$.

8. $y=(1.5+x)\left(80-\dfrac{10x}{0.5}\right)$

9. Initil $\mathrm{PE}=mgh$

Changed $\mathrm{PE}=(2m)(g)\left(\dfrac{1}{2}h\right)=mgh$

Therefore, the answer is (C).

10. $s=v_0t+\dfrac{1}{2}at^2$

$a=\dfrac{2}{t^2}(s-v_0t)$

Therefore, the answer is (D).

III. Absolute Value

1. $4x=8$ or $4x=-8$

$x=2$ or $x=-2 \rightarrow x=-2$ or 2

2. $3x+2=11$ or $3x+2=-11$

$3x=9$ or $3x=-13 \rightarrow x=-\dfrac{13}{3}$ or 3

3. $-10<10x<10 \rightarrow -1<x<1$

4. $|5x-2|>8 \rightarrow 5x-2<-8$ or $5x-2>8$

$5x<-6$ or $5x>10 \rightarrow x<-\dfrac{6}{5}$ or $x>2$

IV. Functions

Exercise

1. (d), (b), (a), (c)

2. Shifts the original graph to the right by 4 units.

SAT Question

1. $\dfrac{3x-5}{2}=5$

$3x-5=10$

$3x=15$

$x=5$

Therefore, the answer is 5.

2. When $x=10, g(x)+5=8, f(x)-3=8$. Use substitution.

Therefore, the answer is (D).

3. The "left" x-intercept is 4 units away from $(-3,\ 0)$ $\rightarrow$ the "right" x-intercept should be 4 units away as well.

$\rightarrow a=1$

Therefore, the answer is (D).

4. Reflecting across the y-axis $\rightarrow$ change x to $-x$

$\rightarrow -2x+5y-4=1$

Therefore, the answer is (C).

5.

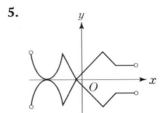

Two points

Therefore, the answer is (C).

V. Powers & Roots

Exercise

1. 225

2. 1

3. 5

4. $6\sqrt{3}$

5. $\dfrac{7}{8}\sqrt{8}=\dfrac{7}{4}\sqrt{2}$

1. $3.005 \times 10^4 = 30050$

$\qquad = 30000 + 5 \times 10^1$

$\qquad = (3 \times 10^4) + (5 \times 10^k)$

$\qquad \rightarrow k = 1$

Therefore, the answer is 1.

2. $3^{t-2} = 3^6$

$t - 2 = 6$

$t = 8$

Therefore, the answer is 8.

3. $7x^3 = 56$

$x^3 = 8$

$7x^6 = 7 \times (x^3)^2 = 7 \times 64$

Therefore, the answer is 448.

4. $3^{11} = 3^{10} \cdot 3 = m^2 \cdot 3$

Therefore, the answer is (D).

5. x^4 cannot be negative $\rightarrow a \leq 0$

Therefore, the answer is (D).

6. Substitute 5^t with a

$5^t + 5^t = a + a = 2a = 2 \cdot 5^t$

Therefore, the answer is (A).

7. $7^x \rightarrow$ Power numbers of 7

Find out the pattern of the unit digits

$\rightarrow \underline{7},\ 4\underline{9},\ 34\underline{3},\ 240\underline{1},\ ...\ \underline{7},\ \underline{9}\ ...$

Unit digits of $7,\ 9,\ 3,\ 1$ repeat.

Therefore, the answer is (D).

8. $3^8 = 3^3 \times 3^3 \times 3^2 = 9x^2 = x \times 3^3 \times 3^2 = 243x$

Therefore, the answer is (B).

Question Answers & Explanations_Chapter 3 | 183

I. Triangles

Exercise

1. $x : y : x = 1 : \sqrt{3} : 2$

2. $x : y : z = 1 : 1 : \sqrt{2}$

3. 4

4. $x = 6$, $y = 9$

SAT Question

1. $z > 95$, $x + y < 85$ (Substitute x with $y + 15$)

$2y + 15 < 85$

$2y < 70$

$y < 35$

$y = 34°$

Therefore, the answer is (D).

2. Apply the special ratio of a right triangle

$1 : \sqrt{3} : 2(30°, 60°, 90°)$

$\overline{PB} = 3$, $\overline{AP} = 1$

Therefore, the answer is 4.

3. $BC = 4$, $QR = 5$

$\overline{OA} : \overline{AP} = \overline{OC} : \overline{CR} \rightarrow 4 : 3 = 12 : \overline{CR}$

$\overline{CR} = 9$

$4 : 3 = 8 : \overline{BQ} \rightarrow \overline{BQ} = 6$

$5 + 4 + 6 + 9 = 24$

Therefore, the answer is (B).

4. $\triangle APC(O)$, $\angle A$, $\angle PCA = 20°$

$\triangle CRQ(O)$, $\angle BQC$, $\angle CRQ = 80°$

$\triangle ABC(O)$, $\angle B$, $\angle C = 80°$

$\triangle BPC(X)$, no $\angle$ match

$\triangle QBC(O)$, $\angle BQC$, $\angle C = 80°$

Therefore, the answer is (D).

5.

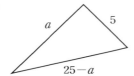

Let the three sides be 5, a, and $25 - a$ and use the Pythagorean Theorem

$a^2 + 5^2 = (25 - a)^2$

$a^2 + 5^2 = 625 - 50a + a^2$

$25 = 625 - 50a$

$50a = 600$

$a = 12$

$25 - 12 = 13$

Therefore, the answer is (D).

6.

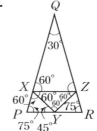

$\angle XYP = 45°$

Therefore, the answer is (C).

II. Polygons

Exercise

1. $a=140°$

$b=140°$

$c=40°$

$d=140°$

$e=90°$

2. $(8-2)\cdot180°=1080$

3. $\dfrac{360°}{8}=45°$

4. $180°$

5. $90°$

6. 3

SAT Question

1. $\angle EOC$ is the opposite angle of x

*Opposite angles always have the same value

$\angle DOC$, $\angle DOE=70°$

$y=70°$

Therefore, the answer is $70°$.

2. $e=2b$

$3b=180°$

$b=60°$

$a=e=c=120°$

(Applying the nature of opposite angles and adjacent angles)

$b=d=60°$

$3b-d=c$ $(180°-60°=120°)$

Therefore, the answer is (C).

3. Sum of the interior angles of the quadrilateral is $360°$

$(180°-x)+y+100+70°=360°$

$y-x+350=360$

$\therefore\ 3y-3x=30$

Therefore, the answer is (D).

4. Sum of the interior angles of a hexagon: $720°$

∵ Polygon Interior Angles Sum Theorem:

$180(n-2)\ \rightarrow\ n=$ the number of vertices

∵ $720-(130+130)=460$

Therefore, the answer is 460.

5.

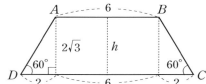

Draw a perpendicular line from A to DC

Use $1:\sqrt{3}:2$ $(30°,\ 60°,\ 90°)$

$\therefore\ \overline{AB}=10-2-2=6$

Therefore, the answer is 6.

6. $125=5\times5\times5$ is the number of small cubes with no paint on them.

$\therefore\ 7\times7\times7=343$ is the total number of cubes

Therefore, the answer is 343.

III. Perimeter and Area

Exercise

1. 24

2. 8

1. $(\overline{AE}+\overline{BF})\overline{AB}/2=160$

$\overline{AE}=28$, $\overline{FG}=24$, $\overline{EG}=10$

Using Pythagorean Theorem,

$\overline{EF}^{2}=\overline{FG}^{2}+\overline{EG}^{2}$ and thus $\overline{EF}=26$

∴ $26+10+24=60$

Therefore, the answer is 60.

2. Each hexagon is equilateral → $\overline{AB}=7\times3=21$

Therefore, the answer is (B).

3. area$=300$, length$=60$

Let width$=x$ → $60x=300$

$x=5$

$120+10=130$

Therefore, the answer is 130m.

4.

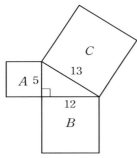

one side of A$=5$

one side of B$=12$

$5^{2}+12^{2}=13^{2}$ → one side of C

$12+5+13=30$

Therefore, the answer is (C).

5.

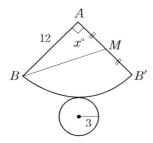

$\overset{\frown}{BB'}=2\pi r=6\pi$

$\qquad =12\times\pi\times2\times\dfrac{x}{360}$

$\qquad =24\pi\times\dfrac{x}{360}$

$\qquad =\dfrac{x}{15}\pi$

$x=90°$, $\overline{AM}=6$

$\overline{BM}=\sqrt{6^{2}+12^{2}}$

$\qquad =\sqrt{180}=6\sqrt{5}$

Therefore, the answer is (B).

IV. Circles

1. area: $9\pi\cdot\dfrac{45}{360}=\dfrac{9}{8}\pi$

arc length: $6\pi\cdot\dfrac{45}{360}=\dfrac{3}{4}\pi$

2. $2r=$diagonal → 8

3. $\dfrac{10}{2}=5$

4. $100-\pi(5^{2})=100-25\pi$

1. $\triangle OXY=$Isosceles triangle

$\angle X$, $\angle Y=30°$, $\angle M=90°$

$\overline{OM}=3$, $\overline{XM}=3\sqrt{3}$

area$=\dfrac{3\times3\sqrt{3}}{2}=\dfrac{9\sqrt{3}}{2}$

Therefore, the answer is (A).

2. $\overline{AD}=3r$, $\overline{AB}=4r$

Perimeter is $14r$.

Therefore, the answer is $14r$.

3. $\dfrac{360}{10}=36 \rightarrow 180-90-36=54$

$\therefore$ 54

Therefore, the answer is 54.

4. radius of small semicircle=2

radius of large semicircle=4

$4\pi \times 2=8\pi$

$8\pi \times 1=8\pi$

$8\pi+8\pi=16\pi$

Therefore, the answer is (C).

5. $2\pi r \times \dfrac{45}{360}=10\pi$

$2\pi r \times \dfrac{1}{8}=10\pi$

$\dfrac{r}{4}=10, \ r=40$

area of a circle$=\pi r^2$

$40 \times 40 \times \pi \times \dfrac{45}{360}=200\pi$

Therefore, the answer is (D).

6. Let small circle's radius be r.

area of semicircle$=\dfrac{\pi r^2}{2}$

3 semicircles$=\dfrac{3\pi r^2}{2}$

1 quarter$-$circles$=\dfrac{\pi r^2}{4}$

$\dfrac{3\pi r^2}{2}+\dfrac{\pi r^2}{4}=\dfrac{7\pi r^2}{4}$

$\therefore \dfrac{7}{4}$ times

Therefore, the answer is $\dfrac{7}{4}$ times.

7.

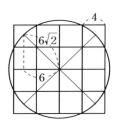

$r=6\sqrt{2} \rightarrow A=\pi r^2=72\pi$

Therefore, the answer is (C).

V. Solids

1.

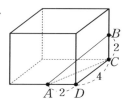

$4^2+2^2=16+4=20$

$\rightarrow (\sqrt{20})^2+3^2=29 \rightarrow d=\sqrt{29}$

2. volume=27

SA=54

3. volume$=\pi \times 4 \times 5=20\pi$

SA$=2(\pi \cdot 2^2)+5(2 \cdot \pi \cdot 2)=8\pi+20\pi=28\pi$

4. $\dfrac{1}{3}(7^2 \times \pi \times 6)=98\pi$

1. $3^2+6^2=\sqrt{45}$

$\sqrt{(\sqrt{45})^2+3^2}=XY$

$\sqrt{45+9}=\sqrt{54}=3\sqrt{6}$

Therefore, the answer is $3\sqrt{6}$.

2.

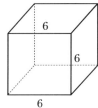

Area of each surface is 36.

$\rightarrow$ There are 6 faces.

Surface Area$=36 \times 6=216$

Therefore, the answer is SA$=216$.

VI. Coordinate Geometry

Exercise

1. $\sqrt{(-3-2)^2+(4+1)^2}=\sqrt{25+25}=5\sqrt{2}$

2. $\left(\dfrac{3+1}{2},\ \dfrac{2+0}{2}\right)=(2,\ 1)$

3. $\dfrac{4-2}{5-3}=\dfrac{2}{2}=1$

4. $\begin{aligned}2&=4m+b\\5&=10m+b\end{aligned}\ \Rightarrow\ \begin{aligned}5&=10m+2.5b\\5&=10m+b\end{aligned}$

$\Rightarrow\ 0=1.5b\ \rightarrow\ b=0$

$\Rightarrow\ m=\dfrac{1}{2}\ \rightarrow\ y=\dfrac{1}{2}x$

SAT Question

1.

B(-1, 6)   A(2, 6)

C(2, 2)

$\overline{AC}=6-2=4$

$\overline{AB}=2-(-1)=3$

$\dfrac{3\times4}{2}=6$

Therefore, the answer is 6.

2.

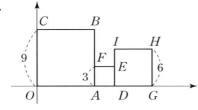

slope of $\overline{OI}=\dfrac{6-0}{12-0}=\dfrac{1}{2}$

slope of $\overline{OH}=\dfrac{6-0}{18-0}=\dfrac{1}{3}$

$\dfrac{1}{2}-\dfrac{1}{3}=\dfrac{1}{6}$

Therefore, the answer is $\dfrac{1}{6}$.

3. $x=20,\ y=80\ \rightarrow\ (20,\ 80)$

$x=120,\ y=140\ \rightarrow\ (120,\ 140)$

$\Rightarrow\ y=mx+c$

$m(slope)=\dfrac{140-80}{120-20}=\dfrac{60}{100}=\dfrac{3}{5}$

$y=0.6x+c(20,\ 80)\ \rightarrow\ c=68$

$y=0.6x+68$

Therefore, the answer is (C).

VII. Circle Equation

Exercise

1. $(x+2)^2+(y-3)^2=36$

2. Center: $(0,\ 0)$

Point: $(3,\ 4)$

Radius

$=\sqrt{\text{distance between center and a point on circumference}}$

$=\sqrt{3^2+4^2}=5$

Therefore, the answer is 5.

SAT Question

1.

T(1, 5) line ℓ

$C\left(\dfrac{11}{5},\ 2\right)$

Slope of line $l=\dfrac{2}{5}$

Slope of $\overline{CT}=\dfrac{-3}{s-1}$

Since the two slopes are perpendicular,

$$\frac{2}{5} \times \frac{-3}{s-1} = -1$$

$$5s - 5 = 6$$

$$5s = 11$$

$$s = \frac{11}{5}$$

Therefore, the answer is $\frac{11}{5}$.

2.

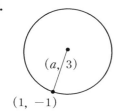

$$(1-a)^2 + (-1-3)^2 = 5^2$$

$$(a-1)^2 + 16 = 25$$

$$(a-1)^2 = 9$$

$$a - 1 = \pm 3$$

$$a = 4, \ -2$$

Since a must be positive,

$$a = 4$$

Therefore, the answer is 4.

3.

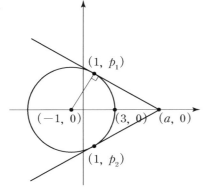

Circle equation:

$$(x+1)^2 + y^2 = 16$$

Plug $x = 1$ into the equation, and you will get p.

$$4 + p^2 = 16.$$

$$p^2 = 12$$

$$p = \pm 2\sqrt{3}$$

It doesn't matter whether p is positive or negative

because the value of a is the same for both cases.

So let's just go with

$$p = 2\sqrt{3}$$

Slope of the segment that connects $(-1, \ 0)$ and $(1, \ 2\sqrt{3})$

$$= \frac{2\sqrt{3} - 0}{1 - (-1)} = \sqrt{3}$$

Since this segment is perpendicular to the tangent line,

$$\sqrt{3} \times \frac{-2\sqrt{3}}{a-1} = -1$$

$$6 = a - 1$$

$$a = 7$$

Therefore, the answer is (C).

4. Center of the circle

$$\left(\frac{7-1}{2}, \ \frac{10-2}{2} \right) = (3, \ 4)$$

Radius

$=$ Distance between center and any point on the circle

$$= \sqrt{(7-3)^2 + (-2-4)^2}$$

$$= \sqrt{4^2 + 6^2}$$

$$= \sqrt{52}$$

Thus, the equation of the circle is

$$(a-3)^2 + (b-4)^2 = 52$$

Therefore, the answer is (D).

VIII. Trigonometry

Exercise

1. π rad $= 180°$

$$\frac{\pi}{180} \text{ rad} = 1°$$

$$200° = 200 \times \frac{\pi}{180} \text{ rad}$$

$$= \frac{10}{9} \pi$$

Therefore, the answer is $\frac{10}{9}\pi$ or 3.49.

2.

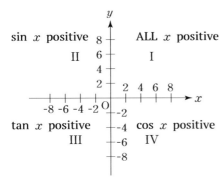

Only $\tan x$ is positive in Quadrant III.

Therefore, the answer is Quadrant III.

3. 2π

1. $\cos(90° - x°) = \sin x°$

$$= \frac{5}{13}$$

Therefore, the answer is $\dfrac{5}{13}$.

2.

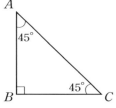

The angles of the triangle stay the same even if it's enlarged.

$\tan 45° = 1$

Therefore, the answer is 1.

IX. Complex Numbers

1. $4 + i - 3 + 8i$

$\quad = 1 + 9i$

Therefore, the answer is $1 + 9i$

2. $3 + 7i - (2i - 3i^2)$

$\quad = 3 + 7i - 2i + 3(-1)$

$\quad = 3 + 5i - 3$

$\quad = 5i$

Therefore, the answer is $5i$

3. $(1+i)(2-i)(1+2i)$

$\quad = (2 - i + 2i + 1)(1 + 2i)$

$\quad = (3 + i)(1 + 2i)$

$\quad = 3 + 6i + i - 2$

$\quad = 1 + 7i$

Therefore, the answer is $1 + 7i$

X. Extra Topics

1. $(4mn^3)^2 - (x - 7) + \sqrt{49l^6}$

$\quad = (16m^2n^6) - (x - 7) + 7l^3$

Therefore, the answer is (B).

2. $\dfrac{3x}{5x + 15} + \dfrac{x + 4}{x^2 + 3x}$

$\quad = \dfrac{3x}{5(x+3)} + \dfrac{x+4}{x(x+3)}$

$\quad = \dfrac{3x^2 + 5x + 20}{5x(x+3)}$

$\quad = \dfrac{3x^2 + 5x + 20}{5x^2 + 15x}$

Therefore, the answer is (A).

3.

$$\frac{45p^2q^4r^5+15p^5q^3r^6-25p^3q^5r^2}{5p^2q^3r^4}$$

$$=\frac{5p^2q^3r^2(9qr^3+3p^3r^4-5pq^2)}{5p^2q^3r^4}$$

$$=\frac{9qr^3+3p^3r^4-5pq^2}{r^2}$$

Therefore, the answer is (D).

4. $(x^2+t^2)^2$

$$=x^4+2x^2t^2+t^4$$

$$=(1+a-b)x^4+2bx^2+ab$$

$1+a-b=1$

$a-b=0$

$\therefore\ a=b$

$2b=2t^2$

$b=t^2$

$\therefore\ a=t^2$

Therefore, the answer is (C).

5. Just because there are more registered members than non−registered members in the swimming team does not mean the former is better at swimming than the latter. The registered members might be more passionate about swimming which may be why they joined the swimming team or they might have joined the team to improve their swimming skills. There is no evidence of relationship between being a member of the swimming pool and being in the swimming team. Therefore, the answer is (D).

6. The researcher is creating a control group and an experimental group by randomly assigning different treatments to the mice. This experiment is called a controlled experiment.
Therefore, the answer is (C).

7. In order for a result of an experiment to be valid, two factors must be met: random sampling and random assignment. In this survey, the researcher only interviewed high school boys and not girls. Hence, the sample was not randomly selected and the result cannot be generalized to the whole population. Therefore, the correct answer is (D).

New SAT Math Practice Tests

Practice Test 1

1. In the figure below, all the circles are the same size. Each one is tangent to the larger square and two or three other circles, except for the one in the middle. The center points of the four corner circles are the vertices of the smaller square. If the smaller square is 16 square inches in area, what is the area of the larger square?

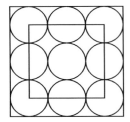

A) 36sq in
B) 48sq in
C) 56sq in
D) 64sq in

2.

x is 4 more than a.

x is 8 less than b.

The numbers a, b, and x have the relationships stated above. If the average (arithmetic mean) of a and b is -20, what is the value of x?

A) -22
B) -21
C) -19
D) -11

3. The figure below shows two circles with radii of $\overline{AO}$ and $\overline{BO}$ each. If the circumference of the inner circle is 12π and the diameter of the outer circle is 30, what is the length of $\overline{AB}$?

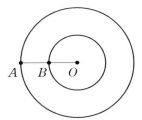

A) 6
B) 8
C) 9
D) 12

4. Points P, Q and R are on a circle with center O shown below such that $\overline{PQ}$ is the diameter. If the length of $\overline{PQ}$ is 9 and $\angle RPQ$ is $20°$, what is the length of minor arc $\overset{\frown}{PR}$?

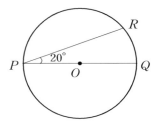

A) $\dfrac{7\pi}{2}$
B) $\dfrac{9}{2}\pi$
C) $\dfrac{11}{2}\pi$
D) 6π

5. The equation $2(2x-3a)(x+3a)=0$ has two solutions for x. Which of the following is the sum of the solutions in terms of a?

A) $\dfrac{2a}{3}$

B) $\dfrac{3a}{2}$

C) $-\dfrac{3a}{2}$

D) $-\dfrac{2a}{3}$

6. The figure below shows an equilateral triangle inscribed in the square. If the area of $\triangle EFG$ is $9\sqrt{3}$, what is the area of $\square ABCD$ equal to?

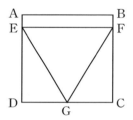

A) 27

B) 36

C) $27\sqrt{3}$

D) $36\sqrt{3}$

7. An equilateral triangle is inscribed in a square. If the length of a side of the equilateral triangle is the same as the length of a side the square, what is the probability that a point in the square is also in the triangle?

A) $\dfrac{1}{2}$

B) $\dfrac{\sqrt{3}}{4}$

C) $\dfrac{3}{4}$

D) 1

8.
$$7,\ 6,\ 13,\ 10,\ 14,\ x$$
The average (arithmetic mean) of the six integers listed above is the same as the mode of the listed numbers. What is the value of x?

x	-2	-1	0	1
$f(x)$	$-\dfrac{3}{4}$	-1	$-\dfrac{3}{2}$	-3

9. The table above shows some corresponding x and y values for the function $f(x)=\dfrac{k}{x-a}$, where a and k are constants. What is the value of $a+k$?

10. If $\dfrac{5}{6}$ of a is 125 and $\dfrac{3}{4}$ of b is 900, what is the value of $2a+b$?

11. The difference between two negative integers x and y is 45. If $\dfrac{x}{2y}=5$, what is the absolute value of x?

12. Let $A=\dfrac{4}{x+y}$ and $\dfrac{1}{A}=\dfrac{3}{2}$. If $x=-3$, what is the value of y?

13. Find the greatest value of x that satisfies the equation $x^2-7x=60$.

14. What is the value of i^3? $(i=\sqrt{-1})$

15. y^2 is directly proportional to $2x-7$, and when x is 8, y is 6. If $x=16$ and $y>0$, what is the value of y?

16. If $\dfrac{4}{x}=\dfrac{7}{x+12}$, what is the value of $\dfrac{x}{4}$?

A) 4
B) 7
C) 11
D) 16

17. If the system of inequalities $y>3x+2$ and $y\le-x+6$ is graphed on the xy-plane, which quadrant contains no solution to the system?

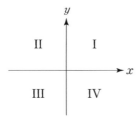

A) Quadrant I
B) Quadrant III
C) Quadrant IV
D) There are solutions for every quadrant.

Questions 18 and 19 refer to the following table.

Material	Specific Heat Capacity (J/kg · °C)
Aluminum	897
Concrete	850
Diamond	509
Glass	840
Helium Gas	5,193
Water	4,186

The chart above shows approximations of the specific heat capacity of the six materials given. Given the specific heat capacity of a material, you can calculate the amount of heat, in Joules (J), needed to raise the temperature of a certain substance by using the formula $Q=cm\triangle T$ (Q is the amount of heat needed; c is the specific heat capacity; m is the mass of the substance and $\triangle T$ is the number of degrees of Celsius). For instance, if the specific heat capacity of Substance A is $1.5 J/kg \cdot °C$ and you want to raise the temperature of 1.5kg of Substance A by 2°C, then you need
$$Q=cm\triangle T=1.5J/kg \cdot 2°C=4.5J$$

18. How much heat is needed to raise the temperature of 3kg of helium gas by 1.2 degrees Celsius?

A) 6,235 J
B) 15,579 J
C) 18,695 J
D) Cannot be determined from the given information.

19. Compared to 7.3kg of diamond, how much more heat do you need in order to raise the same mass of concrete by 3.5 degrees Celsius?

A) $8,\ 713$ J

B) 341 J

C) $2,\ 489$ J

D) 26 J

Practice Test 2

1. Six identical squares are used to make a cube. If the area of each square is 36, what is the sum of all the edges of the cube?

A) 48
B) 60
C) 72
D) 216

2. The figure below consists of one square, $\square$ABCD, and two identical right triangles. If $\overline{BE}=12$ and $\overline{CE}=5$, what is the perimeter of hexagon ABECDF?

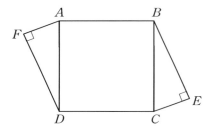

A) 54
B) 60
C) 64
D) 70

3. In the figure below, the big square has sides with a length of 4 and contains one circle, one triangle, and two quarter circles. If A, B, C and D are midpoints of each side of the big square, what is the area of the shaded region?

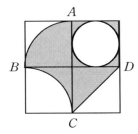

A) 6
B) $6-\pi$
C) $6+\pi$
D) $10-\pi$

4. James collects precious antique stamps. In 2002, he had 155 stamps, and he decided to buy the same number of stamps on the first day of every year, starting from 2003. By the end of 2012, the number of stamp was 235. If he continues at this pace, how many stamps will he have collected by the end of 2020?

5. $\dfrac{4x+y}{3}+\dfrac{2x+2y}{3}=6$ for some numbers x and y.

What is the value of $x+\dfrac{1}{2}y$?

6. A rectangular solid is given below. What is the expression for the total surface area of the solid?

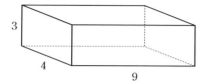

A) $3 \times 4 \times 9$

B) $2(3 \times 4 \times 9)$

C) $2(3+4)+2(3+9)+2(4+9)$

D) $2(3 \times 4)+2(3 \times 9)+2(4 \times 9)$

7. In the figure below, 4 cylinders of the same dimensions are stacked one upon the other in order to make a bigger cylinder. If the height of one of the smaller cylinders is 2.5 inches and the radius of its base is 3 inches, what is the total volume of the figure, in cubic inches?

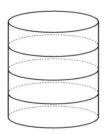

A) 80π

B) 90π

C) 100π

D) 110π

8. 33 people are divided into groups so that each group has 2 to 4 members. If every person must belong to one group, at most how many groups of 4 people can be made?

A) 4

B) 7

C) 8

D) 9

9. The relationship between x and y is that $y=4-x$. Which of the following expressions, in terms of y, is equal to $16-x^2$?

A) y^2

B) $16-y^2$

C) $y(4-y)$

D) $y(8-y)$

10. If $|2-x|<4$, what is a possible value of x?

A) -3

B) -2

C) 2

D) 6

11. If $0.00304=(3.04)10^{2x-5}$, what is the value of x?

12. If $\frac{1}{3}(9^3)^2 = 3^{2x+3}$, what is the value of x?

13. A paper machine in a factory produces 140 pages of paper per minute. If one box contains 80 pages of paper, how many boxes of paper will be produced in 6 hours?

14. Among the expressions below, which is equal to $\frac{3}{a}$ percent of 40 for $a>0$?

A) $6a$

B) $\frac{6a}{5}$

C) $\frac{40a}{3}$

D) $\frac{6}{5a}$

15. Julie is selling thin mints around the city to gather funds for Christmas charity. Starting from September, each month she receives the same amount of thin mints to sell. The number of thin mints left to sell at the end of the month can be estimated with the equation $T=156-5h$, where T is the number of left over thin mints and h is the number of households that bought thin mints. What is the meaning of the value 5 in this equation?

A) Julie sells 5 thin mints per household.

B) Julie sells to 5 households per day.

C) Julie starts each month with 5 thin mints to sell.

D) Julie will be done selling thin mints within 5 days.

16. If $3x-7\geq 6$, what is the minumum possible value for $6x+7$?

A) 16

B) 26

C) 33

D) 36

Questions 17 and 18 refer to the following table.

Items purchased at Sam's record shop

	Genre						
	Rock	R&B	K-Pop	Jazz	Religious	Classical	Total
CD	8	16	9	5	3	8	49
LP	2	3	0	9	1	15	30
Concert DVD	12	6	14	4	3	5	44
Total	22	25	23	18	7	28	123

The table represents the different types of items sold at Sam's record shop in the month of July.

17. What proportion of the purchased items are Jazz LPs?

A) 14.63%

B) 7.32%

C) 50%

D) 3.66%

18. If Amanda bought two CDs, what is the probability that both of them were classical music CDs?

A) 2.38%

B) 16.33%

C) 27.78%

D) 7.72%

Practice Test 3

1. The figure below shows two similar right triangles $\triangle ABC$ and $\triangle DCE$ with the measures of their sides being integers. If $\overline{AC}=6$, $\overline{AB}=10$, and $\overline{CD}=4$, what is the measure of $\overline{CE}$?

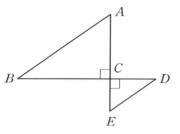

A) 2

B) 3

C) 4

D) 5

2. A rectangular box with a length of 3 inches, a width of 9 inches, and height of 1 inch has the same volume as a cubic box. What is the sum of all the edges of a cubic box, in inches?

3. A piggy bank contains only one kind of coin. Initially, there are 125 coins in the piggy bank. A portion of coins are taken out, and the amount of coins taken is worth $17.50. Now, there are 55 coins left in the piggy bank. What is the value of one coin, in dollars?

4. $3x=2a+1$ and $2y=a-4$. When $x=7$, what is the value of y?

5. In the xy-plane, point P has coordinate $(a, -4)$ and point Q has coordinate $(0, 6)$, where a is a negative integer. If the slope between points P and Q is less than 7 and greater than 4, what is the absolute value of a?

6. The perimeter of one square is 12 and the perimeter of another square is 18. What is the difference in length between the diagonals of these squares? $(\sqrt{2}=1.4)$

7. In a right triangle, 5 times the degree measure of the smallest angle is equal to 3 times the degree measure of the next smallest angle. What is eight times the degree measure of the smallest angle?

8. If $x<0$ and $x-6=-x^2$, what is the value of x^2?

9. If $x^2+y^2=2$ and $x+y=2$, find the value of xy.

10. Simplify $i+i^2+i^3+i^4$ $(i=\sqrt{-1})$.

11. If $(x+y)^2=70$ and $x^2+y^2=40$, what is the value of xy?

A) 22

B) 15

C) 30

D) 16

12. If $y=4(x-2)^2$, which of the following expressions is equal to $3(4-2x)^2$ in terms of y?

A) $-9y^2$

B) $-3y^2$

C) $-9y$

D) $3y$

13. The segment $\overline{OA}$ in the figure below is rotating counterclockwise with point O being fixed. While rotating, the point A passes the x-axis and y-axis. When the point A meets the y-axis for a second time, what is the coordinate of point A?

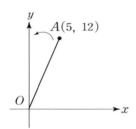

A) $(0, -13)$

B) $(-13, 0)$

C) $(-12, 0)$

D) $(0, -12)$

14. In the xy-coordinate plane below, the coordinates of points A and B are $(-3, 0)$ and $(0, -2)$ respectively. What is the slope of the line passing the points A and B?

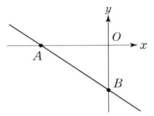

A) -1

B) $-\dfrac{2}{3}$

C) $\dfrac{2}{3}$

D) $-\dfrac{3}{2}$

15. The line $x-3y=-2$ in the xy-coordinate plane is reflected with respect to the y-axis. What is the result of the reflected equation?

A) $x-3y=-2$

B) $x+3y=-2$

C) $x-3y=-2$

D) $x+3y=2$

16. Functions f and g have values according to x as shown below. When $f(-1)=g(x)$, what is the value of x?

x	$f(x)$	$g(x)$
-2	-1	2
-1	-2	-4
0	5	4
1	2	-3
2	1	-2

A) -1

B) 3

C) 2

D) 1

17.
$$7x-(15+4x)=k(x-5)$$
If the equation above has infinitely many solutions and k is a constant, what is the value of k?

A) 2

B) 3

C) 7

D) 11

18.
$$3x-2\leq 4y$$
$$y=\frac{1}{2}x$$

In the system of equations above, what is the maximum possible value for x?

A) -1

B) 0

C) 1

D) 2

Questions 19 and 20 refer to the following graph.

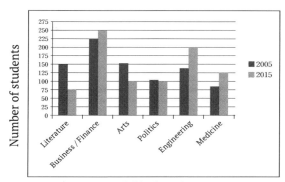

The bar graph above shows the results of a survey, carried out in 2005 and 2015, in which 850 students from a high school were asked to indicate their desired field of study in university.

19. In a scatterplot of this data, where student responses from the year 2005 are plotted along the x-axis and student responses in the year 2015 are plotted along the y-axis for each of the given fields of study, how many data points would lie above the line $y=x$?

A) 0

B) 1

C) 2

D) 3

20. Of the following, which best approximates the percent decrease in the students' interest in the field of literature from year 2005 to year 2015?

A) 150%

B) 75%

C) 50%

D) 25%

Practice Test 4

1. If $x-(2z+3w)=100$ and $x+3y-2z=1000$, what is the value of $y+w$?

2. For a positive number x, if $\frac{30}{x}$ is equal to $\frac{x}{3}$ percent of 40, what is the solution for x?

A) $\frac{3}{4}$

B) $\frac{9}{10}$

C) 10

D) 15

3. The line $x-2y-2=0$ in the xy-coordinate plane is reflected with respect to the x-axis. What is the result of the reflected equation?

A) $x+2y+2=0$

B) $x-2y+2=0$

C) $x-2y-2=0$

D) $x+2y-2=0$

x	$f(x)$	$g(x)$
-2	-4	$\frac{1}{2}$
-1	-2	$\frac{1}{2}$
0	2	3
1	5	2
2	8	1

4. Functions f and g have values according to x as shown above. When $f(0)=2g(x)$, what is the value of x?

A) -1

B) 3

C) 1

D) 2

5. A small amusement park charges each person a $15 entrance fee. A ticket for an all–you–can–ride pass costs an additional $40 per person. On one day, 125 people visited the amusement park and 75 people bought all–ride passes. What was the total income on that day, in dollars? (Disregard the $ sign when gridding your answer.)

6. There are two kinds of candy boxes at a gift shop. One box contains 5 candies, and another box contains 4 candies. If Jeff wants exactly 28 candies, how many boxes containing 5 candies will he need to buy?

7. The three lines in the figure below intersect at a point. What is the value of $-a-b+2d+e+30$?

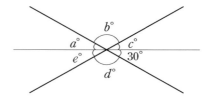

8. John can walk 3 miles in 50 minutes. At the same pace, how many miles would he walk if he walked for 1 hour and 30 minutes?

A) $\dfrac{6}{7}\pi$

B) $\dfrac{7}{6\pi}$

C) $\dfrac{6}{7\pi}$

D) $\dfrac{6}{7}$

9. The figure below shows two lines intersecting each other. The angles created by the lines are also shown. What is the value of y?

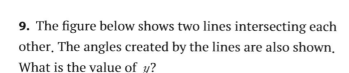

10. Originally, the perimeter of $\triangle ABC$ was 90. Now each side of $\triangle ABC$ has decreased by 10 percent to make a new triangle, $\triangle A'B'C'$. What is the perimeter of $\triangle A'B'C'$?

11. Find the sum of all x that satisfies $2x^2-19x=60$.

12. 12 identical circles with unknown radii are inscribed in the rectangle shown below. Each circle is tangent to the others. If C represents the total circumference of all the circles and P represents the perimeter of the rectangle, what is the value of $\dfrac{P}{C}$?

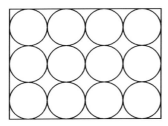

13. One small square and four right triangles measuring 4 inches in height and 3 inches in base are used to make a piece of cloth. If this pattern is used to make a table cloth measuring 21 inches by 28 inches without any leftover cloth, how many right triangles are there?

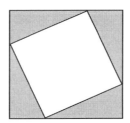

A) 14

B) 21

C) 28

D) 48

14. There are $3x$ boys and $5x$ girls in a classroom. If one student is selected at random, what is the probability of selecting a boy?

15. If x can take the value of any real number between -1 and 4, which of the following expressions represents possible values of x^2?

A) $-1 \le x^2 \le 16$
B) $-1 \le x^2 \le 4$
C) $1 \le x^2 \le 4$
D) $0 \le x^2 \le 16$

16. If $4(y-1) = \dfrac{x}{5} - 4$, what is the value of $\dfrac{x}{y}$?

A) 6
B) 11
C) 20
D) Cannot be determined from the given information.

17. Based on the graph, which of the following is closest to the time the car almost stopped?

A) 12:30 P.M.
B) 1:06 P.M.
C) 2:00 P.M.
D) 2:30 P.M.

18. Which of the following is closest to the total distance traveled by the car?

A) 3,271 miles
B) 108.8 miles
C) 55 miles
D) 75.0 miles

Questions 17, 18, and 19 refer to the following graph.

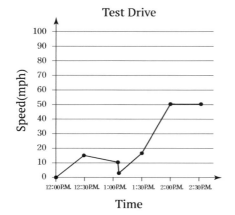

Test Drive

The graph above shows the velocity of an automated car during a test drive. At one point, the car almost came to a sudden halt due to an unknown technical problem.

19. During which interval did the car neither accelerate nor decelerate?

A) 12:00 P.M. $-$ 12:30 P.M.
B) 1:05 P.M. $-$ 1:06 P.M.
C) 2:00 P.M. $-$ 2:30 P.M.
D) There is no such interval

Practice Test 5

1. The sum of x and y is equal to three times z. y is 16 less than three times the sum of x and z. What is the value of x?

2. Simplify the following: $i \times i^3 \times i^5 \times i^7$.

3. The broken clock below has a minute hand and an hour hand. The hour hand turns properly; however, the minute hand turns clockwise at a constant speed of 7 degrees per minute according to a properly functioning watch. How many circles does the minute hand make in actual h hours?

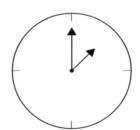

A) $\frac{7h}{6}$

B) $\frac{h}{6}$

C) $\frac{h}{7}$

D) h

4. A sphere is cut into exactly half. If the radius of the sphere was 5 meters, what is the surface area of one of the half spheres?

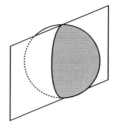

A) $\dfrac{75\pi}{3}$

B) $\dfrac{175\pi}{3}$

C) $\dfrac{500\pi}{3}$

D) 75π

5. If $x>0$, $y^9=x^3y^3$. simplify the expression $\dfrac{x^2y^4}{x^5}$, in terms of y.

A) $\left(\dfrac{1}{y}\right)^4$

B) y^4

C) $\left(\dfrac{1}{y^3}\right)$

D) $\left(\dfrac{1}{y^2}\right)$

6. In a triangle ABC, the angle $A=50°$ and the angle $B=64°$. If $\angle C=2x°$, what is x?

7. A cyclist spent 150 minutes to travel from Huntington city to Ozwell city. A truck driver spent 40 minutes to travel the same distance. By what fraction of an hour was the cyclist's travel time longer than truck driver's travel time?

8. The coordinates of points as shown below are A($-$2, 5), B(-4, 3), C(5, -2), and D(2, -7). If point P lies on any point on $\overline{AB}$, and point Q lies on any point on $\overline{CD}$, what is one possible absolute value of slope of $\overline{PQ}$?

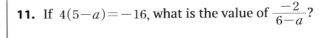

9. If a certain cube has 24 square inches in surface area, what is the volume of the cube in cubic inches?

10. The quadratic equation $3x^2-mx-24=0$ has 4 as one of the solutions. m is the coefficient of x. What is the value of m?

11. If $4(5-a)=-16$, what is the value of $\dfrac{-2}{6-a}$?

12. Find the coordinate $(p,\ q)$ on $x^2+y^2=4$ that makes the distance between $(p,\ q)$ and $x=-5$ the shortest.

13. Find the value of $(i+2)\times(3+4i)$. $(i=\sqrt{-1})$

14. Set A has 5 numbers such that the average (arithmetic mean) of these numbers is 25. When a new number is added to set A, the average increases by 4. What is the value of the new number?

15. A store increased the price of items by 20 percent from the regular price of $500. Because of fewer customers, the store decreased this new price by 20 percent. When an item is sold, a sales tax of 10 percent of the regular price is charged as well. What is the new price including the tax? (Disregard the $ sign when gridding your answer.)

16.
$$3a - rb = 2$$
$$4a - 3b = 5$$

In the system of equations above, r is a constant and a and b are variables. For what value of r will the system of equations have no solution?

A) -7.35

B) 2.25

C) 4.75

D) 9

18. If the land area of Seoul—Incheon is $2,266$ km², what is its population, in millions? (Round your answer to the nearest million.)

19. The population density of Dhaka is what percent higher than the population density of New York? (Round your answer to the nearest whole number.)

Questions 17, 18 and 19 refer to the following table.

City	Population density (per km²)	City	Population density (per km²)
Dhaka, Bangladesh	43,500	Seoul-Incheon, South Korea	10,400
Hyderabad, Pakistan	40,300	Salvador, Brazil	9,100
Mumbai, India	32,400	La Paz, Bolivia	7,000
Hong Kong, China	26,400	Panama City, Panama	6, 800
Hamah, Syria	23,700	Vancouver, Canada	4,800
Mogadishu, Somalia	23,400	New York, USA	4,500

The table lists the population density of 12 cities around the world in 2015.

17. According to the table, what is the mean population density, per km², of the 12 cities? (Round your answer to the nearest whole number.)

Practice Test 6

1. In the xy-coordinate plane below, point A and point C lie on the y-axis and x-axis respectively. If ▢ABCO is a square, which of the following represents the equation of a line that passes through points A and B?

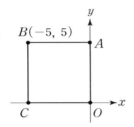

A) $y=x+5$

B) $y=5x$

C) $y=x$

D) $y=5$

2. In a physics lab, 4 students share a ruler, 5 students share a scale, and 10 students share a marker. If the total number of rulers, scales, and markers is k, how many students are in the lab, in terms of k? (Assume that the number of the students is divisible by 20.)

A) $\dfrac{19}{200}k$

B) $\dfrac{200}{19}k$

C) $\dfrac{11}{20}k$

D) $\dfrac{20}{11}k$

3. The function f is defined as $f(x)=\sqrt{3x+4}$. When $f(a)=5$, which of the following is the value of a?

A) -3

B) -5

C) 5

D) 7

4. For positive integers x and y, $x^y=81$. How many different integers can x be?

A) More than three

B) One

C) Two

D) Three

5. There were 15 birds 20 years ago in a zoo. The number of birds increased for 12 years at a constant rate of t birds per year. Then the number of birds decreased until now at the same constant rate. If there are 35 birds now, what was the number of birds 2 years ago?

A) 45

B) 48

C) 50

D) 52

6. In the table below, some x values and corresponding $f(x)$ values are shown. What is the value of $3f(2)+f(5)-4$?

x	$f(x)$
0	2
1	0
2	3
3	6
4	5
5	4

A) 1
B) 2
C) 8
D) 9

7. For positive integers a and b, which of the following is equivalent to $5^{2a} \cdot 3^{(2a+b)}$?

A) $15^{2a} \cdot 3^b$
B) $15^{(4a^2+2ab)}$
C) $225^{2a} \cdot 3^b$
D) $15^{(2a+b)}$

8. $3x+4$ is 2 less than $2y$. When $x=4$, what is the value of y?

9. There are 150 strawberry candies and some chocolate candies in a box. When a candy is chosen from the box randomly, the probability that the candy will be chocolate is $\frac{4}{7}$. How many chocolate candies are in the box?

10. A graph of a function is drawn below. If points A and B are as shown, what is y-coordinate of y-intercept?

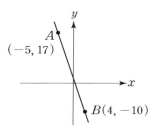

11. In the figure below, $\triangle ABC$ is an isosceles triangle. The coordinates of points are $A(2,\ 6)$, $B(-a,\ 3)$, and $C(5,\ -4)$. What is the value of integer a if $a>0$?

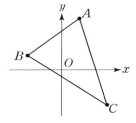

(Note: figure not drawn to scale.)

12. In the xy-coordinate plane shown below, a square and four half circles with their diameters forming each side of the square are drawn. If each mark represents 2 units, what is the total area of the four half circles?

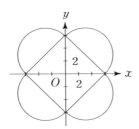

A) 36

B) 36π

C) $24\sqrt{2}\pi$

D) $36\sqrt{2}\pi$

13. In the figure below, four identical circles are inscribed in a bigger equilateral triangle such that they are tangent to one another. If the radius of a circle is 3, what is the height of the bigger equilateral triangle?

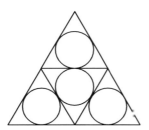

A) $8\sqrt{3}+6$

B) $8\sqrt{3}+8$

C) $12\sqrt{3}+6$

D) 18

14. As shown below, 10% of the students are not in any club. Considering only students who are in clubs, Math club represents what percent of the total students who are in clubs?

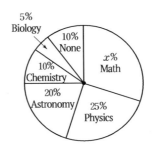

% of students in certain clubs in a high school

A) 30%

B) $33\frac{1}{3}\%$

C) 33.5%

D) 35.5%

15. A furniture store buys wooden desks from a factory at a wholesale price. The store then sells the desks to individual customers at a store. The retail price is 35 percent more than the wholesale price. At a special event, the store gives 20 percent off the retail price for desks. What is the final price at the store if the wholesale price is a?

A) $0.55a$

B) $0.92a$

C) $1.08a$

D) $1.15a$

16.

$$5m - a = 9m - 4$$
$$5n - b = 9n - 4$$

In the equations above, a and b are constants. If b is a minus 8, what is the value of $n - m$?

A) 2
B) 4
C) 8
D) 9

17. Justin is buying bags of nacho chips and jars of queso dip for $3.50 and $2.00, respectively, to prepare for a party. If Justin spent a total of $109.00 from buying a total of 41 nachos and quesos, how many nachos did Justin buy?

A) 11
B) 18
C) 23
D) 30

Questions 18 and 19 refer to the following information.

'Simple interest' is a type of interest that is paid as a fixed percentage of the original amount of money that has been borrowed. If a total of P dollars was lent in the beginning with a rate of R per year, then the amount of interest to be paid, I, after T years is given by the formula $I = PRT$.

Janice is planning to open a vintage shop as a part of her budding fashion business and estimates that she needs an initial budget of $17,000. After one year with no interest, the bank charges a simple interest rate of 0.12 (12%) for the next three years, at the end of which Janice must repay the bank with the original amount borrowed plus interest.

18. Using the simple interest formula given above, how much does Janice need to pay the bank at the end of the four years, in thousands? (Round your answer to the nearest thousand dollar.)

19. Suppose that Janice's vintage shop witnesses burgeoning sales and Janice now thinks that she will be able to repay her loan within two years by making monthly payments. Assuming that the bank still charges a simple interest rate of 0.12 per year after an initial year with no interest, how much is Janice's monthly payment? (Round your answer to the nearest dollar.)

Practice Test 7

1. A nurse has a bottle containing 4.5 liters of Ringer's solution. She has to fill 32 drip bags that must contain exactly 135 milliliters of Ringer's solution. After filling all the drip bags without spilling, how many <u>milliliters</u> of Ringer's solution will she have left in the bottle? (1 liter$=1,\ 000$ milliliters)

2. When $\frac{4}{3}=\frac{2}{a}$ and $\frac{12}{4}=\frac{5}{b}$, what is the value of $\frac{b}{a}$?

A) $\frac{4}{3}$

B) $\frac{9}{4}$

C) $\frac{10}{9}$

D) $\frac{12}{5}$

3. If $(x-6)(y+6)=6$, what is the greatest value of $|y-x|$? $(x>0,\ y<0)$

A) 6

B) 11

C) 13

D) 17

4. If $\frac{1}{3}(5x+2y)=3x$, what is $2x$ in terms of y?

A) y

B) $2y$

C) $\frac{2}{3}y$

D) $\frac{3}{2}y$

5. The distance between x and 4 on a straight line is 3 units. Which of the following expression represents the equation to find the values x?

A) $|x-7|=0$

B) $|x-4|=3$

C) $|x-3|=4$

D) $|x+3|=4$

6. Three identical circles are shown below. Each circle passes through the centers of other two circles and has a radius of 8. What is the total length of the dashed arcs?

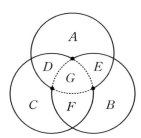

A) 16π

B) $\frac{40}{3}\pi$

C) $\frac{32}{3}\pi$

D) 8π

7. In the figure below, $\triangle ABC$ and $\triangle ACD$ are right triangles. What is the area of $\triangle ABC$?

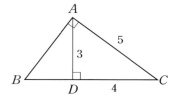

8. If $6x+8 \le 3x+40$, what is the largest possible value of x?

9. When a number is divided by 3 and then decreased by 5, the result is 4. Calculate the number.

10. The figure below shows two lines passing through the origin. If the slope of line a is m and the slope of line b is $-m$, what is the value of x?

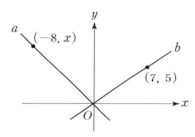

11. $\triangle ABC$ is the triangle given below. If $3x < y < 4x$, what is one possible value of x?

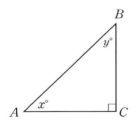

12. The rectangle shown below is divided into 4 different areas. If the area of A is 5, what is the area of D?

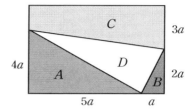

A) $\dfrac{15}{7}$

B) $\dfrac{15}{4}$

C) $\dfrac{7}{2}$

D) 5

13. Two circles with different radii shown below share the same point O as their center. The radius of the smaller circle is a, and the radius of the bigger circle is $a+5$. If the minor arc length of $\overarc{CD}$ is 10, what is the minor arc length of $\overarc{AB}$, in terms of a?

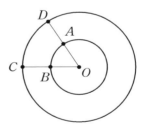

A) $\dfrac{5a\pi}{a+5}$

B) $\dfrac{(a+5)\pi}{10a}$

C) $\dfrac{a+5}{10a}$

D) $\dfrac{10a}{a+5}$

14. A car is driven at a constant speed on a local road. If the driver takes 40 seconds to drive 0.5 miles, how fast was the car driven, in miles per hour?

15. The graph shown below describes the percentages of students in various clubs in a high school. What percent of students are in Math club?

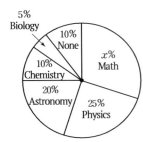

% of students in certain clubs in a high school

A) 30%

B) 25%

C) 20%

D) 15%

16.
$$6x-8\geq 3y$$
$$\frac{1}{2}y=\frac{1}{6}x+2$$

In the system of equations above, what is the minimum possible value of x?

A) 3

B) 4

C) 8

D) 20

17.
$$p=1.38+0.42n$$
$$h=2.91+0.25n$$

In the equations above, p and h represent the price, in dollars, of pens and highlighters, respectively, n days after November 2015. What will be the price of pens when pens and highlighters have the same price?

A) $1.53

B) $5.16

C) $9.00

D) $11.37

Questions 18 and 19 refer to the following table.

Day	Population
1	!
2	51
3	153
4	459
5	1377
6	4,131
7	?

The table above shows the population of fruit flies in a laboratory over the course of a week. A researcher at the lab uses the equation $P=17(r)^{t-1}$ to model the population, P, of fruit flies after t days since the beginning of the experiment.

18. What value should the researcher use for r?

19. What does the researcher believe the population will be at the end of Day 7, in hundreds? (Round your answer to the nearest hundreds.)

Practice Test 8

1. The cost to make a certain number of items in a factory is given as cost$=95000+(15-3x)^2$, where x is the number of items. How many items should the factory produce to minimize the cost?

2. For all values of x, the function f is defined by $f(x)=\dfrac{4-2x}{3}$. What is the value of x when $f(x)=-14$?

3. The equilateral triangle and the circle with radius r shown below have equal areas. If one side of the equilateral triangle is $2\sqrt{3}$, what is the value of r^2?

A) $\dfrac{3\sqrt{3}}{\pi}$

B) $\dfrac{3\sqrt{3}\pi}{4}$

C) $\dfrac{3}{4\pi}$

D) $\dfrac{3\pi}{4}$

4. In the xy-plane, point A$(1,\ 4)$ is reflected across the y-axis to make a new point B. The point B is reflected across the line $y=2$, to make another point

C. What is the perimeter of $\triangle$ABC?

A) $2\sqrt{5}+6$

B) $-2\sqrt{5}+6$

C) 11

D) $4\sqrt{5}+6$

5. Which of the following is the graph of a function f which has exactly four values of x that satisfy the equation $f(x)=0$?

A)

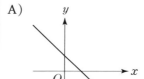

B)

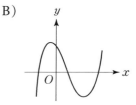

C)

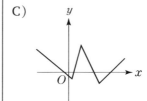

D)

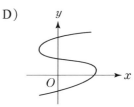

6. If $x>0$ and $x^{\frac{1}{4}}x^{\frac{2}{4}}x^{\frac{5}{4}}=2x^2-3x$, what is the value of x?

A) 1

B) $\sqrt{3}$

C) 0

D) 3

7. Janet has candy and James has chocolates as snacks. If Janet gives James 2 candies, they each have an equal number of snacks. If instead James gives Janet 3 chocolates, the number of candies and chocolates Janet has is twice the number of those James has. How many chocolates does James have in the beginning?

A) 8
B) 9
C) 10
D) 13

8. If $\frac{5x}{3} - \frac{2}{3} = \frac{7x}{6}$, what is the value of x?

9. If $4 < x < 9$ and $15 < y < 40$, where x and y are integers, what is the smallest possible value of $\frac{y}{x}$?

10. The perimeter of a rectangle whose width is 20 is 100. What is the length of the rectangle?

11. 8,000 people live in a town. In this town, 70 percent of the population resides within 2 miles of a bus stop. Half of the residents living more than 2 miles from a bus stop use their cars instead of riding the bus while the rest rides the bus. In the town, how many people have to use the bus and also live more than 2 miles from a bus stop?

12. The figure below consists of two identical right isosceles triangles and one square. If the length of $\overline{AE}$ is $4\sqrt{2}$, what is the total area of the triangles and square?

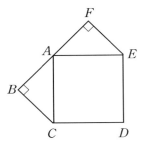

13. In the xy-coordinate plane below, two vertices of a square are as shown. What is the perimeter of the square?

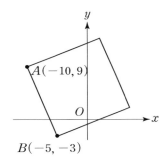

PRICES OF Cookies

Names of packages	Number of cookies	Cost of package
A	6	$0.75
B	10	$1.00
C	18	$1.70
D	25	$2.00

14. The table above shows cookie packages sold at a store. Packages contain different numbers of cookies so that each package has a different price. What is the least amount of money required in order to buy exactly 108 cookies?

A) $9.00
B) $9.70
C) $9.90
D) $0.25

15. The diagram below shows the results of a survey of 90 people who have visited at least one of the three countries. For example, 5 people visited Korea and Japan, but not China. The numbers of people who have visited only Japan or China are unknown. According to the survey, if the number of people who visited Korea is the same as the number of people who visited Japan, how many people in the survey visited only China?

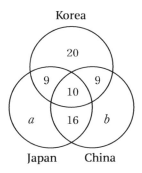

16.
$$7a - 6b = 22$$
$$3a + 3b = 2$$
In the system of equations above, a and b are variables. What is the value of $a + 3b$?

A) -2
B) 0
C) 2
D) 6

17. If the system of inequalities $y \leq x$ and $y > 2x - 3$ is graphed on the xy-plane, which quadrant contains no solution to the system?

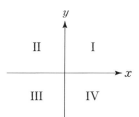

Questions 18 and 19 refer to the following information.

A marine scientist is studying gray whale population in the Pacific Ocean, and the recorded initial population was 16,000. Given the change in population of this species, $\triangle N$, and the initial population, $N_{initial}$, the scientist seeks to find the value of constant K, which is the number of gray whales the environment is able to support, by using the equation below.

$$\triangle N = 0.6 N_{initial} \left(1 - \frac{N_{initial}}{K} \right)$$

18. According to the formula, if $\triangle N$ is 600, what is the value of K?

19. In a study of a different whale species, the scientist found out that the initial population was 16,000 and the value of K is equal to 16,000. If the scientist uses the same equation above, what is the value of $\triangle N$?

Practice Test 9

1. The function $y=c\cdot a^x$, where c and a are both positive integers, is defined for all real values of x. If $x=2$, then $y=12$ and if $x=3$, then $y=24$. When $y=96$, what is the value of x?

2. If the equation $(x^3)^6=x^k$ is satisfied for all real numbers of x, what is the value of k?

3. The figure below is a parallelogram. What is the value of $x+y$?

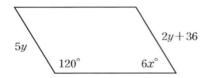

4. In the figure below, what is the area of the quadrilateral?

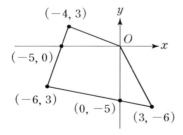

A) 31.5

B) 34

C) 36.5

D) 37.5

5. The equation $x^2+6x+c=(x-m)^2$ is true for all values of x, where c and m are constants. what is the value of $c-m$?

A) -12

B) -6

C) 6

D) 12

6. A delivery company charges a $100 handling fee and $25 for each box it delivers. If an office ordered n number of boxes to deliver, which of the following is the total cost per box, in dollars?

A) $\dfrac{100}{n}+25$

B) $\dfrac{n}{25}+100$

C) $\dfrac{25}{n}+100$

D) $25n+100$

7. A tractor has two small front tires and two large back tires. When the front tire makes 15 revolutions, the large tire makes 9 revolutions on a road. If the radius of the small tire is 30 centimeters, what is the radius of the large tire, in centimeters?

A) 50

B) 65

C) 70

D) 85

8. In the figure below, what is the value of x?

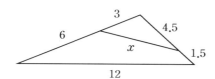

A) 5.5
B) 6
C) 6.5
D) 7

9. In $\triangle ABC$ below, $\overline{AB}=\overline{AC}$ and $\overline{BP}=\overline{AP}$. What is the value of x?

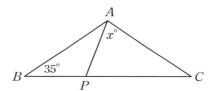

10. $75<5x+5<90$ for some integer x. What is one possible value of x?

11. In $\triangle ABC$ below, what is the value of x?

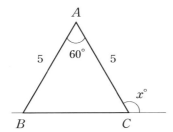

12. An expression, "pair", consists of two numbers that can be written as $(3x^2,\ 5x^3)$ for some integer x. If $(27,\ y)$ is a pair, what is the positive value of y?

13. 27 students are boys in a class of 51 total students. The students are in either the Math club or the Physics club. If 25 students are in the Math club and 16 students among them are boys, how many girls are <u>not</u> in the Math club?

14. An 8% sales tax is added to a price of a candy bar that costs k cents. What number times k is the final cost, in cents?

15. x liters of a sodium chloride solution are to be poured into beakers in a chemistry lab. The first 4 liters of the liquid are poured into one beaker. Then the rest of the liquid is poured in equal amounts into 6 other beakers. What amount of the liquid is in one of those 6 beakers?

A) $\dfrac{x-4}{6}$

B) $4-\dfrac{x}{6}$

C) $\dfrac{4-x}{6}$

D) $\dfrac{x}{6}+4$

16.

$$42x - 81 = 21 + y$$

$$\frac{y}{x} = 6$$

In the system of equations above, what is the value of y?

17. Conan bought a pickup truck at a dealership that gave a 15 percent discount off its original price. The total amount he paid to the car salesman was c dollars, including an 11 percent sales tax on the discounted price. Which of the following represents the original price of the car in terms of c?

A) $0.76c$

B) $\dfrac{c}{0.76}$

C) $(0.85)(1.11)c$

D) $\dfrac{c}{(0.85)(1.11)}$

Questions 18 and 19 refer to the following graph.

Urbanization and per capita GDP-2010

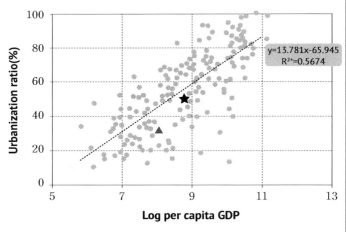

The scatterplot above shows the urbanization ratio and log per capita GDP for various countries around the world in the year 2010. The line of best fit is also shown and has equation $y = 13.781x - 65.945$. The star-shaped dot represents China, and the triangular dot represents India.

18. Which of the following best explains how the number 13.781 in the equation relates to the scatterplot?

A) In 2010, India's lowest urbanization ratio was 13.781.

B) In 2010, India's urbanization ratio was about 13.781% of that of China.

C) According to the line of best fit, a country is likely to experience a 13.781 unit increase in urbanization ratio for every unit increase in log per capita GDP.

D) According to the line of best fit, a country is likely to experience 13.781 unit decrease in urbanization ratio for every unit increase in log per capita GDP.

19. According to the line of best fit, the urbanization ratio of a country with log per capita GDP of 10 is likely to be about

A) 70%

B) 75%

C) 59%

D) 80%

Practice Test 10

1. The function y is defined as $y=f(x)=2ax-5b$ for constants a and b. The graph of the function passes through two points A and B, and the coordinates of A and B are $(30,\ 400)$ and $(70,\ 800)$ respectively. What is the sum of $-a$ and $-b$?

2. An amusement park sells entrance tickets at the rate of $150 for adults and $75 for children under 12 years-old. Yesterday the ratio of the number of entrance tickets sold to adults to the number sold to children under the age of 12 was 5 : 3. If the amusement park earned total of $48,750 from yesterday's entrance fees, how many people bought entrance tickets yesterday?

3. A cyclist wants to go on a bicycle trip from Punster City to Wells City. On average, she can ride d kilometers in t minutes. If the distance between the two cities is 120km, in terms of d and t, how many minutes does she have to ride from Punster to Wells?

A) $\dfrac{120t}{d}$

B) $\dfrac{t}{d}$

C) $\dfrac{d}{t}$

D) $\dfrac{t}{120d}$

4. In the xy-plane below, points A and B are on the x-axis and y-axis respectively. If the line is a graph of function $y=-\dfrac{1}{2}x-5$, what is the coordinate of point A?

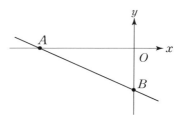

A) $(-10,\ 0)$

B) $(-5,\ 0)$

C) $(5,\ 0)$

D) $(0,\ -5)$

5. In the figure below, two circles are concentric. If the radius of the smaller circle is 4 and the area of the shaded region is 112π, what is the radius of the larger circle?

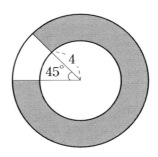

A) 18

B) 16

C) 14

D) 12

6. The graph of the function f is shown below. As seen, the x-intercepts are -4 and 4. If the function is $f(x) = -x^2 + bx + c$, what is the value of c?

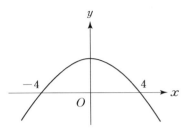

A) 6

B) 7

C) 8

D) 16

7. A square is inscribed in a circle. What is the ratio of the areas of the circle to the square?

A) $\pi : 1$

B) $\pi : 2$

C) $\pi : 3$

D) $2\pi : 3$

8. In the figure below, $\triangle ABC$ and $\triangle CDE$ are congruent triangles such that $\overline{BC} = \overline{CD}$ and $\overline{AB} = \overline{ED}$. If $\overline{AB} = 6$ and the area of triangle ABC is 15, what is the length of PQ?

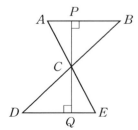

A) 7

B) 8

C) 9

D) 10

9. If x is an integer and $|2x-5| \leq 1$, what is the number of solutions that satisfy the inequality?

10. A square with vertices A, B, C, and D is drawn in an xy-coordinate plane. Point A$(3, -2)$ and C$(-5, 6)$ are opposite vertices. If point E is on line segment $\overline{AB}$ such that $\overline{AE} : \overline{BE} = 2 : 3$, what is the area of $\triangle CDE$?

11. For extra credit in a physics class in which 25 students are enrolled, students have to conduct at least two different experiments or at most three different experiments. After the semester, a total of 63 experiment reports have been turned in. How many students have conducted three experiments?

12. Simplify $\frac{(i^4)(i^3)}{(i^{11} + i^3)}$.

13. If $3x = 2y$ and $4y = 5z$, what is $2x + 3z$ in terms of y?

A) $\frac{9}{2}y$

B) $\frac{15}{56}y$

C) $\frac{56}{15}y$

D) $\frac{12}{61}y$

14. A postal service charges $25 for a handling fee and $7 for every two letters sent. Even if there are 3 letters, the cost would be the same as the cost of four letters. How much is the total cost in dollars for n number of letters, where n is odd?

A) $25 + 7\left(\dfrac{n}{2} - 1\right)$

B) $25 + \dfrac{7}{2}(n-1)$

C) $25 + \dfrac{7}{2}(n+1)$

D) $25 + \dfrac{7}{2}n$

15. $5x$ is less than or equal to 21

           $4x$ is greater than or equal to 5

How many integer values of x satisfy the inequalities above?

16. A line on the xy-plane passes through the origin and has a slope of -3. Which of the following points DOES NOT lie on the line?

A) $(1, -3)$
B) $(-1, 3)$
C) $(2, -6)$
D) $(-2, -6)$

17. A line on the xy-plane passes through coordinates $(2, 2)$ and has a slope of $\dfrac{1}{2}$. Which of the following points DOES NOT lie on the line?

A) $(0, 1)$
B) $(1, 0)$
C) $(4, 3)$
D) $(3, 2.5)$

Questions 18 and 19 refer to the following graph.

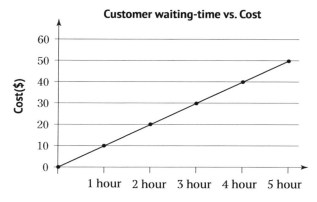

Customer waiting-time vs. Cost

The owner of Giotto's Gelato Shop estimates that the cost of customer waiting time, in terms of customer dissatisfaction and lost goodwill, can be graphed as above.

18. Which of the following represents the relationship between customer waiting-time and cost?

A) $y = x + 10$
B) $y = x$
C) $y = 10x$
D) $y = 5x + 5$

19. If Giotto's Gelato Shop has approximately 120 customers per day and the average customer has a 10-minute waiting time, what is the estimated customer waiting-time cost, per day, according to the graph?

Practice Test 11

1. A train 200 meters long was about to cross a bridge that is 3,200 meters. When the head of the train entered the bridge, a stopwatch was started from zero. When the tail of the train left the bridge, the watch was stopped. According to the stopwatch, the train took 80 seconds to cross the bridge completely. If the speed of the train was constant, what was the speed of the train?

A) 42.5m/s

B) 40m/s

C) 37.5m/s

D) 27.2m/s

Preference in Food

Food	Number of people
Burgers	6,300
Pizza	2,850
Steak	3,420

2. The results of a survey about people's food preferences is shown above. What is the fewest number of people who would need to change their preference in order for the number of people who chose pizza to be more than the number of people who chose burgers?

3. In the figure below, the values of all sides of a triangle are integers. If $\overline{AB}=5$ and $\overline{AC}=8$, what is the smallest possible value of $\overline{BC}$?

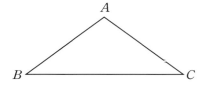

4. If the value of $\cos x$ is $\frac{3}{4}$, what is the value of $\sin(90°-x)$?

5. In the xy-plane, two lines f and g are perpendicular to each other. If the function $f(x)=mx+n$, where m and n are constants and $g(x)=-4x+3$, what is the value of m?

A) 4

B) $-\frac{1}{4}$

C) 0

D) $\frac{1}{4}$

6. In the right triangle below, point M lies on $\overline{AB}$. If $\overline{AC}=5$, $\overline{BC}=12$, and $\overline{AM}+\overline{AC}=\overline{BM}+\overline{BC}$. What is the value of $\overline{AM}$?

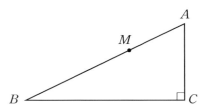

A) 4

B) 5

C) 8

D) 10

7. For positive values of x, $x^{\left(\frac{9}{16}\right)}=(x^n)^2$. What is the value of n?

A) $-\dfrac{3}{4}$

B) $\dfrac{9}{32}$

C) $\dfrac{3}{8}$

D) $\dfrac{3}{4}$

8. $\square$ABCD is a square whose sides are a units long. If $\overline{DE}=\overline{CE}$ and the area of $\triangle$CEF is $\dfrac{1}{5}$ the area of the square, what is the length of $\overline{BF}$ in terms of a?

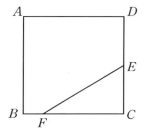

A) $\dfrac{a}{5}$

B) $\dfrac{a}{4}$

C) $\dfrac{a}{3}$

D) $\dfrac{2a}{5}$

9. Complete graphs of $f(x)$ and $g(x)$ are shown below. How many solutions of x satisfy the condition $f(x)=g(x)$?

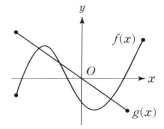

A) One

B) Two

C) Three

D) Four

10. Which of the following expressions is the same as $25^3 \cdot 5^{2x}$ for all values of x?

A) 5^{6+2x}

B) 5^{12x}

C) 5^{6x}

D) 5^{10x}

11. $(8x)^a=x^{4a}$ for nonzero integers x and a. If a is an even number, what is the value of x?

A) 2

B) 3

C) 4

D) 8

12. A circle C has a diameter of 10, and a chord $\overline{AB}$ whose length is 6. Chord $\overline{AB}$ is bisected at point D. If right triangle $\triangle BCD$ is formed, what is the value of $\sin B$?

13. In the xy-coordinate plane, two lines intersect each other perpendicularly. The slope and x-intercept of one line are 1 and 5 respectively. The x-intercept of the other line is 1. What is the equation of the other line?

A) $y=-x+1$

B) $y=-x+5$

C) $y=-\dfrac{1}{5}x+5$

D) $y=5x-\dfrac{1}{5}$

14. If $ab=2$ and $a^2b=18$, what is the value of $\dfrac{2a}{b}$?

A) $\dfrac{9}{2}$

B) 3

C) 6

D) 81

15.
$$2x+y=0$$
$$3x-2y=a$$
The solution for the system of equations above is $(3,\ n)$. What is the value of a?

A) $9+2n$

B) 0

C) 15

D) 21

16. What is one possible value of x that satisfies $5x<6$ and $7x>8$?

17.
$$x+2y+3z=10$$
$$3x-2y+z=6$$
$$x+2y-z=6$$
The relations among x, y, and z are given by the three equations above. If the numbers are real numbers, what is the value of $3x+2y+z$?

A) -20

B) -14

C) 7

D) 14

18. A small boat on a river will sink if the total weight of the boat exceeds 5500 pounds. A shepherd is trying to move s number of sheep that weigh 21 pounds each across the river using this boat. If the combined weight of the empty boat and the boat driver is 2000 pounds, what is the maximum possible number of sheep s that will keep the boat, boat driver, and sheep afloat on the river?

Questions 19 and 20 refer to the following data.

Enzymes A and B are left in a culture at 40°C. As time passes, the enzymes denature and lose capability. The following table shows each enzyme's capacitance as a percentage over time.

Time(Minutes)	Enzyme A (%)	Enzyme B (%)
0	96.8	97.4
10	94.7	95.2
20	90.4	93.8
30	85.6	92.4
40	78.3	90.7
50	71.1	89.1
60	70.4	86.9
70	70.1	84.2

19. If enzyme A had been able to break down 130mg of amino acids at time 0, how much amino acid, in grams, is it able to break down after an hour in the culture? (Round to the nearest thousandth.)

A) 0.095
B) 0.112
C) 0.089
D) 0.173

20. What does the data tell you about the durability of each enzyme?

A) Enzyme A denatures at a constant rate.
B) Enzyme A and B denature at a constant rate.
C) At 40°C, Enzyme B has denatured less than Enzyme A has.
D) Cannot be determined from the given information.

Practice Test 12

1. The average (arithmetic mean) number of apples from 6 boxes containing different numbers of apples is 15. When a box that contains 8 apples is added, the average number of apples from 7 boxes becomes k. What is the value of k?

2. In the xy-plane below, the graph of a quadratic function f passes the x-axis as shown. To get the maximum value of this function, what must be the value of x?

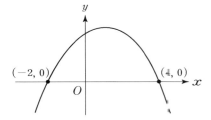

3. Simplify $\dfrac{3+4i}{2+5i}$.

A) $\dfrac{26-7i}{29}$

B) $\dfrac{26+7i}{29}$

C) $\dfrac{3+4i}{29}$

D) $\dfrac{26-7i}{2+5i}$

4.
$$0.4073 = \frac{3}{10^x} + \frac{4}{10^y} + \frac{7}{10^z}$$

In the expression above, x, y, and z are positive integers. What is the value of $x+y+z$?

5. The average (arithmetic mean) of 5 numbers is $3a$. What is the average of these 5 numbers and x in terms of a and x?

A) $\dfrac{3a+x}{6}$

B) $\dfrac{15a+x}{6}$

C) $\dfrac{5a+x}{2}$

D) $\dfrac{3a+x}{2}$

6. The radius of a circle is 3, and a square is inscribed in the circle. What is the area of the square?

A) 9

B) $9\sqrt{2}$

C) 6π

D) 18

7. At a movie theater, the prices of tickets are $15, $10, $7 for an adult, a senior over 65, and a child under 12 respectively. In an hour, total sales were $1,960. In this hour, three times as many $15 tickets were sold as $10 tickets, and seven times as many $10 tickets were sold as $7 tickets. How many adults entered the movie theater?

8. In the right triangle shown below, point M is the midpoint between A and B. If $\triangle MBC = 30°$, what is the measure of x?

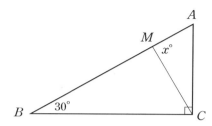

(Note: figure not drawn to scale.)

9. Right triangle $\triangle ABC$ is similar to right triangle $\triangle DEF$. The perimeter of triangle $\triangle ABC$ is 12, and the perimeter of triangle $\triangle DEF$ is 48. If $\sin A = \dfrac{3}{5}$, what is the value of $\cos D$?

10. A convenience store sells bread in a bag. Each day, the store buys 15 bags, each containing 10 pieces of bread. One bag costs \$18.00 at a wholesale price from the bakery and each piece of bread costs \$2.25 at the retail price of the store. If the store sells x pieces of bread on one day, what is the daily profit in terms of x?

A) $2.25x - 270$
B) $2.25x + 270$
C) $18 - 2.25x$
D) $270 - 2.25x$

11. If $3x$ is 6 less than twice y, which of the following is $2x$ in terms of y?

A) $\dfrac{2}{3}y - 4$

B) $\dfrac{4}{3}y - 4$

C) $\dfrac{2}{3}x + 4$

D) $\dfrac{4}{3}y + 6$

12. What number is 5 less than $\dfrac{3}{2}$ of itself?

A) 4
B) -6
C) 6
D) 10

13. The volumes of two cubes are 1 to 27 in ratio. If the length of a side of the smaller cube is a, which of the following expression in terms of a is the total surface area of the larger cube?

A) $9a^2$
B) $27a^3$
C) $45a^2$
D) $54a^2$

14. Points P and Q are in the xy-coordinate plane such that the slope of a line passing through P and Q is $\dfrac{1}{3}$. If the y-coordinate of P is 5 less than the y-coordinate of Q, how much less is the x-coordinate of P than the x-coordinate of Q?

15. If $a=-1$, then $b<21$

If the statement above is true, which of the following is also true?

A) If $a<21$, then $b=-1$
B) If $b>21$, then $a=-1$
C) If $a\neq-1$, then $b\neq21$
D) If $b\geq21$, then $a\neq-1$

16.
$$-3a+5b=9$$
$$6a-2b=6$$

If $(a,\ b)$ is the solution to the system of equations above, what is the value of a?

Questions 17, 18, and 19 refer to the following data.

The following graph shows the beak lengths of *Aepyornis Medius* after the divided populations migrated to different parts of the island of Microwen. (The species of *Aepyornis Medius* is extinct.)

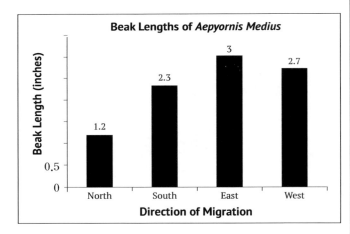

17. What does the y-axis of the graph indicate?

A) Body length of *Aepyornis Medius*
B) Mass of *Aepyornis Medius*
C) Beak length of *Aepyornis Medius*
D) Cannot be determined from the given information.

18. If the species originated from the center of the island, with a beak length of 0.8 inches, which direction of migration caused the biggest change in beak length?

A) East
B) West
C) South
D) North

19. According to the chart, what would birds from north of Microwen be able to eat?

A) Seeds, cricket eggs
B) Worms, beetles
C) Mosquitoes, seeds, cricket eggs
D) Worms, seeds, cricket eggs

Type of Food	Distance from Surface
Worms	1.5 in., down
Seeds	0.8 in., down
Beetles	2.5 in., down
Cricket Eggs	0.5 in., down
Mosquitoes	0~5 ft., up

Table 1. Food Availability for the Island of Microwen

Practice Test 13

1. If $3x=4$, what is the value of $\dfrac{9x^3}{4}$?

2. If $a^{13}=5000$ and $\dfrac{a^{11}}{b^2}=50$ for positive numbers a and b, what is the value of $\dfrac{20}{ab}$?

3. What is absolute value of the sum of all values of x that satisfy the equation $-5x^2-x+1=0$?

4. Last month, an ice-cream cafe sold green tea flavored ice-cream alone for $1,200 of sales and strawberry flavored ice-cream alone for $1,500 of sales. According to the graph shown below, what is the total sales of all flavors?

A) $6,300
B) $7,000
C) $8,300
D) $9,000

5. At a restaurant, tables have either 4 chairs or 5 chairs. A tour group of 34 people arrives at the restaurant. If two people have no chair available to sit after all the table seating has been assigned and there is at least one table with 5 chairs, how many tables are at the restaurant?

6. In the figure shown below, $\overline{DE}$ and $\overline{BC}$ are parallel, and $\triangle ABC$ and $\triangle ADE$ are right triangles. It is given that $\overline{DE}=5$ and $\overline{BC}=9$. If $\overline{AC}=15$, what is the length of $\overline{AD}$?

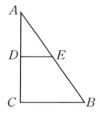

7. A delivery company charges $0.5 for the first 1 kilogram and $0.8 for each additional kilogram. If a customer pays $12.5 for a box, how many kilograms does the box weigh?

8. In a zoo, three years ago, 10 rabbits lived in 'Happy Rabbit Land'. Now, 24 rabbits live there. At the same rate, in how many years from now will there be 164 rabbits living in 'Happy Rabbit Land'?

9. Two cyclists rode their bicycles along a biking trail. They started from each end of the trail and traveled toward each other. James rode at a constant speed of 8 miles per hour, and Patrick rode at a constant speed of 7 miles per hour. The distance along the coast was 45 miles. If they departed at the same time and rode without resting, how many miles did James ride before their first encounter?

10. If the value of $\sin x$ is $\frac{4}{5}$, what is the value of $\cos (90° - x)$?

11. On the xy-plane below, what is the value of a?

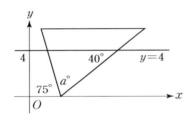

A) 60
B) 65
C) 70
D) 75

12. The price of pencils is $2 per dozen or $45 for 25 dozens. How much more is the price per pencil at the rate for 1 dozen than at the rate for 25 dozens?

A) $0.17
B) $0.27
C) $0.01
D) $0.017

13. In the xy-plane below, points A, B, C, and D lie on lines. If $\angle COD$ is 65°, what is the measure of $\angle AOD$ in degrees?

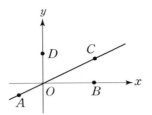

14. If the area of an equilateral triangle is $16\sqrt{3}$, what is the length of one side of the triangle?

15. A rectangle is divided into 4 areas as shown below. What is the value of x?

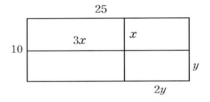

16. $a^2 b = 1 + a$, where a is a positive integer. Which statement cannot be true?

I. $b = a$.
II. b is an integer.
III. $b = \frac{1}{a^2} + \frac{1}{a}$.

A) I only
B) III only
C) I and II only
D) I and III only

17.

$$\frac{y}{x}=4$$

$$2(x+6)=y$$

If $(x,\ y)$ is the solution set to the system of equations above, what is the value of y?

A) 6

B) 12

C) 24

D) 30

Questions 18 and 19 refer to the following graph.

The following graph shows the relationship between volume and pressure, as defined by Boyle's Law.

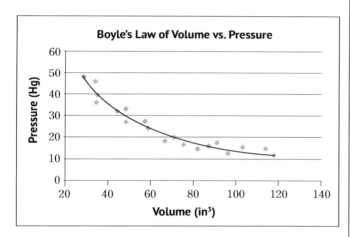

18. At a volume of about 40 in^3, what would be the best estimate of the pressure in Hg?

A) 40 Hg

B) 35 Hg

C) 30 Hg

D) Cannot be determined from the given information.

19. What happens to pressure as volume keeps increasing?

A) Increases

B) Decreases

C) Insignificant change

D) Cannot be determined from the given information.

Practice Test 14

1. Simplify $\frac{4+2i}{3+7i}$.

A) $\frac{-11i+13}{29}$

B) $\frac{-11i-13}{29}$

C) $\frac{4+2i}{29}$

D) $\frac{-11i+13}{3+7i}$

2. If $a^{\frac{1}{3}}a^{\frac{4}{3}}a^{-\frac{2}{3}}=2$, what is the value of 3^a?

3.
$$x^2+2x-3=0$$
How many solutions of x satisfy the equation above?

A) none

B) one

C) two

D) more than two

4.   46, 98, 51, 78, 69, 85, x

Above is a list of test scores from a math midterm. If the median of the test scores is 69, what is the greatest possible integer value of x?

5. If the solutions of an equation are $x=\frac{-7\pm\sqrt{37}}{6}$, then what is the value of $a+b$, where the equation is equal to ax^2+bx+c?

6. If $\frac{a}{b}-3=2-\frac{a}{b}$, what is $\frac{5b}{2a}$ equal to?

A) $\frac{2}{5}$

B) $-\frac{2}{5}$

C) 1

D) $\frac{2}{3}$

7. 2 liters of soy sauce are added to 5 liters of liquid honey for cooking at a restaurant. What fraction of this solution is liquid honey by volume?

8. In minutes, how long is a drive that is 2.4 hours long?

9. If x and y are related by $3x-5y=21$ and $x=4y$, what is the value of $2x+3y$?

10. In the figure below, what is the value of $x+y-z$?

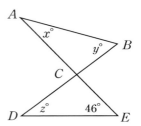

11. In the xy-plane, the graph of the equation $mx+ny=10$ for constant numbers m and n intersects the x-axis at $x=5$. What is the value of m?

12. Point P is one vertex of a cube and point Q is another vertex which is the farthest from point P. If the distance between P and Q is $2\sqrt{3}$, what is the surface area of the cube?

A) 24

B) 12

C) $24\sqrt{3}$

D) $8\sqrt{3}$

13. In $\triangle$BDC shown below, $\angle$BDC$=130°$, and $\overline{AB}=\overline{AC}$. If $\overline{BD}$ and $\overline{CD}$ bisect the angles $\angle$ABC and $\angle$ACB respectively, what is the value of x?

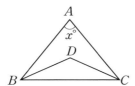

A) 50

B) 55

C) 60

D) 80

14. Points A, B, C, and O form a rectangle in the plane below. If the slope of the line passing through the origin and point B is $-\dfrac{3}{4}$, what is the area of the rectangle?

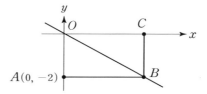

A) $\dfrac{3}{2}$

B) $\dfrac{9}{2}$

C) $\dfrac{15}{3}$

D) $\dfrac{16}{3}$

15. The figure below shows $\triangle$ABC with $\overline{AB}=\overline{AC}$, and points D, A, and C lie on a line. If $\angle$BAD is $110°$, what is the value of $\angle$ABC?

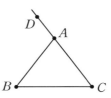

16.
$$-2<2x-3<5$$
$$3<3y+2<13$$

The inequalities shown above are true for some integers x and y. What is the greatest value of xy?

17.

$$2n-r=5n+9$$
$$4m-k=7m+9$$

In the equations above, r and k are constants. If r is 6 more than k, what is the value of $m-n$?

A) 2

B) 3

C) 5

D) 6

19. If 6 more buildings, with heights of 8, 9, 24, 46, 46, and 26 were built, what could be the median height of the buildings?

A) 46

B) 51

C) 39

D) 22

Questions 18 and 19 refer to the following graph.

The following graph represents the heights of 64 buildings in Kevin's city.

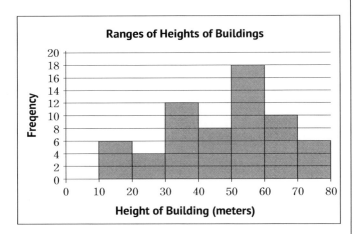

18. Which of the following could be the median height of the buildings?

A) 59

B) 49

C) 61

D) 62

Practice Test 15

1. Simplify $\dfrac{i^6 + i^2}{(i^2)^4}$.

2.
$$x^2 - 8x + n = (x + m)^2$$
For constants m and n, the equation above is true for any real number x. What is the value of $n + m$?

A) 2
B) 4
C) 12
D) 16

3. The graph of the parabola below shows that the line of symmetry is $x = -1$. The coordinates of x-intercepts are $(3,\ 0)$ and $(a,\ 0)$. What is the value of a?

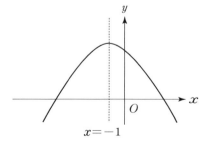

A) -7
B) -6
C) -5
D) -4

4. For all real numbers of x, the function $g(x)$ is defined by $g(x) = 3x - k$, where k is a constant. If $g(4) = 15$, what is the value of $-k$?

5. $\dfrac{x}{3} = \dfrac{2y}{5}$ for non-zero numbers x and y. What is the value of $\dfrac{10x}{3y}$?

A) $\dfrac{1}{20}$
B) $\dfrac{2}{5}$
C) $\dfrac{5}{4}$
D) 4

6. A cup of chocolate ice-cream costs x cents. If a person pays y dollars for 12 cups of ice-cream, how much is the change in terms of x and y, in cents?

A) $y - 12x$
B) $y + 12x$
C) $100y - 12x$
D) $100y + 12x$

7. To build a long fence, a farmer digs 25 holes in a straight line. If the center points of the holes are equally spaced by $4\frac{1}{2}$ feet, what is the total distance between the centers of the first and last holes?

A) 112.5 ft
B) 108 ft
C) 103.5 ft
D) 99 ft

8. The population of rabbits at a zoo triples every 6 months. If there were 4 rabbits initially, which of the following expressions represents the population of rabbits after t years?

A) 4×3^{2t}
B) 4×3^{t}
C) $4 \times 3t$
D) 4^{3t}

9. In the figure below, a triangle ABC is inscribed in a circle. If $\overline{BO}=\overline{BC}=4$, what is the perimeter of $\triangle ABC$?

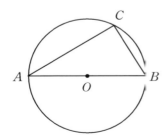

A) 18
B) 20
C) $16\sqrt{3}$
D) $12+4\sqrt{3}$

10. A cylinder with radius 5 and height 10 is shown below. What is the total surface area of the cylinder?

A) 50π
B) 100π
C) 120π
D) 150π

11. The rectangle below shows points M and N which are the midpoints of their respective sides. If the lengths of $\overline{BD}$ and $\overline{CD}$ are 8 and 4 respectively, what is the area of the unshaded region?

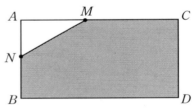

(Note: figure not drawn to scale.)

A) 4
B) 6
C) 8
D) 16

12. The perimeter of a rectangle is 20. If the length and width of the rectangle are integers, what is one possible value of the area of the rectangle?

13. In the xy-plane below, three lines intersect one another at points B, C, and D. If $\angle DEF = 34°$ and $\angle BDC = 103°$, what is the measure of $\angle ABC$?

$$(\overline{BC} /\!/ \overline{EF})$$

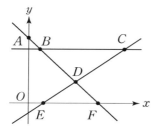

14. The average (arithmetic mean) of $2a$ and b is -3. What is the value of $\dfrac{b}{-3-a}$?

A) -3

B) -2

C) 1

D) 2

15.
$$8 \text{ sapphires} = 1 \text{ gold bar}$$
$$20 \text{ diamonds} = 3 \text{ gold bars}$$

A mining company sets the prices of sapphires and diamonds as shown above. How many diamonds are equal to 600 sapphires?

16. Two people ride bicycles with different sizes of wheels. The radius of the bigger wheel is 100 centimeters and the radius of the smaller wheel is 45 centimeters. When the bigger wheel makes 18 revolutions, how many revolutions does the smaller wheel make?

17.
$$3a + 8 = 2b + 2$$
$$\frac{1}{2}b = \frac{1}{4}a + 1$$

In the system of equations above, what is the value of b?

A) -2

B) -1

C) 1.5

D) 3

Questions 18 and 19 refer to the following graph.

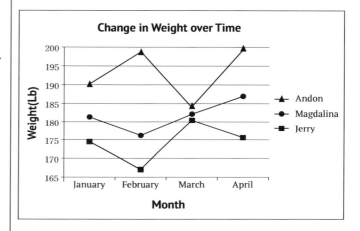

18. Whose weight changed the most from January to April?

A) Jerry

B) Magdalina

C) Andon

D) Cannot be determined from the given information.

19. Who experienced the most weight gain during 1-month-interval, and in which months?

A) Jerry; from March to April

B) Magdalina; from February to March

C) Jerry; from February to March

D) Andon; from March to April

Practice Test 16

1. Everyday, Jin makes wooden cubic boxes and cylinders. The number of boxes, y, that he can produce in one day is inversely proportional to the square of the number of cylinders produced, x, by the equation $y = \dfrac{k}{x^2}$. If he can make 100 cubic boxes and 8 cylinders in one day, how many cubic boxes can he make after producing 10 cylinders?

A) 64

B) 80

C) 640

D) 800

2. If $3^x \cdot 5^y = 15^{26}$ for positive integers x and y, what is the value of $2x - y$?

A) 8

B) 13

C) 15

D) 26

3. A pizza delivery person gets \$1.60 as a tip for each delivery. One day he had delivered 25 pizzas by $2{:}00$ P.M. and by the end of the day had made a total of \$72.00. How many deliveries did he make after $2{:}00$ P.M. that day?

4. On a straight walking trail, three emergency shelters A, B, and C are located such that the distance between A and B is 15 miles and the distance between B and C is 9.3 miles. What is the difference in the least and greatest possible distance between A and C?

5. Two mine companies exchange their gems. Company A has 36 sapphires, and company B has 48 diamonds. If they begin the transaction by trading 2 sapphires for 3 diamonds, after how many exchanges does each company possess an equal number of gems?

6. For real values of $x > 1$ and y, $y = x^3$. If $x^6 = y^{8-3k}$, what is the value of k?

7. In a math class of 15 students, 3 problems are assigned as homework. 3 students each submitted 2 additional problems for extra points. 5 students each submitted 3 more problems as punishment for tardiness. 2 students submitted only 2 problems. How many problems were submitted?

8. The number of rabbits in 'Happy Rabbit Land' in t years is expressed by $3 \times 2^t + 10$. How many rabbits will there be in Happy Rabbit Land in 5 years?

9. In the figure below, five squares fit into one large square. Squares A and E are identical and squares B and D are identical. If the lengths of sides of A, B, and C are 1, 2, and 3 respectively, what is the perimeter of the shaded region?

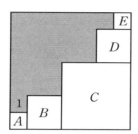

(Note: figure not drawn to scale)

10. In the xy-plane, the coordinates of the center of a circle are $(3, -4)$. If the circle passes through the origin, what is the x-coordinate of the x-intercept besides 0?

11. A manufacturing company wants to produce a cylinder to contain exactly 3 ping-pong balls as shown below. If the radius of one ping-pong ball is 20 millimeters, what is the volume of the cylinder, in cubic millimeters?

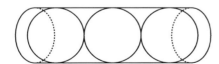

A) 48π

B) 480π

C) 4800π

D) 48000π

12. Isosceles triangle ABC is drawn on a coordinate plane. Point A lies on x-axis, base $\overline{BC}$ is perpendicular to x-axis, and $\overline{AB}=\overline{AC}$. If the coordinates of point B are $(-4, 3)$, what are the coordinates of point C?

A) $(-4, -3)$

B) $(4, -3)$

C) $(4, 3)$

D) $(-4, 4)$

13. One side of a triangle is 10 and one other side of the same triangle is 4. What is the largest possible integer value for the length of the remaining side?

A) 11

B) 12

C) 13

D) 14

Nationalities of International students at Anaheim H.S.

14. The graph above shows the percentages of international students from five countries in Europe. If 130 students are from France, how many more students are from Germany than from Spain?

A) 17

B) 21

C) 25

D) 26

15. The table below shows the total number of students and the number of students in Physics club in each high school. The Education Committee requires that each school have the same percentage of students in Physics club. What is the value of $a+b$?

School	A	B	C
Physics	105	a	b
Total	700	800	1100

A) 120

B) 155

C) 165

D) 285

Questions 16 and 17 refer to the following image.

Spinning Wheel

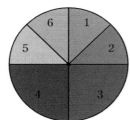

16. The spinning wheel above has 6 different sections, with 1, 2, 5, and 6 in equal parts, and 3 and 4 in equal parts. If a dart is thrown randomly, how much more likely is it to land on 3 than 6?

A) 2 times as likely

B) no difference

C) 0.5 times as likely

D) 1.5 times as likely

17. If each of the parts of the spinning wheel were to be halved and the numbers were redistributed, starting from 2, going clockwise from 12 o'clock, what is the probability of a dart landing on 7 or 12?

A) $\frac{1}{8}$

B) $\frac{1}{16}$

C) $\frac{3}{16}$

D) $\frac{1}{4}$

Questions 18 and 19 refer to the following table.

The following table shows the relationship between x, $f(x)$, and $g(x)$.

x	$f(x)$	$g(x)$
0	6	3
1	4	9
2	2	1
3	7	2
4	3	5

18. What is the value of $f(3)+2g(1)$?

A) 25

B) 11

C) 15

D) 20

19. What is the value of $\dfrac{f(3)-2g(2)}{[g(4)]^2}$?

A) 0

B) 1

C) 0.2

D) -1

Practice Test 17

1. If $\dfrac{3}{a} = \dfrac{7}{b}$ and $\dfrac{6}{c} = \dfrac{5}{b}$, then $\dfrac{c}{a} =$

2. The total cost of 6 pens and 5 pencils is the same as the total cost of 3 pens and 14 pencils. If one pen costs m times the cost of one pencil, what is m?

3. If $a = \dfrac{2x+3y}{x}$ and $b = \dfrac{y}{2x}$ for positive numbers x and y, which of the following expresses a in terms of b?

A) $4+6b$

B) $2+6b$

C) $6-2b$

D) $6-4b$

4. If $2x+3 \geq -7$ and $2x-1 \leq 11$, which of the following is the range of x?

A) $-5 \leq x \leq 6$

B) $-5 \leq x \leq 7$

C) $-4 \leq x \leq 6$

D) $4 \leq x \leq 6$

5. The equation $x^2 - mx - n = 0$, where m and n are constants, has two solutions $x = -2$ and $x = 6$. What is the value of $m+n$?

A) -16

B) -12

C) 12

D) 16

6. If x satisfies the inequality $2 < |3-x| < 4$, what is a possible value of x?

A) -3.2

B) -1.7

C) 1.7

D) 5.3

7. What is the solution for the equation $5^{2x-3} = 5^{-x+4}$?

8. If $0 < a < 7$ and $-6 < b < 0$ where a and b are integers, what is the maximum value of $\dfrac{4}{|a-b|}$?

9. The table below shows some values of functions f and g for some x values. What is the value of $f(g(3))$?

x	$f(x)$	$g(x)$
1	2	5
2	4	3
3	3	4
4	1	1
5	5	2

A) 2
B) 3
C) 5
D) 1

10. A rectangular box has three different lengths of edges, and the lengths are all integers. If the area of one of the biggest surfaces is 20 and the area of one of the smallest surfaces is 8, what is the volume of the box?

A) 160
B) 80
C) 40
D) 20

11. Two lines are passing through the origin in the xy-coordinate plane below. The angle between line m and the positive x-axis is $7°$, and the angle between line ℓ and the negative y-axis is $15°$. What is the greater value of the angles between two lines?

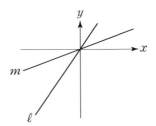

A) 98°
B) 105°
C) 112°
D) 122°

12. What is the circumference of a circle whose area is 6.25π? $(\pi = 3.14)$

13. In the figure below, what is the value of $-w + x + y - z$?

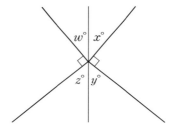

14. If point $A(-2,\ 2)$ is on a circle whose center is $(2,\ -1)$, what is the radius of the circle?

15. A person drove a car at 110 kilometers per hour for 4 hours. For the next 6 hours, the person drove at 60 kilometers per hour. What was the average (arithmetic mean) speed of the entire trip, in kilometers per hour?

Percent of tour locations

16. In a survey, 300 people provided the location of their first visit to Asia. How many people chose Korea as their first visit to Asia?

Questions 17 and 18 refer to the following graph.

The following graph shows the number of stars in each temperature range in Galaxy XY.

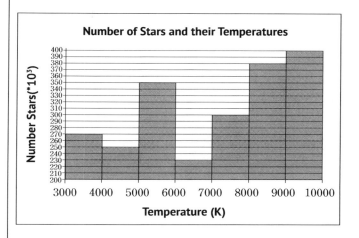

17. What range of temperature do most stars belong to?

A) 5000K to 6000K
B) 6000K to 7000K
C) 8000K to 9000K
D) 9000K to 10000K

18. Stars of about 5000K to 6000K show a color of orange. Stars of about 9000K to 10000K show a color of white. How many stars in Galaxy XY show a color of orange or white?

A) 7.5×10^2
B) 7.3×10^2
C) 7.5×10^5
D) 730×10^5

Practice Test 18

1. If a is 5 less than b and c is 2 more than b, what is the value of $c-a$?

A) 7

B) 3

C) 0

D) -3

2. The front wheel of a bicycle has a mark. When the mark on the wheel was on the ground, the bicyclist began a trip. After the mark rotated 35000 times, the distance on the map indicated 49πkm from the starting point. What is the radius of the front wheel, in meters?

3. There are chocolate bars and candy bars at a sweet store. For a special sale day, 30 percent of chocolate bars and 70 percent of candy bars are on sale. If the store has 300 chocolate and candy bars, 60 percent of which are candy bars, how many chocolate bars are on sale?

4. Two car dealers, A and B, are selling identical cars at different discount rates. Dealer A gives a 17 percent discount, and dealer B gives a 23 percent discount. If the original price of a car is $25,000$ dollars, what is the difference between the two pieces offered by dealer A and B, in dollars?

5. In an isosceles triangle ABC, $\overline{AB}=\overline{AC}$ and one of the base angles is $30°$. If three lines that bisect the angles of $\triangle ABC$ intersect at point D, what is angle ADB in degree measure?

A) 85

B) 95

C) 105

D) 115

6. For positive numbers x and y, $7^{(2x+3)}=49y$. What is the expression $7^{(4x+3)}$ in terms of y?

A) $\dfrac{y^2}{49}$

B) $\dfrac{y^2}{7}$

C) y^2

D) $7y^2$

7. If the equation $4x=9x^3$ has only non-zero solutions, what is the value of x^2?

A) $\dfrac{4}{9}$

B) $\dfrac{9}{4}$

C) $\dfrac{2}{3}$

D) $\dfrac{3}{2}$

8.
$$|2x-5|=3$$
To satisfy the equation above, how many solutions of x exist?

A) No solution
B) One
C) Two
D) Three

9. The lengths of the sides of a triangle are all integers. If the lengths of two sides are 3 and 9 respectively, what is the greatest possible length of the remaining side?

10. A cube box without a top was lain flat as shown by the solid lines in the figure below. To make the box bigger, 1-inch of width is added to the eight edges as shown by the dotted lines. Before these were added, the volume of the box was 64 cubic inches. After their addition, what is the volume of the new box?

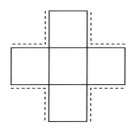

11. In the figure below, lines a and b are parallel, and lines ℓ and m are also parallel. What is the value of $x-y$?

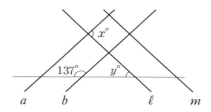

12. Lines ℓ and m are tangent to a circle as shown above. Line n passes through the center of the circle. If $\overline{AC}=8$ and $\overline{OC}=5$, what is the length of $\overline{BE}$?

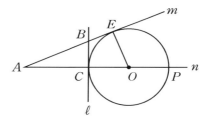

13. If $xy=20$ and $x-y=8$, where x and y are negative integers, what is the value of $-(x+y)$?

14. In a survey, 100 people said that they have visited Russia. Among these, 55 people have also visited Mongolia. 222 people said that they have visited either Russia or Mongolia. How many people have visited Mongolia?

15. Let the functions f and g be defined by $f(x)=2x^2+x+8$ and $g(x)=2\sqrt{f(x)}-8$ for all real numbers. What is the value of $g(8)$?

A) 4

B) 7

C) 14

D) 16

Ice−cream Sales

Flavor	Percent (%)
Chocolate	35
Vanilla	28
Strawberry	21
Green Tea	16

16. On a certain day, an ice-cream store sold four flavors according to the table. If 42 strawberry flavors were sold, how many vanilla flavors were sold?

17. A triangle has one of its vertices on a square. At most, how many intersections between the triangle and the square could be made?

A) 2

B) 3

C) 4

D) 5

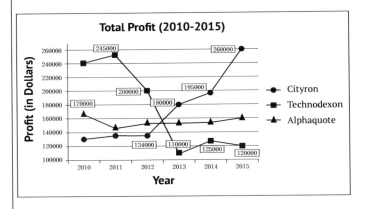

18. Which company experienced a continual growth in profit? By how much did the company's profit increase, from 2010 to 2015?

A) Cityron; by about 100%

B) Technodexon; by about 104%

C) Cityron; by about 33%

D) Technodexon; by about 100%

19. Which company experienced the most dramatic change in profit from year 2012 to 2013?

A) Cityron

B) Technodexon

C) Alphaquote

D) Cannot be determined from the given information.

Practice Test 19

1. For real numbers x, y and z, if $x-z=27$ and $xy-yz=9$, what is the value of y?

2. If $34<\dfrac{2x-5}{4}<37$, what is one possible integer value of $\dfrac{2x-5}{6}$?

3. x is 65 percent of y, and y is 140 percent of z, where x, y and z are positive numbers. What percent of z is x?

A) 46%
B) 75%
C) 91%
D) 95%

4. A container is 70% full when 21 liters of water are added. How many more liters of water must be added to fill the container completely?

A) 7
B) 8
C) 9
D) 10

5. If $a^2-b^2=9$ and $a^2+b^2=9$ for positive number a, what is the value of a?

A) $\sqrt{3}$
B) $3\sqrt{2}$
C) 3
D) 9

6. The volumes of two right circular cylinders A and B shown below are equal. If the height of cylinder A is four times the height of cylinder B, what is the ratio of the radius of cylinder B to the radius of cylinder A?

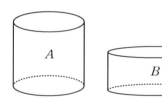

A) $1:2$
B) $1:1$
C) $4:1$
D) $2:1$

7. x and y are related as $(x-y)(x^2-y^2)=0$. If $x>y$ and $y=-4$, what is the value of x?

8. If $(1.25-2x)(3x-10.2)$ is bigger than zero, what is one possible integer value of x?

9. In the figure below, the four lines intersect one another. What is the value of $\frac{x}{2}+y$?

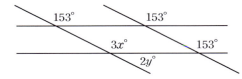

10. The square of x is less than three times x. If the inequality is true for some integer x, what is one possible value for x?

11. Five angles are shown below. If $x=35$, what is the value of y?

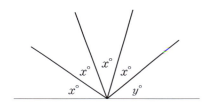

12. A certain integer x is decreased by 5, and the sum of x and the new number is tripled. If the result is 9 more than 2 times the number x, what is the value of x?

13. In the xy-coordinate plane below, if $a=155$, what is the value of b?

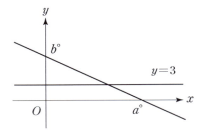

A) 110
B) 115
C) 130
D) 145

14. Two points, A and B, are marked on a circle with a center marked O, such that points A, B, and O as vertices form an equilateral triangle. If the circumference of the circle is 36π, what is the length of major arc $\overset{\frown}{AB}$?

A) 6π
B) 15π
C) 24π
D) 30π

Plans during Thanksgiving Day

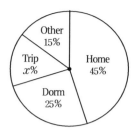

15. In a survey about plans during Thanksgiving, 2500 college students answered that they want to go home, stay in a dormitory, take a trip, or do something else. How many students want to take a trip?

16. In a survey about a country or countries which people want to visit, 200 people said they wanted to visit Korea. 100 people wanted to visit Japan. 300 people wanted to visit China. Some people answered more than one country. If 500 people answered the survey, at most how many people said that they do NOT want to visit any of the countries?

Questions 17 and 18 refer to the following graph.

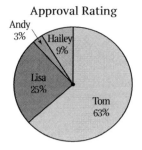

Approval Rating

17. The poll took about 6340 people's opinions into account. Approximately how many people voted for Tom? Round to the nearest whole number.

A) 3994

B) 3969

C) 3780

D) 2346

18. Next month, Tom's rating fell to 46%, and Hailey gained all the votes he lost. In percentage, approximately how much more votes did Tom receive compared with Hailey? Round to the nearest tenth.

A) 76.9%

B) 42.9%

C) 37.0%

D) 27.0%

Practice Test 20

1. A novelist writes words at a rate of k words per every 35 seconds. If he spends 28 minutes to complete a short story, which of the following expressions correctly represents the number of words he writes?

A) $\dfrac{5k}{4}$

B) $\dfrac{49k}{3}$

C) $15k$

D) $48k$

2. In the xy-plane, the line $5x+4y=-16$ is perpendicular to the line $y=mx-5$. What is the value of m?

A) $-\dfrac{5}{4}$

B) -1

C) $\dfrac{1}{4}$

D) $\dfrac{4}{5}$

3. $y=\left\{\dfrac{1}{3}x\right\}$

$$\left\{\;\;\right\}=\text{rounded to nearest greater or equal whole number.}$$

The equation above is used to calculate y, the cost of x number of candy boxes in dollars. The candy shop accepts dollar bills only and does not give changes. For example, to purchase 11 candy boxes, 4 dollars need to be paid. If 31 candy boxes are to be purchased, what is the dollar amount that needs to be paid?

4. Starting at 8 A.M., a clock is set to beep once every 15 minutes. Between $10:05$ A.M. and $1:55$ P.M. on the same day, how many times does the clock beep?

A) 12

B) 13

C) 14

D) 15

5. In the xy plane below, the coordinate of point A lying on a line passing through the origin is $(-4\sqrt{3},\ 4)$. If point B lies on the x-axis, what is the measure of $\angle \text{AOB}$?

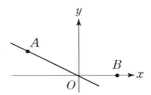

A) $120°$

B) $135°$

C) $150°$

D) $165°$

6. The function f is defined as $f(x)=-2x^3+25$, and the function g is defined as $g(x)=4x^2$. If $f(a)=9$, what is the value of $g(a)$?

A) 44

B) 23

C) 16

D) 9

7. If $(a-b)^2-(a+b)^2=40$ for integers a and b, which of the following is <u>not</u> a possible value of $a-b$?

A) -11
B) -7
C) 7
D) 9

8. When the square root of x is divided by 2, the result is 18. What is the value of x?

A) -1296
B) -3
C) 36
D) 1296

9. Students in a math class share rulers. If 2 students share one ruler, 5 students do not have rulers. If 3 students share one ruler, 5 rulers remain unused. How many rulers are in the math class?

10. Mike collects quarters, which are worth 25 cents each. If he has more than $\$31.00$ in total, what is the least number of quarters he can have?

11. In the figure below, the smallest circle is contained in the middle circle which is in the biggest circle. Each inner circle passes through the center of its outer circle as shown. If the area of the smallest circle is 4π, what is the diameter of the biggest circle?

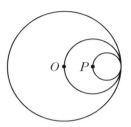

12. The sum of 10 and 6 is multiplied by 3. The result equals the product of 4 and x. What is the value of x?

13. A rectangle has a perimeter of 34 and an area of 30. What is the length of the shorter side of the rectangle?

14. Vertices of three right triangles meet at point A on line ℓ as shown below. If $\angle PAB=30°$, $\angle CAD=18°$, $\angle EAF=12°$, and $\angle GAQ=35°$, what is the sum of $\angle B$, $\angle D$, and $\angle F$ in degrees?

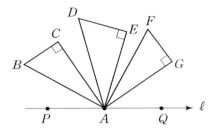

15.
$$S(t)=100\times2^{6t}$$
The function above is used to estimate the data size, S, of a virus file in kilobytes t hours after the file has launched. What is the value of the data size of the virus file in kilobytes 40 minutes after the file has launched?

16. The sides of a triangle are all different integers x, y, and z. If the perimeter of the triangle is less than 20, what is the greatest number that one side could be?

A) 5

B) 6

C) 8

D) 9

17. If $a=3^b$ and $c=b+2$, what is $9a$ in terms of c?

A) 3^c

B) $3+c$

C) $9+2c$

D) 3^{c-2}

Questions 18 and 19 refer to the following table.

Annual Revenue for Different Product Groups at Floorgreens, 2011 to 2014

Product Groups	Year			
	2011	2012	2013	2014
Hygiene, health, and beauty	231,045	348,875	654,840	678,053
Cigarettes / Cigars	501,514	548,487	402,153	305,845
Groceries	1,799,865	1,859,548	1,987,516	2,408,977
Non-alcoholic Beverages	15,484,654	16,845, 448	18,165, 445	20,514,842
Alcoholic Beverages	5,468,484	6,154,945	6,518,632	7,618,531
Electronics	489,484	523,654	651,848	704,854

*The table above lists the annual revenue, in thousands of dollars, for each of the six product groups from 2011 to 2014.

18. Which of the following best approximates the average rate of change in the annual revenue for Electronics from 2011 to 2013?

A) $34,000,000 per year

B) $81,000,000 per year

C) $94,000,000 per year

D) $162,364,000 per year

19. Of the following, which product group's ratio of its 2011 revenue to its 2014 revenue is closest to the Non-alcoholic Beverages group's ratio of its 2011 revenue to its 2014 revenue?

A) Hygiene, health, and beauty
B) Cigarettes / Cigars
C) Groceries
D) Alcoholic Beverages

New SAT Math Practice Tests Explanations

New SAT Practice Test 1 Explanations

1. $16=4^2$

$r=1$

Length of one side of the bigger square

$=6$ inch

Area$=6^2=36$ inch^2

$\therefore$ A

2. $x=a+4$, $x=b-8$

$\dfrac{a+b}{2}=-20$

$a+b=-40$

$2x=a+b-4=-44$

$x=-22$

$\therefore$ A

3. Radius of the smaller circle：r

Radius of the bigger circle：R

$2\pi r=12\pi \rightarrow r=6$

$2R=30 \rightarrow R=15$

$\overline{AB}=\overline{AO}-\overline{BO}=9$

$\therefore$ C

4.

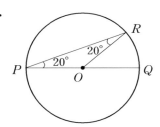

$\angle P=\angle R=20°$

$\angle POR=180-40=140°$

$r=\dfrac{1}{2}\times 9$

$\overparen{PR}=2\pi\dfrac{9}{2}\times\dfrac{140}{360}=\dfrac{7}{2}\pi$

$\therefore$ A

5. $x=\dfrac{3a}{2},\ -3a$

$\dfrac{3a}{2}+(-3a)=-\dfrac{3}{2}a$

$\therefore$ C

6. Area of the equilateral triangle：

$\dfrac{\sqrt{3}}{4}a^2\ (a=\overline{AB})$

$\dfrac{\sqrt{3}}{4}a^2=9\sqrt{3}$

$a^2=36,\ a=6$

$\rightarrow$ Area of the square：$6^2=36$

$\therefore$ B

7. One side of the square：a

Area of the square：a^2

Area of the triangle：$\dfrac{\sqrt{3}}{4}a^2$

$\dfrac{Area\ of\ the\ \triangle}{Area\ of\ the\ Square}=\dfrac{\dfrac{\sqrt{3}}{4}a^2}{a^2}=\dfrac{\sqrt{3}}{4}$

$\therefore$ B

tip. The question is asking for $\dfrac{Area\ of\ the\ \triangle}{Area\ of\ the\ Square}$

8. $\dfrac{50+x}{6}=x$

$6x=x+50$

$5x=50$

$\therefore\ x=10$

Tip. Because the mode cannot exist whout x, x must be the mode and arithmetic mean.

9. Supposing $x=1$: $-3=\dfrac{k}{1-a}$

$\rightarrow -3+3a=k$

Supposing $x=0$: $-\dfrac{3}{2}=\dfrac{k}{-a}$

$\rightarrow 3a=2k$

Substitute $3a$ in the above equation with $2k$:

$-3+2k=k$

$k=3,\ a=2$

$\therefore\ 5$

10. $\dfrac{5}{6}a=125$

$a=125\times\dfrac{6}{5}=25\times6=150$

$\dfrac{3}{4}b=900$

$b=1200$

$\therefore\ 2a+b=1500$

11. $|x-y|=45$

$\dfrac{x}{2y}=5$

$x=10y$

$|9y|=45$

$y=-5$

$x=-50$

$\therefore\ |x|=50$

12. $3A=2$

$A=\dfrac{2}{3}=\dfrac{4}{x+y}=\dfrac{4}{-3+y}$

$-6+2y=12$

$2y=18$

$y=9$

13. $x^2-7x-60=0$

$(x-12)(x+5)=0$

$x=12\ or\ -5$

$\therefore\ x=12$

14. $i=\sqrt{-1}$

$i^3=i\times i^2=-1\times i=-i$

$\therefore\ i^3=-i$

15. $y^2=k(2x-7)$

$36=k\times9$

$k=4$

$y^2=4(2x-7)$

$\quad=4(32-7)$

$\quad=4\times25$

$\quad=100$

$\therefore\ y=10$

16. $\dfrac{4}{x}=\dfrac{7}{x+12}$

$4(x+12)=7x$

$4x+48=7x$

$3x=48$

$x=16$

$\dfrac{x}{4}=4$

$\therefore\ A$

17.

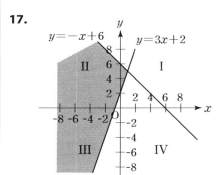

Above is the given system of inequalies drawn on the xy-plane. The colored area shows the solution set for the system of inequalities. There are no solutions in Quadrant IV.

$\therefore\ C$

18. $Q = cm\triangle T$

$\quad = 5,193 J/kg \cdot 3kg \times 1.2°C$

$\quad = 18,694.8J$

$\quad \approx 18,695J$

$\therefore$ C

19. $Q_{diamond} = cm\triangle T$

$\quad = 509 J/kg \cdot °C \times 7.3kg \times 3.5°C$

$\quad = 13,004.95J$

$Q_{concrete} = cm\triangle T$

$\quad = 850 J/kg \cdot °C \times 7.3kg \times 3.5°C$

$\quad = 21,717.5J$

$\therefore$ A

New SAT Practice Test 2 Explanations

1. Let one side of the square be x

$x^2 = 36, \ x = 6$

$6 \times 12 = 72$

$\therefore$ C

2. $\overline{BC} = \sqrt{12^2 + 5^2} = 13$

$2(12 + 5 + 13) = 60$

$\therefore$ B

3.

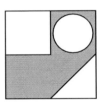

$2^2 + \dfrac{1}{2} 2^2 + (2^2 - \pi)$

$= 10 - \pi$

$\therefore$ D

4. $155 + 10x = 235$

$10x = 80$

$x = 8$

$235 + 8 \times 8 = 235 + 64 = 299$

5. $6x + 3y = 18$

$x + \dfrac{1}{2}y = 3$

$\therefore$ 3

6. The areas of the two sides of a cuboid facing each other are equal

$2(3\times 4)+2(3\times 9)+2(4\times 9)$

$\therefore$ D

7.

$\mathrm{v}=\pi r^2 h$

$\mathrm{v}=\pi\times 3^2\times 10=90\pi$

$\therefore$ B

8. $33=4\times 8+1$

        (a group of one person cannot be formed)

    $=4\times 7+5$

    $=4\times 7+(2+3)$

$\therefore$ B

9. $16-x^2=(4-x)(4+x)$

$x=4-y$

$4+x=8-y$

$16-x^2=(8-y)y$

$\therefore$ D

10. $-4<2-x<4$

$-2<x<6$

$\therefore$ C

11. $2x-5=-3$

$2x=2$

$\therefore\ x=1$

12. $\dfrac{1}{3}\times 3^{12}=3^{2x+3}$

$3^{-1}\times 3^{12}=3^{2x+3}$

$3^{12-1}=3^{2x+3}$

$2x+3=11$

$2x=8$

$\therefore\ x=4$

13. $\dfrac{140\times 6\times 60}{80}=630$

Tip. $6\ \text{hours}=6\times 60\ \text{minutes}$

$\therefore\ 630$

14. $40\times\dfrac{\frac{3}{a}}{100}=\dfrac{2}{5}\times\dfrac{3}{a}=\dfrac{6}{5a}$

$\therefore$ D

15. In the given equation $T=156-5h$,

T represents the number of leftover thin mints to sell and h is the number of households that bought thin mints.

We can infer that 156 is the initial amount of thin mints given to Julie at the start of the month, therefore, 5 being the mumber of thin mints Julie sells at each household.

$\therefore$ A

16. $3x - 7 \geq 6$

$3x \geq 13$

$6x \geq 26$

$\therefore \ 6x + 7 \geq 26 + 7 = 33$

$\therefore \ $ C

17. Proportion of Jazz LPs $= \dfrac{\text{number of Jazz LPs}}{\text{total number of items}}$

$$= \dfrac{9}{123} \approx 0.0732 = 7.32\%$$

$\therefore \ $ B

18. Probability of 1 CD being a classical music CD

$= \dfrac{\text{number of classical music CDs}}{\text{number of CDs}}$

$= \dfrac{8}{49} \approx 0.163$

Probability of both CDs being classical music CDs

$= \dfrac{8}{49} \times \dfrac{7}{48} \approx 0.02381 \approx 2.38\%$

$\therefore \ $ A

New SAT Practice Test 3 Explanations

1. $BC = \sqrt{\overline{AB}^2 - \overline{AC}^2} = 8$

$\triangle ABC$ and $\triangle DCE$ are similar triangles

$\overline{CD} : \overline{BC} = \overline{CE} : \overline{AC}$

$\rightarrow \ 4 : 8 = x : 6$

$x = 3$

$\therefore \ $ B

2. $3 \times 9 \times 1 = 27 = x^3$

$\rightarrow \ x = 3$

$\therefore \ 3 \times 12 = 36$

3. $70x = 17.5$

$\therefore \ x = 0.25$

4. $21 = 2a + 1$

$a = 10$

$2y = 10 - 4 = 6$

$y = 3$

$\therefore \ 3$

5. $\text{slope} = \dfrac{6 - (-4)}{0 - a} = \dfrac{10}{-a}$

$7 > \dfrac{10}{-a}$

$-7 < \dfrac{10}{a}$

$-7a > 10$ (since a is negative, $<$ is changed to $>$)

$a < -\dfrac{10}{7}$

$4 < -\dfrac{10}{a}$

$-4 > \dfrac{10}{a}$

$-4a < 10$ (since a is negative, $>$ is changed to $<$)

$a > -\dfrac{10}{4}$

$-\dfrac{10}{4} < a < -\dfrac{10}{7}$

$a = -2$

$\therefore \ |a| = 2$

9. $x^2 + y^2 = (x+y)^2 - 2xy$

$2 = 2^2 - 2xy$

$2xy = 2$

$\therefore \ xy = 1$

10. $i^2 = -1$

$i^3 = -i$

$i^4 = i^2 \times i^2 = 1$

$i + i^2 + i^3 + i^4 = i + (-1) + (-i) + 1 = 0$

$\therefore \ 0$

6.

$\dfrac{18\sqrt{2}}{4} - \dfrac{12\sqrt{2}}{4} = \dfrac{3\sqrt{2}}{2} = \dfrac{4.2}{2} = 2.1$

$\therefore \ 2.1$

11. $(x+y)^2 = x^2 + 2xy + y^2 = 70$

$40 + 2xy = 70$

$xy = 15$

$\therefore \ \text{B}$

12. $3(4 - 2x)^2 = 3 \times 2^2 (2 - x)^2$

$= 12(x - 2)^2$

$= 3y$

$\therefore \ \text{D}$

7. $a + b = 90$

$5a = 3b \ \left(b = \dfrac{5}{3} a \right)$

$\dfrac{8}{3} a = 90$

$a = \dfrac{270}{8} = \dfrac{135}{4}$

$\therefore \ \dfrac{135}{4} \times 8 = 270$

13. When the point A meets the y-axis, its x-coordinate is 0

$\overline{OA} = \sqrt{5^2 + 12^2} = 13$

First time: $(0, \ 13)$

Second time: $(0, \ -13)$

$\therefore \ \text{A}$

8. $x^2 + x - 6 = 0$

$(x - 2)(x + 3) = 0$

$x = -3$

$\therefore \ x^2 = 9$

14. $\dfrac{0 - (-2)}{-3 - 0} = \dfrac{2}{-3}$

$\therefore \ \text{B}$

15. tip. Reflected with respect to y-axis → Sign of x-coordinate becomes its opposite

$-x-3y=-2$

$x+3y=2$

∴ D

16. $f(-1)=-2$

$g(2)=-2$

∴ C

17. $7x-(15+4x)=k(x-5)$

$7x-15-4x=kx-5k$

$3x-15=kx-5k$

For x to have infinitely many solutions, both sides of the equation must be equal.

If $k=3$

$3x-15=3x-15$

$k=3$

∴ B

18. Plug in the second equation to the inequality.

$3x-2\leq 4\left(\dfrac{1}{2}x\right)$

$3x-2\leq 2x$

$x\leq 2$

∴ D

19. A data point is 'above the line $y=x$' when the y value is greater than the x value.

The question is asking how many fields received more student responses in year 2015 than compared wh year 2005.

There are only 3 fields that apply: Business/Finance, Engineering, and Medicine.

∴ D

20. In year 2015, there were 150 students for Literature.

In year 2005, there were only 75.

Decrease in students wishing to study Literature

$=150-75=75$

Percent decrease$=\dfrac{\text{amount of decrease}}{\text{original amount}}$

$=\dfrac{75}{150}=50\%$

∴ C

New SAT Practice Test 4 Explanations

1. $x-2z-3w=100-(1)$

$x+3y-2z=1000-(2)$

$(2)-(1)=3y+3w=900$

$\therefore\ y+w=300$

2. $\dfrac{30}{x}=40\times\dfrac{\frac{x}{3}}{100}=\dfrac{4x}{30}$

$x^2=225,\ x=15$

$\therefore$ D

3. tip. Reflected with respect to x-axis $\rightarrow$ Sign of y-coordinate becomes its opposite

$x-2y-2=0$

$x+2y-2=0$

$\therefore$ D

4. $f(0)=2$

$g(2)=1$

$\therefore$ D

5. $125\times15+75\times40$

$=1875+3000$

$=4875$

$\therefore$ 4875

6. $5x+4y=28$

$x=4,\ y=2$

or $x=0,\ y=7$

$\therefore$ 4 or 0

7. $-a-b+2d+e+30$

$=-a+d+e+30$ ($\because b=d$, Vertical angles)

$=d+e$ ($\because a=30$, Vertical angles)

$=150$

$\therefore$ 150

8. $3:50=x:90$

$50x=270$

$\therefore\ x=\dfrac{27}{5}$ miles

9. $5x+x=180°$

$x=30°$

$y=5x$(Since they are vertical angles)

$\therefore\ y=150°$

10. $a+b+c=90$

$0.9a+0.9b+0.9c=0.9(a+b+c)$

$0.9\times90=81$

$\therefore$ 81

11. $2x^2-19x-60=0$

$(2x+5)(x-12)=0$

$x=-\dfrac{5}{2},\ 12$

$-\dfrac{5}{2}+12=\dfrac{19}{2}$

$\therefore\ \dfrac{19}{2}$

12. Let the radius of the circle be r

$C=2\pi r\times 12=24\pi r$

$P=2(8r+6r)=28r$

$\dfrac{P}{C}=\dfrac{7}{6\pi}$

$\therefore$ B

13. One side : $4+3=7$

$21\div 7=3$

$28\div 7=4$

4 triangles fit in the square

$4\times 3\times 4=48$

$\therefore$ D

14. Probability of selecting a boy

$=\dfrac{\text{number of boys}}{\text{total number}}=\dfrac{3x}{8x}=\dfrac{3}{8}$

$\therefore\ \dfrac{3}{8}$

15. Any squared number must be greater than (or at least equal to) zero.

So $x^2\geq 0$.

Greatest value of x is 4, so

$x^2\leq 16$

$\therefore$ D

16. $4(y-1)=\dfrac{x}{5}-4$

$4y-4=\dfrac{x}{5}-4$

$4y=\dfrac{x}{5}$

$20y=x$

$\dfrac{x}{y}=20$

$\therefore$ C

17. When the car almost stopped, its velocity should have dropped to almost zero all of a sudden. The only point that satisfies this condition is the point at 1:06 P.M.

$\therefore$ B

18. Distance$=$speed$\times$time$=$Area under the graph! You can calculate the total area under the graph by calculating the area of 5 different sections and adding them up:

Section 1 (12:00P.M. $-$ 12:30 P.M.)

This area is in the shape of a triangle.

Area of a triangle$=\dfrac{1}{2}\times$ base $\times$ height

Area of Section $1=\dfrac{1}{2}\times 0.5\times 14=3.5$

*Note that although 30 minutes passed from 12:00 P.M. to 12:30 P.M., you should convert minutes into hours because the speed was given in miles per hour!!!

Section 2 (12:30 P.M. $-$ 1:06P.M.)

This area is in the shape of a trapezoid.

Area of trapezoid$=\dfrac{1}{2}\times$ (Sum of the lengths of 2 parallel sides)$\times$ height

Area of Section $2=\dfrac{1}{2}\times(14+10)\times\dfrac{36}{60}=7.2$

Section 3 (1:06 P.M. $-$ 1:30 P.M.)

This area is in the shape of a triangle.

Area of Section $3=\dfrac{1}{2}\times\dfrac{24}{60}\times 16=3.2$

Section 4 (1:30 P.M. $-$ 2:00 P.M.)

This area is in the shape of a trapezoid.

Area of Section $4=\dfrac{1}{2}\times(16+50)\times\dfrac{50}{60}=16.5$

Section 5 (2:00 P.M. − 2:30 P.M.)

This one is a rectangle.

Area of Section $5 = \dfrac{30}{60} \times 50 = 16.5$

Now add these all up:

total area = Area 1 + Area 2 + Area 3 + Area 4 + Area 5

$= 3.5 + 7.2 + 3.2 + 16.5 + 25 = 55.4$ miles

∴ C

19. 'Neither accelerate nor decelerate' means that the speed stays the same.

Only the interval 2:00 P.M. − 2:30 P.M. satisfies this condition.

∴ C

New SAT Practice Test 5 Explanations

1. $x + y = 3z$

$y = 3(x + z) - 16$

① $x = 3z - y$

② $3x = y - 3z + 16$

$4x = 16$ (add ① and ②)

$x = 4$

∴ 4

2. $i^2 = -1$

$i \times i^3 \times i^5 \times i^7 = i^{16} = (i^2)^8 = (-1)^8 = 1$

3. $7 : \dfrac{1}{60} = x : h$

$x = 420h$

$\dfrac{420h}{360} = \dfrac{7h}{6}$

∴ A

4. Surface area of the sphere : $4\pi r^2$

$4 \times \pi \times 5^2 \times \dfrac{1}{2} = 50\pi$

$5^2\pi + 50\pi = 75\pi$

∴ D

5. $\dfrac{y^9}{y^3} = x^3,\ y^6 = x^3$

$y^2 = x$

$\dfrac{x^2 x^2}{x^5} = \dfrac{1}{x} = \dfrac{1}{y^2}$

∴ D

6. $2x = 180 - 114 = 66$

$\therefore\ x = 33$

7. 150 minutes $= \dfrac{5}{2}$ hours

40 minutes $= \dfrac{2}{3}$ hours

$\therefore\ \dfrac{15}{6} - \dfrac{4}{6} = \dfrac{11}{6}$

8. slope of $\overline{AD} \leq$ slope of $\overline{PQ} \leq$ slope of $\overline{BC}$

$\dfrac{-7-5}{2-(-2)} \leq$ slope of $\overline{PQ} \leq \dfrac{3-(-2)}{-4-5}$

$-3 \leq$ slope of $\overline{PQ} \leq -\dfrac{5}{9}$

$\therefore\ \dfrac{5}{9} \leq |\,\text{slope of } \overline{PQ}\,| \leq 3$

9. Area of one surface : $24 \div 6 = 4$ inch^2

Length of one side : $\sqrt{4} = 2$ inch

$V = 2^3 = 8$ inch^3

$\therefore\ 8$ inch^3

10. Substitute x with 4

$3(4)^2 - 4m - 24 = 0$

$48 - 24 = 4m$

$\therefore\ m = 6$

11. $5 - a = -4$

$a = 9$

$\dfrac{-2}{6-a} = \dfrac{-2}{6-9}$

$\therefore\ \dfrac{-2}{6-a} = \dfrac{2}{3}$

12.

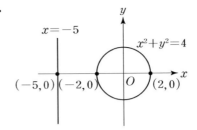

The point closest to line $x = -5$ is $(-2,\ 0)$.

$\therefore\ (-2,\ 0)$

13. $(i+2) \times (3+4i)$

$\quad = 3i + 4i^2 + 6 + 8i$

$\quad = 11i + 2$

$\therefore\ 11i + 2$

14. $\dfrac{\text{Sum of numbers} \in \text{set A}}{5} = 25$

Sum of numbers $\in$ set A $= 125$

$\dfrac{\text{Sum of numbers} \in \text{set A} + x}{6} = 29$

$x = 29 \times 6 - 125$

$\therefore\ x = 49$

15. $500 \times \dfrac{120}{100} \times \dfrac{80}{100} + 500 \times \dfrac{10}{100}$

$\quad = 480 + 50$

$\quad = 530$

$\therefore\ 530$

16. $3a-rb=2 \rightarrow$ ①

$4a-3b=5 \rightarrow$ ②

①$\times 4$: $12a-4rb=8$

②$\times 3$: $12a-9b=15$

①$\times 4-$②$\times 3$:

$(9-4r)b=-7$

For the system of equations to have no solution, the equation above must be false.

$\therefore \ 9=4r$

Therefore, $r=\dfrac{9}{4}=2.25$

$\therefore \ B$

17. Mean $=\dfrac{\text{Sum of all values}}{\text{number of values}}$

$=\dfrac{232,300}{12} \approx 19,358$

$\therefore \ 19,358$

18. Population density $=\dfrac{\text{Population}}{\text{Area}}$

$\therefore$ Population $=$ Population density $\times$ Area

$=10,400 \times 2,266 = 23,566,400$

≈ 24 million

$\therefore \ 24$

19. Percent difference

$=\dfrac{\text{Population density of Dhaka} - \text{Population density of New York}}{\text{Population density of New York}}$

$=\dfrac{43,500-4,500}{4,500} \approx 8.67 = 867\%$

$\therefore \ 867\%.$

1. A is a point on y-axis $\rightarrow$ x-coordinate is 0

$A(0, 5), \ B(-5, 5)$

$\dfrac{0}{5}=0$

$y=5$

$\therefore \ D$

2. The number of people : x

$r=\dfrac{x}{4}, \ s=\dfrac{x}{5}, \ m=\dfrac{x}{10}$

$\dfrac{x}{4}+\dfrac{x}{5}+\dfrac{x}{10}=\dfrac{11x}{20}=k$

$x=\dfrac{20}{11}k$

$\therefore \ D$

3. $f(a)=\sqrt{3a+4}=5$

$3a+4=25$

$a=7$

$\therefore \ D$

4. $3^4, \ 9^2, \ 81^1$

3

$\therefore \ D$

5. $15+12t-8t=15+4t=35$

$4t=20$

$t=5$

$35+5\times 2=45$

$\therefore \ A$

6. $3f(2)=9$

$f(5)=4$

$9+4-4=9$

$\therefore$ D

7. $5^{2a} \cdot 3^{(2a+b)} = 5^{2a} \cdot 3^{2a} \cdot 3^b$

$=(5 \times 3)^{2a} \times 3^b = 15^{2a} \times 3^b$

$\therefore$ A

8. $3x+4=2y-2$

$y = \dfrac{3}{2}x + 3$

$= \dfrac{3}{2} \times 4 + 3$

$= 9$

$\therefore y = 9$

9. $\dfrac{x}{150+x} = \dfrac{4}{7}$

$7x = 600 + 4x$

$3x = 600$

$\therefore x = 200$

10. slope $= \dfrac{-27}{9} = -3$

$y = -3(x-4) - 10 = -3x + 2$

$\therefore$ y-intercept $= 2$

11. Although $\triangle ABC$ is an isosceles triangle, we do not know which two sides have the same lengths.

1) $\overline{AB} = \overline{AC}$

$\sqrt{(2+a)^2 + (6-3)^2} = \sqrt{(5-2)^2 + (-4-6)^2}$

$4 + 4a + a^2 + 9 = 9 + 100$

$a^2 + 4a - 96 = 0$

$a = -12$ or 8 $(a > 0)$

$a = 8$

2) $\overline{BC} = \overline{AC}$

This equation does not result in an integer value of

a

3) $\overline{BC} = \overline{AB}$ also has the same problem as 2)

$\therefore$ 8

12. $\sqrt{6^2 + 6^2} = 6\sqrt{2}$

Radius of the semicircle : $\dfrac{6\sqrt{2}}{2} = 3\sqrt{2}$

Sum of the areas : $3\sqrt{2} \times 3\sqrt{2} \times \pi \times 2 = 36\pi$

$\therefore$ B

13.

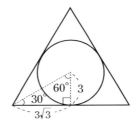

The diagram above shows one of the smaller possible triangles.

Using the special ratio of $1 : 2\sqrt{3}$ when the ratio of interior angles of a triangle are $30 : 60 : 90$, side of a bigger triangle $= 3\sqrt{3} \times 4$

$\qquad\qquad\qquad = 12\sqrt{3}$

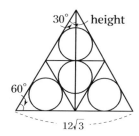

$$\text{height}=\frac{12\sqrt{3}}{2}\times\sqrt{3}=18$$

∴ D

14. $\dfrac{30}{90}\times100=\dfrac{100}{3}$

∴ B

15. $a\times\dfrac{135}{100}\times\dfrac{80}{100}$

$\dfrac{108a}{100}=1.08a$

∴ C

16. $5m-a=9m-4 \Rightarrow 4m+a=4$

$5n-b=9b-4 \Rightarrow 4n+b=4$

∴ $4m+a=4n+b$

Since it is given that $b=a-8$,

$4n-4m=a-b$

$4(n-m)=8$

∴ $n-m=2$

∴ A

17. Nachos : n

Queso : q

It is given that

$n+q=41$

$3.50n+2.00q=109.00$

From $n+q=41,\ q=41-n$

Plug $q=41-n$ into the other equation.

$3.50n+2.00(41-n)=109.00$

$3.50n+82.00-2.00n=109.00$

$1.50n=27.00$

$n=18$

∴ B

18. $I=PRT=\$17,000\times0.12\times3=\$6,120$

Amount due$=$Loan$+$Interest

$\qquad\qquad=\$17,000+\$6,120=\$23,120$

∴ 23

19. Monthly payment$=\dfrac{\text{Amount due}}{24\text{ months}}$

$\qquad\qquad=\dfrac{\text{Loan}+\text{Interest}}{24\text{ months}}$

$\qquad\qquad=\dfrac{\$17,000+\$17,000\times0.12\times1}{24\text{ months}}$

$\qquad\qquad=\dfrac{\$19,040}{24\text{ months}}$

$\qquad\qquad\approx\$793\text{ per month}$

∴ 793

New SAT Practice Test 7 Explanations

1. $135 \times 32 = 4320$

$4500 - 4320 = 180$

$\therefore$ 180

2. $4a = 6$, $12b = 20$

$a = \dfrac{3}{2}$, $b = \dfrac{5}{3}$

$\dfrac{b}{a} = \dfrac{10}{9}$

$\therefore$ C

3. Since both x and y are integers, $(x-6)$ and $(y+6)$ are also integers.

In order to get the greatest value of $y - x|$ for $x > 0$ and $y < 0$, y must be the smallest possible value and x must be the greatest possible value.

This gives you two choices:

① $(x-6) = 6$ and $(y+6) = 1$

② $(x-6) = -1$ and $(y+6) = -6$

→ ① $x = 12$, $y = -5$

→ ② $x = 5$, $y = -12$

In both cases, $|y - x| = 17$

$\therefore$ D

4. $5x + 2y = 9x$

$4x = 2y$

$2x = y$

$\therefore$ A

5. Distance may mean both 4 to and 4 from

$|x - 4| = 3$

$\therefore$ B

6. $16\pi \times \dfrac{1}{6} \times 3 = 16\pi \times \dfrac{1}{2} = 8\pi$

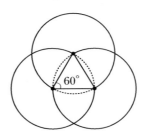

The sides of a triangle shown above are equal to the lengths of the radii. Therefore, the triangle is equilateral with each angle of $60°$.

length of one dashed arc:

$2\pi(8) \times \dfrac{60°}{360°} = \dfrac{8}{3}\pi$

total length of three dashed arcs:

$\dfrac{8}{3}\pi \times 3 = 8\pi$

$\therefore$ D

7. $\angle ABD + \angle BAD = 90°$, $\angle BAD + \angle CAD = 90°$

→ $\angle ABD = \angle CAD$, $\angle BAD = \angle ACD$

since their angles are the same,

$\triangle ABD$ and $\triangle CAD$ are similar triangles

$\overline{BD} : \overline{AD} = \overline{AD} : \overline{CD}$

$\overline{BD} : 3 = 3 : 4$

$4\overline{BD} = 9$

$\overline{BD} = \dfrac{9}{4}$

$\dfrac{1}{2} \times 3 \times \left(\dfrac{9}{4} + 4\right) = \dfrac{1}{2} \times 3 \times \dfrac{25}{4} = \dfrac{75}{8}$

$\therefore \dfrac{75}{8}$

8. $3x \leq 32$

$x \leq \dfrac{32}{3}$

∴ The largest possible value of x is $x = \dfrac{32}{3}$

9. $x \div 3 - 5 = 4$

$(4 + 5) \times 3 = 27$

∴ 27

10. Slope : $\dfrac{\triangle y}{\triangle x}$

Since $-m = \dfrac{7}{5}$,

$m = -\dfrac{x}{8} = -\dfrac{5}{7}$

$7x = 40$

∴ $x = \dfrac{40}{7}$

11. $x + y = 90$

$4x < x + y < 5x$

$4x < 90 < 5x$

$18 < x < \dfrac{90}{4}$

∴ $18 < x < \dfrac{90}{4}$

12. $A = \dfrac{1}{2} \times 4a \times 5a = 10a^2 = 5 \rightarrow a^2 = \dfrac{1}{2}$

$B = \dfrac{1}{2} \times a \times 2a = a^2$

$C = \dfrac{1}{2} \times 6a \times (a + 3a) = 12a^2$

$D = 5a \times 6a - (5 + a^2 + 12a^2) = 17a^2 - 5 = \dfrac{7}{2}$

∴ C

13. $a : a + 5 = x : 10$

$x = \dfrac{10a}{a + 5}$

∴ D

14. Speed $= \dfrac{\text{Distance}}{\text{Time}}$

$\dfrac{0.5}{40}$ miles/sec

Since we need to find out miles per hour, not second,

$\dfrac{0.5}{40} \times 60 \times 60 = 45$

∴ 45 miles/hr

15. $100 - (25 + 20 + 10 + 5 + 10) = 30$

∴ A

16. $6x - 8 \geq 3y \Rightarrow$ ①

$\dfrac{1}{2}y = \dfrac{1}{6}x + 2 \Rightarrow$ ②

② × 6 :

$3y = x + 12$

Plug in ② × 6 into ①

$6x - 8 \geq (x + 12)$

$5x \geq 20$

$x \geq 4$

∴ B

17. If the prices of pens and highlighters are the same,

$1.38+0.42n=2.91+0.25n$

$0.17n=1.53$

$n=9$

Therefore, the price of pens when the prices are the same is :

$1.38+(0.42\times9)$

$=1.38+3.78=5.16$

$\therefore$ B

18. $r=\dfrac{153}{51}=3$

$\therefore$ 3

19. $P=17\times3^{t-1}=17\times3^6=12,393\approx12,400$

$\therefore$ 124

New SAT Practice Test 8 Explanations

1. $95000+(15-3x)^2$

$=95000+(3x-15)^2$

$=95000+9(x-5)^2$

$\therefore$ $x=5$

2. $\dfrac{4-2x}{3}=-14$

$4-2x=-42$

$2x=46$

$\therefore$ $x=23$

3.

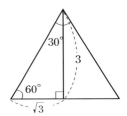

The area of the triangle :

$\dfrac{1}{2}\times2\sqrt{3}\times3=r^2\pi=3\sqrt{3}$

$r^2\pi=3\sqrt{3}$

$r^2=\dfrac{3\sqrt{3}}{\pi}$

$\therefore$ A

4.

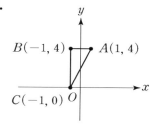

$\overline{AC}^2=\sqrt{2^2+4^2}=20$

$\overline{AC}=2\sqrt{5}$

Perimeter of $\triangle ABC=2+4+2\sqrt{5}=6+2\sqrt{5}$

$\therefore$ A

5. The graph should intersect x-axis exactly 4 times.

$\therefore$ C

6. $x^{\frac{1}{4}+\frac{2}{4}+\frac{5}{4}}=x^{\frac{8}{4}}=2x^2-3x$

$x^2=2x^2-3x$

$x^2-3x=0$

$x(x-3)=0$

$x=0$ or 3 (but $x>0$)

$\therefore$ D

7. Let $a=$ number of candies, $b=$ number of chocolates.

$a-2=b+2$

$a-b=4$

$2(b-3)=a+3$

$a-2b=-9$

$b=13$

$\therefore$ D

8. $\dfrac{3}{6}x=\dfrac{2}{3}$

$\dfrac{1}{2}x=\dfrac{2}{3}$

$\therefore$ $x=\dfrac{4}{3}$

9. For a fraction to have the minimum value, y must have the minimum value and x must have the maximum value

$x=8,\ y=16$

$\dfrac{16}{8}=2$

$\therefore$ 2

10.

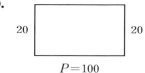

$50-20=30$

$\therefore$ 30

11. $8000\times\dfrac{30}{100}\times\dfrac{1}{2}$

$=1200$

$\therefore$ 1200 (people)

12. $\triangle AFE\equiv CBA$, and both triangles are isosceles triangles.

Since the ratio of the sides of a isosceles triangle is $1:1:\sqrt{2}$,

$\overline{AF}=4$

$\triangle AFE=\triangle CBA=4\times4\times\dfrac{1}{2}=8$

$\square AEDC=4\sqrt{2}\times4\sqrt{2}=32$

$\therefore$ The area of the shape$=8+8+32=48$

13. $\overline{AB}=\sqrt{(-5+10)^2+(-3-9)^2}=13$

$13\times4=52$

$\therefore\ 52$

14. $108=25\times2+18\times1+10\times4$

$\quad\quad\quad (2\times2)\quad (1.7\times1)\quad (1\times4)$

$4+1.7+4=9.7$

$\therefore\ B$

15. The number of people who visited Korea:

$20+5+9+10=44$

The number of people who visited Japan:

$5+10+16+a=44$

$a=13$

$20+5+9+10+13+16+b=90$

$\therefore\ b=17$

16. $7a-6b=22\ \Rightarrow\ ①$

$3a+3b=2\ \Rightarrow\ ②$

$②\times2:$

$6a+6b=4$

$①+②\times2:$

$13a=26$

$a=2$

Plug $a=2$ into $②$.

$3\times2+3b=2$

$3b=-4$

$a+3b=2-4=-2$

$\therefore\ A$

17.

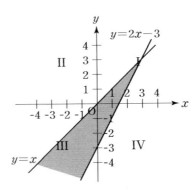

Above is the given system of inequalities drawn on the xy-plane. The colored area shows the solution set to the system of inequalities. There are no solutions in Quadrant II.

$\therefore\ $ Quadrant II

18. $\triangle N=0.6N_{initial}\left(1-\dfrac{N_{initial}}{K}\right)$

$600=0.6\times16,000\left(1-\dfrac{16,000}{K}\right)$

$600=9,600\left(1-\dfrac{16,000}{K}\right)$

Solving for K yields

$K=\dfrac{16,000\times16}{15}\approx17,067$

$\therefore\ 17,067$

19. $\triangle N=0.6N_{initial}\left(1-\dfrac{N_{initial}}{K}\right)$

$\triangle N=0.6\times16,00\left(1-\dfrac{16,000}{16,000}\right)$

$\quad\quad =0.6\times16,000\times0$

$\quad\quad =0$

$\therefore\ 0$

New SAT Practice Test 9 Explanations

1. tip. Find out the value of the unknown first using substitution.

(1) $12 = c \times a^2$

(2) $24 = c \times a^3$

$(2) \div (1) = a = 2$

$c = \dfrac{12}{a^2} = 3$

$\rightarrow y = 3 \times 2^x$

$96 = 3 \times 2^x$

$2^x = 32$

$\therefore x = 5$

2. $x^{18} = x^k$

$\therefore k = 18$

3. $6x = 60, \ x = 10$

$5y = 2y + 36$

$3y = 36, \ y = 12$

$\therefore x + y = 22$

4.

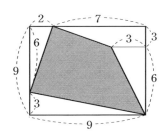

$9 \times 9 - (6 + 13.5 + 15 + 9)$

$= 81 - 43.5$

$= 37.5$

$\therefore$ D

5. $x^2 + 6x + c = x^2 - 2mx + m^2$

$m = -3, \ c = 9$

$9 - (-3) = 12$

$\therefore$ D

6. $\dfrac{total\ cost}{number\ of\ boxes} = \dfrac{100 + 25n}{n} = \dfrac{100}{n} + 25$

$\therefore$ A

7. The distance that the front tires travel =

The distance that the back tires travel

Front tires : $60\pi \times 15rev = 900\pi$

Back tires : $2\pi r \times 9rev = 18\pi r$

$900\pi = 18\pi r$

$r = 50$

$\therefore$ A

8.

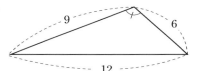 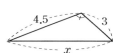

$3 : 6 = 4.5 : 9$, the angle between two sides is the same for both triangles.

The two triangles are similar.

$3 : 6 = x : 12$

$x = 6$

$\therefore$ B

9.

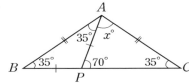

$\therefore$ 75

10. $70 < 5x < 85$

$14 < x < 17$

$\therefore$ 15, 16

11. $\angle B + \angle C = 180° - 60° = 120°$

$\angle B = \angle C = 60°$

$\therefore$ $x = 180 - 60 = 120°$

12. $3x^2 = 27$

$x = \pm 3$

$5^3 = 135,\ -135$

Need to find out a positive value of y

$\therefore$ $y = 135$

13. The number of girls : $51 - 27 = 24$

The number of girls in Math club : $25 - 16 = 9$

$24 - 9 = 15$

$\therefore$ 15

14. $\left(1 + \dfrac{8}{100}\right)k$

$\therefore$ 1.08

15. amount of the liquid after the first pour

$= x - 4$

after pouring into 6 beakers $= \dfrac{x-4}{6}$

$\therefore$ A

16. From $\dfrac{y}{x} = 6$, $y = 6x$

Plug in $y = 6x$ into the first equation.

$42x - 81 = 21 + (6x)$

$36x = 102$

$6x = 17$

$y = 6x = 17$

$\therefore$ 17

17. Original price of car : x

Car price with discount :

$(1.00 - 0.15)x = 0.85x$

Car price with discount plus sales tax :

$(1.00 + 0.11)0.85x$

$= (1.11)(0.85)x = c$

$x = \dfrac{c}{(0.85)(1.11)}$

$\therefore$ D

18. 13.781 is the slope of the line of best fit, which means that there is a 13.781 increase y-value for every unit increase in x-value.

$\therefore$ C

19. Simply find a point along the line of best fit at which the x-value, log per capita GDP, equals 10. When x-value is 10, y-value is closest to 70.

$\therefore$ A

New SAT Practice Test 10 Explanations

1. $f(30)=60a-5b=400$

$f(70)=140a-5b=800$

$80a=400,\ a=5$

$f(x)=10x-5b$

$400=300-5b$

$b=-20$

$-a-b=-5+20=15$

$\therefore\ 15$

2. Let $x=$ number of adults, $y=$ number of children under the age of 12.

$x:y=5:3$

$3x=5y\ \Rightarrow\ x=\dfrac{5y}{3}$

$150x+75y=48,750$

plug in $x=\dfrac{5y}{3}$

$250y+75y=48,750$

$y=150$

$x=\dfrac{5}{3}(150)=250$

number of people $=150+250=400$

$\therefore\ 400$

3. takes $\dfrac{t}{d}$ minutes to travel 1km.

$120\times\dfrac{t}{d}=\dfrac{120t}{d}$

$\therefore\ A$

4.

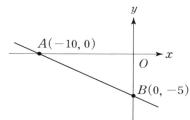

$y=-\dfrac{1}{2}x-5$

$0=-\dfrac{1}{2}x-5$

$\dfrac{1}{2}x=-5$

$x=-10$

$(-10,\ 0)$

$\therefore\ A$

5. Let $r=$ radius of the larger circle.

$(\pi r^2-\pi 4^2)\times\dfrac{315°}{360°}=112\pi$

$r^2=144$

$r=12$

$\therefore\ D$

6. $y=-1(x+4)(x-4)=-x^2+16$

$\therefore\ D$

7.

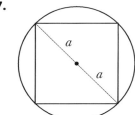

The area of the square : $\left(\dfrac{2a}{\sqrt{2}}\right)^2=\dfrac{4a^2}{2}=2a^2$

The area of the circle : $a^2\pi$

$a^2\pi:2a^2=\pi:2$

$\therefore\ B$

8. $15 = \dfrac{1}{2} \times 6h$

$h = 5$

$5 \times 2 = 10$

$\therefore$ D

9. $|2x - 5| \leq 1$

$-1 \leq 2x - 5 \leq 1$

$\therefore 2 \leq x \leq 3$

$\therefore 2$

10. $C(-5, 6)$ $B(3, 6)$

E

$D(-5, -2)$ $A(3, -2)$

$\overline{CD} = 6 - (-2) = 8$

The height of $\triangle CDE$: $\overline{CB} = 3 - (-5) = 8$

$\triangle CDE = 8 \times 8 \times \dfrac{1}{2} = 32$

$\therefore 32$

11. a : the number of students who conducted 2 experiments

b : the number of students who conducted 3 experiments

$a + b = 25$

$2a + 3b = 63$

$b = 13, \ a = 12$

$\therefore 13$

12. $\dfrac{(i^2)^3 \times i}{(i^2)^5 \times i + i^2 \times i}$

$= \dfrac{-1 \times i}{(-1 \times i) + (-1 \times i)}$

$= \dfrac{-i}{-2i}$

$= \dfrac{1}{2}$

13. $2x = 2y \times \dfrac{2}{3} = \dfrac{4}{3}y$

$3z = 4y \times \dfrac{3}{5} = \dfrac{12}{5}y$

$2x + 3z = \dfrac{20}{15}y + \dfrac{36}{15}y = \dfrac{56}{15}y$

$\therefore$ C

14. any odd number of letters would be rounded to the nearest greater even number

$\Rightarrow n + 1$

\$7 per 2 letter $\Rightarrow \dfrac{7}{2} \times (n + 1)$

total cost: $25 + 7\dfrac{(n+1)}{2}$

$\therefore$ C

15. $5x \leq 21, \ 4x \geq 5$

$\dfrac{5}{4} \leq x \leq \dfrac{21}{5}$

$x = 2, \ 3, \ 4$

$\therefore 3$

16. The slope of the line is -3, and the line passes the origin.

Therefore, the line equation is : $y = -3x$

Plug in the answers into the equation.

A) $-3 = -3 \times 1$

  This point is the line.

B) $3 = -3 \times 1$

  This point is the line.

C) $-6 = -3 \times 2$

  This point is the line.

D) $-6 \neq -3 \times -2$

  This point is NOT on the line.

∴ D

17. The slope of the line is $\frac{1}{2} \Rightarrow y = \frac{1}{2}x + b$

Since the line passes the point $(2, \ 2)$

$2 = \frac{1}{2} \times 2 + b$

∴ $b = 1$

Therefore, the line equation is : $y = \frac{1}{2}x + 1$

Plug in the answers into the equation.

A) $1 = \frac{1}{2} \times 0 + 1$

  This point is on the line.

B) $0 \neq \frac{1}{2} \times 1 + 1$

  This point is NOT on the line.

C) $3 = \frac{1}{2} \times 4 + 1$

  This point is on the line.

D) $2.5 = \frac{1}{2} \times 3 + 1$

  This point is on the line.

∴ B

18. The graph shows a directly proportional relationship between y-value and x-value.

For 1 unit increase in x-value, there is a 10 unit increase in y-value, so the slope is 10.

∴ C

19. $\dfrac{120 \text{ customers}}{\text{day}} \times \dfrac{10 \text{ minutes}}{\text{customers}} \times \dfrac{1 \text{ hour}}{60 \text{ minutes}}$

$= \dfrac{20 \text{ hour}}{\text{day}}$

$\dfrac{20 \text{ hour}}{\text{day}} \times \dfrac{\$10}{\text{hour}} = \dfrac{\$200}{\text{day}}$

∴ 200

New SAT Practice Test 11 Explanations

1. $\text{Speed} = \dfrac{\text{Distance}}{\text{Time}}$

$3400 \div 80 = 42.5$

$\therefore$ A

2. $2850 + x > 6300 - x$

$2x > 3450$

$x > 1725$

$\therefore$ 1726

3. $5 + x > 8$

$x > 3$

$\therefore$ $x = 4$

4. $\sin(90° - x) = \cos x = \dfrac{3}{4}$

$\therefore$ $\dfrac{3}{4}$

5. $-4 \times m = -1$

$m = \dfrac{1}{4}$

$\therefore$ D

6. $\overline{AB} = 13$ (Pythagorean theorem)

$\overline{AM} = x$, $\overline{BM} = 13 - x$

$x + 5 = (13 - x) + 12$

$2x = 20$

$x = 10$

$\therefore$ D

7. $x^{\frac{9}{16}} = x^{2n}$

$2n = \dfrac{9}{16}$

$n = \dfrac{9}{32}$

$\therefore$ B

8. Let $x = $ length of $\overline{CF}$

$\dfrac{1}{2} \times \dfrac{1}{2} a \times x = \dfrac{1}{5} a^2$

$\dfrac{1}{4} ax = \dfrac{1}{5} a^2$

$x = \dfrac{a^2}{5} \times \dfrac{4}{a} = \dfrac{4a}{5}$

$\overline{BF} = a - x = \dfrac{a}{5}$

$\therefore$ A

9. number of solutions = number of intersecting points between $f(x)$ and $g(x)$

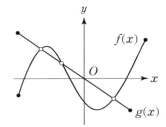

$\therefore$ C

10. $25^3 = (5^2)^3 = 5^6$

$5^6 \times 5^{2x} = 5^{6+2x}$

$\therefore$ A

11. $8^a \times x^a = x^{4a}$

$8^a = x^{3a}$

$8 = x^3$

$x = 2$

$\therefore$ A

12.

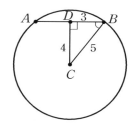

Refer to the picture above.

$\therefore \quad \sin B = \dfrac{4}{5}$

13. The product of the slopes of two perpendicular lines $= -1$

slope of the other line $= \dfrac{-1}{1} = -1$

$\Rightarrow y = -x + b$

since x-intercept is 1, plug in $(1, 0)$.

$\Rightarrow 0 = -1 + b \Rightarrow b = 1$

$y = -x + 1$

$\therefore \quad A$

14. $\dfrac{a^2 b}{ab} = a = \dfrac{18}{2}$

$a = 9, \quad b = \dfrac{2}{9}$

$\dfrac{2a}{b} = \dfrac{9 \times 2}{\dfrac{2}{9}} = 18 \times \dfrac{9}{2} = 81$

$\therefore \quad D$

15. $6 + n = 0$

$n = -6$

$9 - 2n = a$

$a = 21$

$\therefore \quad D$

16. $x < \dfrac{6}{5}, \quad x > \dfrac{8}{7}$

$\dfrac{8}{7} < x < \dfrac{6}{5}$

$\therefore \quad$ Any value within this range can be the answer.

17. $(1) + (2)$

$4x + 4z = 16$

$x + z = 4$

$(2) + (3)$

$4x = 12$

$x = 3$

$z = 1, \quad y = 2$

$3x + 2y + z = 9 + 4 + 1 = 14$

$\therefore \quad D$

18. Take the given information and establish an inequality.

$21s + 2000 \le 5500$

$21x \le 3500$

$3x \le 500$

$x \le 166.67$

$\therefore \quad 166$

19. Let $x =$ initial amount of amino acids.

$x \times \dfrac{96.8}{100} = 130 \text{mg}$

$x = 130 \times \dfrac{100}{96.8} = 134.297... \text{mg}$

At 60 min, capacitance of enzyme $A = 70.4\%$

$134.297... \text{mg} \times \dfrac{70.4}{100} \approx 94.55 \text{mg} \approx 0.095 \text{g}$

$\therefore \quad A$

20. At $40°C$, the capacitance of Enzyme B is 90.7%, while the capacitance of Enzyme A is 78.3%. Thus, Enzyme B has denatured less than Enzyme A.

$\therefore \quad C$

New SAT Practice Test 12 Explanations

1. $15 \times 6 = 90$

$\dfrac{90+8}{7} = 14$

$\therefore \; k = 14$

2. The maximum value of a quadratic function exists at the midpoint of the two x-intercepts.

$x = \dfrac{(-2+4)}{2} = 1$

$\therefore \; 1$

3. $\dfrac{3+4i}{2+5i}$

$= \dfrac{(3+4i)(2-5i)}{(2+5i)(2-5i)}$

$= \dfrac{6-7i+20}{4-25i^2}$

$= \dfrac{26-7i}{29}$

$\therefore \; A$

4. $4 \times 10^{-1} + 7 \times 10^{-3} + 3 \times 10^{-4} = \dfrac{3}{10^4} + \dfrac{4}{10^1} + \dfrac{7}{10^3}$

$4+1+3=8$

$\therefore \; 8$

5. $\dfrac{\text{Sum of All Numbers}}{5} = 3a$

Sum $= 15a$

New average: $\dfrac{15a+x}{6}$

$\therefore \; B$

6.

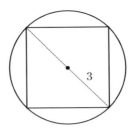

Diameter $= 6$

The length of one side of the square $= \dfrac{6}{\sqrt{2}}$

$\left(\dfrac{6}{\sqrt{2}}\right)^2 = \dfrac{36}{2} = 18$

$\therefore \; D$

7. Adult：x, Senior over 65：y, Child under 12：z

$y = \dfrac{1}{3}x, \; z = \dfrac{1}{7}y = \dfrac{1}{21}x$

$15x + 10y + 7z = 1960$

$15x + \dfrac{10}{3}x + 7 \times \dfrac{1}{21}x = 1960$

$\therefore \; x = 105$

8. $\angle A = 180 - (90+30) = 60$

$\overline{AC} = a, \; \overline{AB} = 2a, \; \overline{AM} = a$

$\triangle AMC$ is an equilateral triangle

$\therefore \; x = 60$

9.

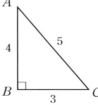

Since $\triangle ABC$ and $\triangle DEF$ are similar

$\cos D = \cos A = \dfrac{4}{5}$

$\therefore \; \dfrac{4}{5}$

10. $18 \times 15 = 270$

2.25 for 1 piece of bread

$2.25x - 270$ (total cost of the bags)

$\therefore$ A

11. $3x = 2y - 6$

$2x = (2y - 6) \times \dfrac{2}{3} = \dfrac{4}{3}y - 4$

$\therefore$ B

12. $\dfrac{3}{2}x - 5 = x$

$\dfrac{1}{2}x = 5$

$x = 10$

$\therefore$ D

13. $a^3 : x^3 = 1 : 27$

$a : x = 1 : 3$

$x = 3a$

Surface area $= 6(3a)^2 = 54a^2$

$\therefore$ D

14. P$(a, y-5)$, Q(x, y)

slope $= \dfrac{y - (y-5)}{x - a}$

$\dfrac{5}{x - a} = \dfrac{1}{3}$

$x - a = 15$

$\therefore$ 15

15. Logically, although $b < 21$, it cannot be concluded that $a = -1$. Whenever $a = -1$, b must be less than 21.

Therefore, when b is greater than or equal to 21, a cannot be -1. Only (D) can be true.

$\therefore$ D

16. $-3a + 5b = 9 \Rightarrow$ ①

$6a - 2b = 6 \Rightarrow$ ②

① $\times 2$:

$-6a + 10b = 18$

① $\times 2 + $ ② :

$8b = 24$

$b = 3$

Plug $b = 3$ into ②.

$6a - 6 = 6$

$6a = 12$

$\therefore a = 2$

$\therefore$ 2

17. The title of the graph tells you the answer: "Beak Lengths of *Aepyornis Medius*".

$\therefore$ C

18. From the graph, beak length is the greatest ($= 3$ inches) for populations that migrated east.

Thus, eastward migration caused the greatest increase in beak length.

$\therefore$ A

19. Birds from north of Microwen had a beak length of 1.2 inches.

The types of food with distance from the surface of less than 1.2 inches are: Seeds, cricket eggs, and mosquitos.

$\therefore$ C

New SAT Practice Test 13 Explanations

1. $x = \dfrac{4}{3}$

$9x^3 = 9 \times \dfrac{64}{27} = \dfrac{64}{3}$

$\dfrac{9x^3}{4} = \dfrac{64}{3} \times \dfrac{1}{4} = \dfrac{16}{3}$

$\therefore \quad \dfrac{16}{3}$

2. $\dfrac{a^{11}}{b^2} \times \dfrac{1}{a^{13}} = \left(\dfrac{1}{ab}\right)^2 = \dfrac{1}{100}$

$\dfrac{1}{ab} = \dfrac{1}{10}$

$\therefore \quad \dfrac{20}{ab} = 2$

3. For any equation $ax^2 + bx + c = 0$,

Sum of roots $= -\dfrac{b}{a}$

$\qquad\qquad = -\dfrac{-1}{-5} = -\dfrac{1}{5}$

$\therefore \quad \dfrac{1}{5}$

4. $1200 + 1500 = $ Total sales of all flavors $\times \dfrac{30}{100}$

$2700 \times \dfrac{10}{3} = 9000$

$\therefore \quad$ D

5. $32 = 4a + 5b$

$a = 3, \ b = 4$

$a + b = 7$

$\therefore \quad 7$

6. All the angles of the two triangles are the same.

$\triangle ABC$ and $\triangle AED$ are similar.

$\overline{DE} : \overline{CB} = \overline{AD} : \overline{AC}$

$5 : 9 = x : 15$

$9x = 75$

$\therefore \quad x = \dfrac{25}{3}$

7. $\dfrac{(12.5 - 0.5)}{0.8} = 15$

$15 + 1 = 16$

$\therefore \quad 16$

8. rate $= +14$ rabbits per 3 years

$10(+14)24(+14)38\cdots$

$(164 - 24) \div 14 = 10$

$10 \times 3 = 30$

$\therefore \quad 30$

9. $8t + 7t = 45$

$15t = 45$

$t = 3$

$8 \times 3 = 24$

$\therefore \quad 24$

10. $\cos(90 - x) = \sin x = \dfrac{4}{5}$

$\therefore \quad \dfrac{4}{5}$

11.

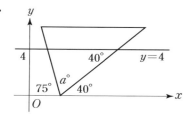

$a = 180 - 40 - 75$
$= 65$
∴ B

12. A pencil costs $0.1666 if a dozen costs $2.
$(2 \div 12 = \$0.1666\cdots \approx \$0.167)$
A pencil costs $0.15 if 25 dozens cost $45.
$(25 \times 12 = 300, \ 45 \div 300 = \$0.15)$
Thus $0.167 - 0.15 = 0.017$
∴ D

13. $\angle AOD = 180 - 65$
∴ 115

14.

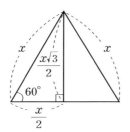

$30° - 60° - 90°$ triangle can be constructed as shown above and the height of the triangle is $\dfrac{x\sqrt{3}}{2}$.

$\text{area} = x \times \dfrac{x\sqrt{3}}{2} \times \dfrac{1}{2} = \dfrac{x^2\sqrt{3}}{4}$

$\dfrac{x^2\sqrt{3}}{4} = 16\sqrt{3}$

$x^2 = 64$

$x = 8$

∴ 8

15. (1) $x + y = 10$
(2) $3x + 2y = 25$
$2 \times (1) \ 2x + 2y = 20$
$(2) - 2(1) x = 5$
∴ 5

16. (1) $a^3 = 1 + a$
If $a = 1 : 1^2 \neq 1 + 1$
If $a = 2 : 2^3 = 8 = 1 + 2$
If $a = 3 : 3^3 = 27 \neq 1 + 3$
As a increases, a^3 becomes much larger than $1 + a$. (1) cannot be true.
(2) $a = 1, \ b = 2$
$a^2 b = 2, \ 1 + a = 2$, (2) can be true.
(3) $a^2 b = 1 + a \Rightarrow b = \dfrac{1+a}{a^2} = \dfrac{1}{a^2} + \dfrac{1}{a}$,
(3) is always true.
Only (1) cannot be true.
∴ A

17. From $\dfrac{y}{x} = 4$, $y = 4x$
Plug $y = 4x$ into the second equation.
$2(x + 6) = (4x)$
$2x + 12 = 4x$
$2x = 12$
∴ $y = 4x = 24$
∴ C

18. Find the location on the best-fit curve at which the x-value equals 40.
→ When volume is 40, pressure is roughly 35.
∴ B

19. The best-fit curve shows that as volume increases, pressure decreases.
∴ B

New SAT Practice Test 14 Explanations

1. $\dfrac{4+2i}{3+7i}$

$=\dfrac{(4+2i)(3-7i)}{(3+7i)(3-7i)}$

$=\dfrac{12-28i+6i-14i^2}{9-49i^2}$

$=\dfrac{-22i+26}{58}$

$=\dfrac{-11i+13}{29}$

$\therefore$ A

2. $a^{\frac{1}{3}+\frac{4}{3}-\frac{2}{3}}=2$

$a=2,\ 3^2=9$

$\therefore$ 9

3. $x^2+2x-3=0$

$b^2-4ac=4+12>0$

$\therefore$ two different real roots

$(x+3)(x-1)=0,\ x=1,\ -3$

$\therefore$ C

4. Rearrange the scores in ascending order so that the median score is 69.

46, 51, x, 69, 78, 85, 98

Median score will still be 69 even if $x=69$.

Thus, the maximum integer value of x is 69.

$\therefore$ 69

5. Quadratic formula:

$$x=\frac{-b\pm\sqrt{b^2-4ac}}{2a}$$

The question tells us that $x=\dfrac{-7\pm\sqrt{37}}{6}$

So $b=7$ and $a=3$

$\therefore\ a+b=10$

6. $2\dfrac{a}{b}=5$

$\dfrac{5b}{2a}=1$

$\therefore$ C

7. $\dfrac{5}{5+2}=\dfrac{5}{7}$

$\therefore\ \dfrac{5}{7}$

8. $2.4\times 60=144$

$\therefore$ 144

9. $x=4y,\ 3x-5y=12y-5y=21$

$\rightarrow\ y=3,\ x=12$

$\therefore\ 2x+3y=33$

10.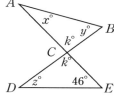

Supposing $\angle ACB = k°$

$k = 180 - (x + y)$

$z = 180 - 46 - k$

$\quad = 180 - 46 - (180 - (x + y))$

$\quad = -46 + x + y$

$x + y - z = x + y - (-46 + x + y)$

$\therefore\ 46$

11. $m \times 5 + n \times 0 = 10$

$\therefore\ m = 2$

12.

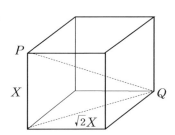

$x^2 + (\sqrt{2}x)^2 = (2\sqrt{3})^2$

$3x^2 = 12$

$x^2 = 4$

$x = 2$

$2^2 \times 6 = 24$

$\therefore\ A$

13. Since $\angle DBC = \angle DCB$, $\triangle BDC$ is an isosceles triangle.

$\angle DBC = \angle DCB = (180 - 130) \times \dfrac{1}{2} = 25$

$\angle ABC = \angle ACB = 25 \times 2 = 50$

$x = 180 - (2 \times 50) = 80$

$\therefore\ D$

14. $B(x, -2)$

$\dfrac{-2}{x} = -\dfrac{3}{4}$

$3x = 8,\ x = \dfrac{8}{3}$

$\text{Area} = \dfrac{8}{3} \times 2 = \dfrac{16}{3}$

$\therefore\ D$

15. $\angle BAC = 70°$

$\angle B = \angle C = \dfrac{1}{2}(180 - 70) = 55$

$\therefore\ 55°$

16. $1 < 2x < 8$

$\dfrac{1}{2} < x < 4$

$\Rightarrow$ 3 is the biggest possible value of x

$1 < 3y < 11$

$\dfrac{1}{3} < y < \dfrac{11}{3}$

$\Rightarrow$ 3 is the biggest possible value of y

$\therefore\ xy = 9$

17. $2n-r=5n+9 \Rightarrow -3n-r=9$

$4m-k=7m+9 \Rightarrow -3m-k=9$

$\therefore -3n-r=-3m-k$

Since it is given that $r=k+6$

$-3n-(k+6)=-3m-k$

$3m-3n=r-k$

$3(m-n)=6$

$\therefore m-n=2$

$\therefore$ A

18. The median is the number that lies in the middle of the data points.

In this case, there are 64 buildings. So the median is the average of the 32nd number and 33rd number, and the histogram tells us that their values lie between $50 \sim 60$.

Thus, the median should belong to the $50 \sim 60$ range as well.

Among all the answer choices, 59 is the only number that satisfies this condition.

$\therefore$ A

19. Since 6 new numbers were added, we now have 70 numbers. So the median is the average of the 35th number and 36th number.

Take into account the 6 new numbers and study the histogram again:

The values of the 35th and 36th number must lie between $40 \sim 50$.

Among the answer choices, 46 is the only number that satisfies this condition.

$\therefore$ A

1. $\dfrac{(i^2)^3+i^2}{(i^2)^4}$

$= \dfrac{-1-1}{1}$

$= -2$

$\therefore -2$

2. $x^2-8x+n=x^2+2mx+m^2$

$m=-4, \ n=16$

$\therefore$ C

3. Distances between the line of symmetry and each x-intercept must be equal.

$\rightarrow$ Add -4 to the x-coordinate of the line of symmetry.

$a=-5$

$\therefore$ C

4. $g(4)=12-k=15$

$k=-3$

$\therefore -k=3$

5. $5x=6y$

$10x=12y$

$\dfrac{12y}{3y}=4$

$\therefore$ D

6. Price of 12 ice-creams: $12x$

1 dollar $= 100$ cents

$100y - 12x$

$\therefore$ C

7. $24 \times 4\frac{1}{2} = 12 \times 9 = 108$

$\therefore$ B

8. 6 months $\times 2 = 1$ year

after 1 year: $4 \times 3 \times 3 = 4 \times 3^2$

after 2 years: $4 \times 3 \times 3 \times 3 \times 3 = 4 \times 3^4$

after t years: 4×3^{2t}

$\therefore$ A

9.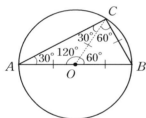

$\triangle$BOC is an equilateral triangle.

$\angle$AOC $= 180° - 60° = 120°$

$\angle$ACO $= \angle$CAO $= \dfrac{(180° - 120°)}{2} = 30°$

$\angle$ACB $= 90°$

Using Pythagorean theorem:

$\overline{AC} = \sqrt{8^2 - 4^2} = \sqrt{48} = 4\sqrt{3}$

Perimeter of $\triangle$ABC:

$4\sqrt{3} + 8 + 4 = 12 + 4\sqrt{3}$

$\therefore$ D

10. $25\pi \times 2 + 10\pi \times 10$

$= 50\pi + 100\pi$

$= 150\pi$

$\therefore$ D

11. $\overline{AM} = \frac{1}{2}\overline{AC} = 4$, $\overline{AN} = \frac{1}{2}\overline{AB} = 2$

The area of the part not shaded: $4 \times 2 \times \dfrac{1}{2} = 4$

$\therefore$ A

12. Let the lengths of the two sides be x, y

$x + y = 10$

$1 \times 9 = 9$

$2 \times 8 = 16$

$3 \times 7 = 21$

$4 \times 6 = 24$

$5 \times 5 = 25$

$\therefore$ 9, 16, 21, 24, 25

13. $\angle$DEF $= \angle$BCD $= 34°$

$\angle$BDC $= 103°$

$\angle$CBD $= 180 - (103 + 34) = 43°$

$\angle$ABC $= 180 - \angle$CBD $= 137°$

$\therefore$ 137°

14. $\dfrac{2a + b}{2} = -3$

$2a + b = -6$

$b = -2a - 6$

$\dfrac{-2a - 6}{-a - 3} = 2$

$\therefore$ D

15. $8s = 1g = \dfrac{20}{3}d$

$8 : \dfrac{20}{3} = 600 : x$

$8x = 4000$

$\therefore\ x = 500$

16. Total distance: $200\pi \times 18 = 3,600\pi\,\text{cm}$

Number of revolutions of the smaller wheel:

$3,600\pi \div 90\pi = 40$

$\therefore\ 40$

17. $3a + 8 = 2b + 2 \Rightarrow$ ①

$\dfrac{1}{2}b = \dfrac{1}{4}a + 1 \Rightarrow$ ②

② $\times 4$:

$2b = a + 4$

Plug ② $\times 4$ into ①.

$3a + 8 = (a + 4) + 2$

$3a + 8 = a + 6$

$2a = -2$

$a = -1$

$\therefore\ b = 1.5$

$\therefore\ \text{C}$

18. Change in weight

Andon: about 10

Magdalina: about 6

Jerry: about 1

$\therefore\ \text{C}$

19. From March to April, Andon gained 16 pounds - which is more than anybody else during any 1-month interval.

$\therefore\ \text{D}$

New SAT Practice Test 16 Explanations

1. $100 = \dfrac{k}{8^2}$

$k = 6{,}400$

$y = \dfrac{6{,}400}{10^2} = 64$

$\therefore\ \text{A}$

2. $15^{26} = (3 \times 5)^{26} = 3^{26} \times 5^{26}$

$x = 26,\ y = 26$

$2x - y = 52 - 26 = 26$

$\therefore\ \text{D}$

3. $1.6 \times 25 = 40$

$72 - 40 = 32$

$32 \div 1.6 = 20$

$\therefore\ 20$

4.

$\overline{AC} = 15 + 9.3 = 24.3$

$\overline{AC} = 15 - 9.3 = 5.7$

Difference $= 24.3 - 5.7 = 18.6$

$\therefore\ 18.6$

5. $36 - 2t + 3t = 48 - 3t + 2t$

$36 + t = 48 - t$

$\therefore\ t = 6$

6. $x^6 = y^2$

$y^2 = y^{8-3k}$

$2 = 8 - 3k$

$3k = 6, \ k = 2$

$\therefore \ 2$

7. $3 \times 5 + 5 \times 6 + 2 \times 2 + (15 - 10) \times 3$

$= 15 + 30 + 4 + 15$

$= 64$

$\therefore \ 64$

8. $3 \times 2^5 + 10$

$= 3 \times 32 + 10$

$= 96 + 10$

$\therefore \ 106$

9.

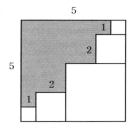

$5 + 5 + 1 + 1 + 2 + 1 + 1 + 2 + 1 + 1 = 20$

$\therefore \ 20$

10.

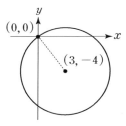

$r =$ distance between $(0, \ 0)$ and $(3, \ -4)$

$= \sqrt{3^2 + (-4)^2}$

$= 5$

Coordinates of the other x-intercept: $(a, \ 0)$

$\sqrt{(3-a)^2 + (-4)^2} = 5$

$(3-a)^2 = 9$

$a = 6$

$\therefore \ 6$

11. $h = 120$

$\pi r^2 h = \pi 20^2 \times 120$

$\qquad = \pi \times 400 \times 120$

$\qquad = 48000\pi$

$\therefore \ D$

12.

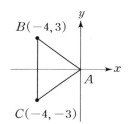

C is symmetrical with B with respect to the $x-$axis.

$\therefore \ A$

13. 1) Length of a side of a triangle must be shorter than the sum of the lengths of the two other sides.

2) Let the remaining side be x: $10 + 4 > x$

$\qquad x < 14$

The largest possible value of the integer x is 13.

$\therefore \ C$

14. Total number of students : $130 \times \dfrac{100}{20} = 650$

$$650\left(\dfrac{18}{100} - \dfrac{14}{100}\right) = 650 \times \dfrac{4}{100}$$
$$= 6.5 \times 4$$
$$= 26$$

$\therefore$ D

15. $\dfrac{105}{700} = \dfrac{a}{800} = \dfrac{b}{1100}$

$a = 120$

$b = 165$

$a + b = 285$

$\therefore$ D

16. Probability of landing on $3 = \dfrac{1}{4}$

Probability of landing on $6 = \dfrac{1}{8}$

$\therefore$ A

17. Probability of landing on $7 = \dfrac{1}{8}$

Probability of landing on $12 = \dfrac{1}{16}$

Probability of landing on 7 or 12

$= \dfrac{1}{8} + \dfrac{1}{16} = \dfrac{3}{16}$

$\therefore$ C

18. $f(3) = 7$

$g(1) = 9$

$f(3) + 2g(1) = 7 + 18 = 25$

$\therefore$ A

19. $\dfrac{f(3) - 2g(2)}{[g(4)]^2}$

$= \dfrac{7 - 2}{25} = \dfrac{1}{5} = 0.2$

$\therefore$ C

New SAT Practice Test 17 Explanations

1. $7a = 3b$

$a = \dfrac{3}{7}b$

$6b = 5c$

$c = \dfrac{6}{5}b$

$\dfrac{c}{a} = \dfrac{\frac{6}{5}}{\frac{3}{7}} = \dfrac{6}{5} \times \dfrac{7}{3} = \dfrac{14}{5}$

$\therefore$ $\dfrac{14}{5}$

2. Supposing $y = $ pen's cost and $x = $ pencil's cost,

$y = mx$

$6y + 5x = 3y + 14x$

$y = mx$

$3y = 9x$

$y = 3x$

$\therefore$ $m = 3$

3. $a = 2 + \dfrac{3y}{x} = 2 + \dfrac{y}{2x} \times 6 = 2 + 6b$

$\therefore$ B

4. $2x \geq -10$

$2x \leq 12$

$-5 \leq x \leq 6$

$\therefore$ A

5. $(x + 2)(x - 6) = x^2 - 4x - 12$

$m = 4, \ n = 12$

$m + n = 16$

$\therefore$ D

6. $2 < 3-x < 4 \Rightarrow -1 < x < 1$

$-4 < 3-x < -2 \Rightarrow 5 < x < 7$

$\therefore$ D

7. $5^{2x-3} = 5^{-x+4}$

$2x-3 = -x+4$

$3x = 7$

$\therefore x = \dfrac{7}{3}$

8. $|a-b|$ must be the smallest number

$a=1, \ b=-1$

$|a-b| = 2$

$\dfrac{4}{2} = 2$

$\therefore 2$

9. $g(3) = 4, \ f(4) = 1$

$\therefore$ D

10.

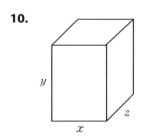

The possible surface area must be a combination of $xy, \ xz, \ yz$. Thus the three sides must be common factors of 20 and 8.

Common factors of 20 and 8 : $1, \ 2, \ 4$.

Let $20 = xy, \ 8 = xz$.

If $x=1, \ yz = 160$

$\Rightarrow 160 > 20$, not an answer.

If $x=2, \ yz = 40$

$\Rightarrow 40 > 20$, not an answer.

If $x=4, \ yz = 10$

$\Rightarrow 20 > 10 > 8$, answer.

$V = 4 \times 5 \times 2 = 40$

$\therefore$ C

11.

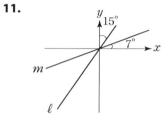

Smaller $\angle = 90 - (7+15) = 68$

Bigger $\angle = 180 - 68 = 112$

$\therefore$ C

12. $r^2\pi = 6.25\pi$

$\sqrt{6.25} = 2.5 = $ r

$2\pi r = 5\pi$

$\therefore 5\pi = 15.7$

13. $x+y = 90$

$w+z = 90$

$90 - 90 = 0$

$\therefore 0$

14. $\sqrt{(-2-2)^2 + (2+1)^2} = \sqrt{4^2 + 3^2} = 5$

$\therefore 5$

15. Speed $=\dfrac{\text{distance}}{\text{time}}$

$\dfrac{110\times4+60\times6}{10}$

$=\dfrac{800}{10}=80$

$\therefore$ 80

16. $2x=100-47-24-11$

$x=9$

$300\times\dfrac{9}{100}=27$

$\therefore$ 27

17. The highest bar is the one on the far right, and the x-axis shows that the temperature ranges between $9{,}000\sim10{,}000$ K.

$\therefore$ D

18. 'How many stars show a color of orange or white?' $=$ 'How many stars have temperatures of $5{,}000\sim6{,}000$K or $9{,}000\sim10{,}000$K?'

$350\times10^3+400\times10^3$

$=750\times10^3$

$=7.5\times10^5$

$\therefore$ C

New SAT Practice Test 18 Explanations

1. $a=b-5,\ c=b+2$

$c-a=(b+2)-(b-5)=7$

$\therefore$ A

2. $49\pi\,\text{km}=49000\pi\,\text{m}$

$49000\pi=35000\times2\pi r$

$r=\dfrac{49000\pi}{70000\pi}=\dfrac{7}{10}$

$\therefore\ \dfrac{7}{10}$

3. $300\times\dfrac{40}{100}\times\dfrac{30}{100}=300\times\dfrac{2}{5}\times\dfrac{3}{10}=36$

$\therefore$ 36

4. $25000\times\dfrac{83}{100}-25000\times\dfrac{77}{100}$

$=25000\times\left(\dfrac{83}{100}-\dfrac{77}{100}\right)$

$=1500$

$\therefore$ 1500

5.

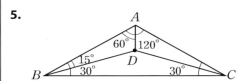

$\angle B=30°=\angle C\,(\because \text{isosceles triangle})$

$\angle A=(180-60)=120°$

$\angle ABD=15°,\ \angle DAB=60°$

$\therefore\ \angle ADB=180°-75°=105°$

$\therefore$ C

6. $7^{4x+3}=7^{2x+3}\times 7^{2x}$

$7^{2x+3}=7^{2x}\times 7^3=49y$

$7^{2x}=\dfrac{y}{7}$

$7^{4x+3}=49y\times\dfrac{y}{7}=7y^2$

$\therefore$ D

7. $4x=9x^3,\ \ 4=9x^2\ \ (\text{since }x\neq 0)$

$x^2=\dfrac{4}{9}$

$\therefore$ A

8. $2x-5=\pm 3$

$2x=8,\ 2$

$x=4,\ 1$

$\therefore$ C

9. $9+3>x\ \rightarrow\ x<12,$

greatest integer smaller than 12 is 11.

$\therefore$ 11

10. Let the length of the original edge be x

$x^3=64\ \rightarrow\ x=4$

$(4+2)\times(4+2)\times(4-1)$

width   length   height

$6\times 6\times 3=36\times 3=108$

$\therefore$ 108

11.

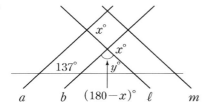

$180-(180-x)-y$

$=x-y=43$

$\therefore$ 43

12.

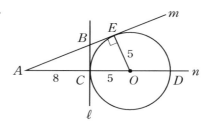

$\overline{AE}=12$ (Pythagorean Theorem $\triangle AOE$)

5, 12, 13

Since $\angle BAC=\angle OAE$ and $\angle ACB=\angle AEO$,

$\triangle ABC$ and $\triangle AOE$ are similar triangles.

$\overline{AB}:\overline{AC}=\overline{AO}:\overline{AE}$

$x:8=13:12$

$\overline{AB}=\dfrac{104}{12}=\dfrac{26}{3}$

$\overline{BE}=12-\dfrac{26}{3}=\dfrac{13}{3}$

$\therefore\ \dfrac{13}{3}$

13. $x=8+y$

$(8+y)y=y^2+8y=20$

$y^2+8y-20=0$

$y=-10\ \text{or}\ 2$

$x=-2\ \text{or}\ 10$

Substitute with the negative values of x and y

$-(x+y)=-(-10+(-2))=12$

$\therefore$ 12

14.

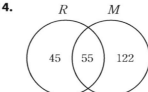

$\therefore$ 177

15. $f(8)=2\times 8^2+8+8=128+16=144$

$g(8)=2\sqrt{144}-8=2\times 12-8=24-8=16$

$\therefore$ D

16. Total sales : $42\times \dfrac{100}{21}=200$

Vanilla flavor sales : $200\times \dfrac{28}{100}=56$

$\therefore$ 56

17.

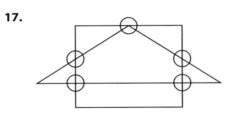

$\therefore$ D

18. Look for the line that showed a continual increase.

Cityron started at a profit of \$130,000 in 2010 and earned \$260,000 in 2015.

Since it earned twice as much as it did in the beginning, Cityron's profits grew by 100%.

$\therefore$ A

19. Technodexon : $-\$90,000$

Cityron : $+\$46,000$

Alphaquote : No change

Thus, during year $2012-2013$, Technodexon went through the most dramatic change.

$\therefore$ B

New SAT Practice Test 19 Explanations

1. $y\times (x-z)=9$

$y\times 27=9$

$\therefore$ $y=\dfrac{1}{3}$

2. $34\times \dfrac{2}{3}<\dfrac{2x-5}{6}<37\times \dfrac{2}{3}$

$\dfrac{68}{3}<\dfrac{2x-5}{6}<\dfrac{74}{3}$

$\therefore$ 23, 24

3. $x=\dfrac{65}{100}y,\ y=\dfrac{140}{100}z$

$x=\dfrac{65}{100}\times \dfrac{140}{100}z=\dfrac{91}{100}z$

$\therefore$ C

4. $0.7:21=1:x$

$x=21\times \dfrac{10}{7}=30$

$30-21=9$

$\therefore$ C

5. ① $a^2+b^2=9$

② $a^2-b^2=9$

add ① and ②

$2a^2=18$

$a^2=9$

$a=3$

$\therefore$ C

6. $V=\pi r^2 h$

radius of $A : r$, radius of $B : R$

height of $A : 4h$, height of $B : h$

$V_A=4hr^2\pi$, $V_B=hR^2\pi$

$4hr^2\pi=hR^2\pi \rightarrow 4r^2=R^2$

$2r=R$

$R : r=2 : 1$

$\therefore$ D

7. $(x+y)(x-y)^2=0$

$y=-4$, $(x-4)(x+4)^2=0$

$x=4$ or $x=-4$

since $x>y$, $x=4$

$\therefore$ $x=4$

8. $(1.25-2x)(3x-10.2)>0$

$(2x-1.25)(3x-10.2)<0$

There are two possible cases.

① $(2x-1.25)<0$ and $(3x-10.2)>0$

$\quad x<0.625$ and $x>3.4$

$\quad 3.4<x<0.625 \Rightarrow$ incorrect inequality

② $(2x-1.25)>0$ and $(3x-10.2)<0$

$\quad x>0.625$ and $x<3.4$

$\quad 0.625<x<3.4$

$\therefore$ $x=1, 2, 3$

9. Given that it is a corresponding angle,

$3x=153$, $x=51$

$180-3x=2y$, $2y=27$

$\dfrac{x}{2}+y=\dfrac{51}{2}+\dfrac{27}{2}=\dfrac{78}{2}=39$

$\therefore$ 39

10. $x^2<3x$

$x^2-3x<0$

$x(x-3)<0$

$0<x<3$

$\therefore$ $x=1, 2$

11. $4x=4\times35=140$

$y=180-140=40$

$\therefore$ 40

12. $3(x-5+x)=2x+9$

$3(2x-5)=2x+9$

$6x-15=2x+9$

$4x=24$

$\therefore$ $x=6$

13.

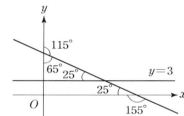

$\therefore$ B

14.

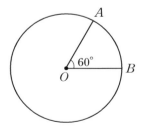

circumference of the circle$=36\pi$

$\angle AOB=60°$

major arc $\overgroup{AB}=$ larger arc with an angle $300°$

$\overgroup{AB}=36\pi\times\dfrac{300}{360}=30\pi$

$\therefore$ D

15. $x = 100\% - (45\% + 25\% + 15\%) = 15\%$

$2{,}500 \times \dfrac{15}{100} = 25 \times 15 = 375$

$\therefore\ 375$

16.

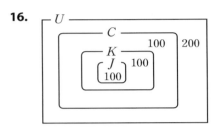

$\therefore\ 200$

17. $6340 \times 0.63 = 3994.2$

$\therefore\ A$

18. Tom's new rating is 46%.

Tom's rating decreased by 17%.

Hailey's rating rose to $9 + 17 = 26\%$.

Compare Tom and Hailey:

$\dfrac{46}{26} = 1.769 = 176.9\%$

This means that Tom's rating is 176.9 percent of Hailey's rating, which means that Tom's rating is 76.9% higher than Hailey's.

$\therefore\ A$

New SAT Practice Test 20 Explanations

1. 28 minutes $= 28 \times 60 = 1680$ seconds

$1{,}680\ \text{sec} \times \dfrac{k\ \text{words}}{35\text{sec}} = 48k\ \text{words}$

$\therefore\ D$

2. $5x + 4y = -16$

$y = -\dfrac{5}{4}x - 4$

$-\dfrac{5}{4} \times m = -1$ (perpendicular lines)

$m = \dfrac{4}{5}$

$\therefore\ D$

3. $y = \dfrac{31}{3} = 10.\times\times\times\times\times$. Round up to 11.

$\therefore\ 11$

4. $60 \div 15 = 4$

The clock chimes four times per hour.

12 times $10{:}05$ to $1{:}05$ (3 hours)

3 times $1{:}05$ to $1{:}50$ (at $1{:}15$, $1{:}30$ and $1{:}45$)

$\rightarrow$ Total 15 times

$\therefore\ D$

5.

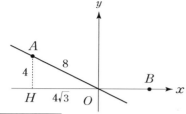

$$\sqrt{\overline{AH}^2+\overline{OH}^2}=\overline{OA}=8$$

The ratio among the lengths of the sides

$1:2:\sqrt{3} \;\rightarrow\; \angle AOH=30°$

$\angle AOB=180-30=150$

$\therefore\; C$

6. $f(\alpha)=-2\alpha^3+25=9$

$\alpha^3=8,\; \alpha=2$

$g(\alpha)=4(2)^2=16$

$\therefore\; C$

7. $(a^2+b^2-2ab)-(a^2+b^2+2ab)=40$

$-2ab-2ab=40$

$ab=-10$

a	b
1	-10
2	-5
5	-2
10	-1

a	b
-10	1
-5	2
-2	5
-1	10

$a-b=11,\; 7,\; -11,\; -7$

$\therefore\; D$

8. $\dfrac{\sqrt{x}}{2}=18$

$\sqrt{x}=36,\; x=36^2=1{,}296$

$\therefore\; D$

9. $N=$ number of students, $n=$ number of rulers

$\dfrac{N-5}{2}=n$

(1) $N=2n+5$

$n-5=\dfrac{N}{3}$

(2) $N=3n-15$

$(2)-(1)=n-20=0$

$\therefore\; n=20$

10. $0.25x>31$

$x>\dfrac{31}{0.25}$

$x>124$

$x=125$

$\therefore\; 125$

11.

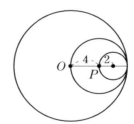

$\therefore\; 16$

12. $16\times3=48=4x$

$x=12$

$\therefore\; 12$

13. Let x=length of one side, y=length of the other side.

$2x+2y=34$

$x+y=17$ ⋯ ①

$xy=30$, $x=\dfrac{30}{y}$ ⋯ ②

plug ② into ①

$\dfrac{30}{y}+y=17$

$30+y^2=17y$

$y^2-17y+30=(y-15)(y-2)=0$

$y=15$, $x=2$ or $y=2$, $x=15$

the length of the shorter side is 2.

∴ 2

14. $\angle\mathrm{BAC}+\angle\mathrm{DAE}+\angle\mathrm{EAG}$

$\quad =180-95$

$\quad =85$

$\angle\mathrm{B}+\angle\mathrm{D}+\angle\mathrm{F}=180\times3-(90\times3+85)=185$

∴ 185

15. 40 minutes $=\dfrac{40}{60}=\dfrac{2}{3}$ hour

$S\left(\dfrac{2}{3}\right)=100\times2^{6\times\frac{2}{3}}$

$\quad\quad =100\times2^4$

$\quad\quad =100\times16$

$\quad\quad =1{,}600$

∴ $1{,}600$

16. Let z=length of the longest side. In order to get the maximum value of z, the perimeter must be greatest.

$x+y+z=19 \Rightarrow x+y=19-z$

z must be less than the sum of other two sides.

$x+y>z$

$19-z>z \Rightarrow 19>2z$

$\dfrac{19}{2}>z$

The greatest value of z is 9.

∴ D

17. $b=c-2$

$a=3^{c-2}$

$9a=3^{c-2}\times3^2=3^{(c-2+2)}$

$9a=3^c$

∴ A

18. $\dfrac{\$651{,}848{,}000-\$489{,}484{,}000}{2\text{ years}}$

$=\dfrac{\$81{,}182{,}000}{\text{years}}$

∴ B

19. Ratio of 2011 revenue to 2014 revenue

Non-alcoholic Beverages:

$\dfrac{20{,}514{,}842}{15{,}484{,}654}=1.325$

Hygiene, health, and beauty:

$\dfrac{678{,}053}{231{,}045}=2.935$

Cigarettes / Cigars:

$\dfrac{305{,}845}{501{,}514}=0.6098$

Groceries:

$\dfrac{2{,}408{,}977}{1{,}799{,}865}=1.338$

Alcoholic Beverages:

$\dfrac{7{,}618{,}531}{5{,}468{,}484}=1.393$

Electronics:

$\dfrac{704{,}854}{489{,}484}=1.440$

The ratio for non-alcoholic beverages is closest to the ratio for groceries.

∴ C

29966253R00172

Printed in Poland
by Amazon Fulfillment
Poland Sp. z o.o., Wrocław